FROM COP TO
SERIAL KILLER

The David Middleton Murders

Jeff Kaye

We who have seen death
will forever see it in our dreams.
Those who have never seen death
will never understand this. Nor will
they understand why we envy them…

-The Author

Dedication

This book is dedicated to all the victims and survivors of evil in our society and to the Dragon Slayers who go into the night to chase the beast and keep us safe from those evils. But it is specifically dedicated to one victim who, to this day, calls to us from her grave for justice against the beast who cut her life short at the young age of eighteen on November 21, 1993.

Rest in peace, Buffy Rice-Donohue. We've got your six…

Author's Note

I FIRST BECAME involved in the David Middleton case on a cold February night in 1995 while working as a sergeant in the Patrol Division of the Reno Police Department. From the moment I arrived at the site where Middleton's first victim was discovered, I knew this was not an ordinary homicide case. The following three years of investigation and prosecution proved my initial hunch to be correct. It also showed me this was a story that someday needed to be told until justice was done for the forgotten victims.

I first wrote *"Beware of the Cable Guy: From Cop to Serial Killer"* in 2007. After the book's release in 2009, I was contacted by numerous people who were either familiar with David Middleton or whose encounters with him had altered their lives forever—and not in a good way…

Among those who contacted me were former law enforcement partners, law enforcement officers, and jurists from jurisdictions where Middleton committed crimes, a prior girlfriend who unknowingly was the "next-up" on Middleton's kill list, family members, and friends of victims.

Most importantly, I received a contact from a sixteen-year-old victim whom he let go after kidnapping and sexually assaulting her in 1989 in the backseat of his unmarked police car in a deserted Florida field while he was wearing his police uniform. This young woman carries with her a burden that is unfathomable to me, and regrettably, she blames herself for the murders of Middleton's subsequent victims because she came forward and testified against him, and her act of courage sent him to prison. To this day, she feels Middleton learned through her acts that dead victims can never testify against him, so he never left a victim of his perverse and heinous crimes to tell their story again.

The day I met and spoke to this young woman, I knew I had to update this book with new information, and this is a story that cannot be forgotten. The original book raised several questions about law enforcement investigations, courtroom procedures, possible law enforcement negligence or malfeasance, and other cause-and-effect issues in the criminal justice system that allowed David Middleton to continue committing crimes until he was eventually caught and arrested in Reno, NV. in 1995.

Ten years after the first release of this book, these questions and others remain unanswered. The last chapters of this revised book will revisit those questions. The most important of which is: why has the killer of Buffy Rice-Donohue never been charged with her murder, even though we know where he is and we know what he did?

This is not the story of David Middleton. I would not justify his existence by making this a story about him. It is a true story about heinous crimes committed by a man whom people trusted and allowed into the inner circles of their lives. My initial research uncovered allegations of possible police malfeasance that occurred before David Middleton ever reached Reno. Because of this, I knew I could not accurately write this book while still being an active member of the law enforcement community. I began writing this book on October 1, 2006—the day I retired from a twenty-five-year law enforcement career with the Reno, NV. Police Department.

When the book was first released, I received negative pushback from some people involved in law enforcement because some agencies appeared to be possibly inept or maybe even not on the straight-and-narrow path in terms of investigating crimes. This negative pushback involved some members of my own agency who were involved in the Middleton investigation. Those who do not believe in the "Blue Wall of Silence" have never worn a badge. Fortunately, those who practice this form of selective silence are the minority in our noble profession.

Some law enforcement officials from Colorado questioned the validity of some of the information in the original book. This was done in print in local newspapers, but to this date, I have not received personal contact from any of these persons, despite my requests for contact. This includes the Detective Lieutenant from the Montrose Police Department in charge of the Buffy Rice-Donohue murder investigation and the District Attorney, who refused to prosecute the case against David Middleton for murdering her. The Lieutenant subsequently ended up being the department's Chief of Police, and the District Attorney ended up being an Assistant United States Attorney. My initial requests for contact regarding any information contained in this book will always stand, and any information deemed to be non-factual will be corrected or retracted if proof of inaccuracy is provided to me. To this date, no facts to contradict any information in this book have been presented to me.

Research for this book was done by sifting through the voluminous collection of police reports and legal documents available as public records in the states of Nevada, Colorado, and Florida. Countless hours of interviews with persons involved in this case were also used to authenticate facts contained in the documentation. Names marked with an asterisk are pseudonyms used to protect confidentiality. In all other instances, real names are used either with permission or as a matter of public record.

David Middleton was removed from society due to the diligent work of the men and women from the Reno and Sparks Nevada Police Departments, the Washoe County Sherriff's Office, and the Washoe County District Attorney's Office. These agencies were very helpful in providing the information used to put this story together. The San Miguel County Colorado Sheriff's office was also particularly helpful with research on the Colorado aspects of this case. Sheriff Bill Masters, the longest serving Sheriff in the United States with 45 years of service, took the time to personally talk to me by phone and provide me documentation of the excellent investigation his agency did to tie David Middleton to the murder of Buffy Rice-Donohue. I am grateful for that. Other agencies discussed in this book were not as forthcoming with assistance on this project, and I will let the reader formulate their own opinion for their reasons.

Some of the photos contained in this book are graphic in nature but are necessary to show the killer's degree of dementedness. Crimes such as those described on these pages shock the conscience of a normal person, so photographic evidence of them should be expected to do the same.

My original book was titled *"Beware of the Cable Guy: From Cop to Serial Killer."* To avoid confusion with this updated edition of this story, the new book is titled *"From Cop to Serial Killer."* When the first book was released in 2009, David Middleton was the first known serial killer to have served as a law enforcement officer. Since then, six others have been identified, but the David Middleton crimes and murders remain unique. A legal system that was designed to protect the public from monsters like David Middleton broke down on multiple occasions in multiple jurisdictions and allowed him to continue to be the *beast.* The main premise of this story is how that happened, how we can never let that happen again, and how we protect the inner circle of our lives. Always respectfully question authority when things just don't look right.

Enjoy *"From Cop to Serial Killer"...*

Contents

Chapter 1:
A Small World

People often say it is a small world when paths cross, or there is familiarity with certain circumstances. It is not a small world. It is actually a very big world, but it is comprised of small microcosms that make up the larger part of the whole. Sometimes, these smaller parts wind tightly together, similar to a ball of yarn, and each smaller part can have a positive or negative effect on the larger scheme of the whole. The small piece of yarn at the center of the ball has a direct effect on all outer layers that eventually form the larger ball.

Newton's first law of physics states in part: "An object will remain at rest or in uniform motion in a straight line unless acted upon by an external force." His third law of physics states in part: "Forces result from interactions, and for every action, there is an equal and opposite reaction."[1] David Middleton was the external force that ended and decimated lives in multiple states throughout the U.S. and continues to do so today. It was a microcosmic event that occurred in Boston in 1980 that began the chain of events that would lead to the murderous crime spree eventually committed by the "Cable Guy."

David Middleton was a police cadet for the Boston Police Department, earning $150 dollars a week as a uniformed, non-sworn employee. The cadet program was for persons eighteen and above who were interested in becoming sworn police officers with the department. Cadets received on-the-job training that could assist them in the eventual police testing program. It was also a way for the department to observe performance prior to the cadet taking the police exam.

Middleton was considered to be on the fast track to a full-time position with the Department. His father had been a university Police Officer in Boston, and Middleton planned to settle down in the area while having a career with the Boston Police Department. Those who knew him in the cadet program thought highly of him and figured his appointment to the department to be a sure thing.

---

[1] Newton's Laws of Motion, Harrison Onah, Sciencebod Publishing, 2014

In 1980, the first catalyst of force to move Middleton out of this career path occurred. The City of Boston went into a budget crisis, and there was a major layoff in the police department. No hiring would be done until all laid-off police officers were hired back into the department, and it appeared that would take several years. At the same time, the Miami Police Department was on a nationwide recruiting campaign for police officers due to increased crime and area growth related to the Cuban Mariel Boatlift influx of aliens to the area. The Miami Police Department sent recruiting material to police departments throughout the U.S., and one of these recruiting fliers ended up in the cadet room at the Boston Police Department. With little hope of getting hired on as a police officer in Boston, Middleton and his partner in the cadet program, Frank Armstrong, headed to Miami to test for the department.[2]

Middleton and Armstrong were both subsequently offered jobs with the Miami Police Department, but then the next microcosmic event that contributed to putting Middleton's criminal future in motion occurred. A political scandal rocked Boston, and a second set of budget books was located. There were no actual budget crises, so all police officers who were laid off were reinstated, and normal hiring began again. Frank Armstrong returned to Boston and did not take the position with the Miami Police Department. The Boston Police Department hired him, and when contacted for information related to this book in 2008, Frank was a Captain with twenty-six years of service under his belt.

Middleton remained in Florida and took a position with the Miami Police Department. It seems he got a taste of the warm weather, the fast-paced Miami nightlife, and some of the even faster-paced women who frequented the clubs. He preferred the new "good life" to that of Boston, but he did not return even though he was offered the position with the Boston Police Department. Middleton was well-liked in the Miami Police Department. He earned several commendations in his first two years. He was given a detective position in the department's Warrant Service Division, responsible for arresting persons with warrants and absconders from justice.

Middleton's former partner in the Warrant's Service Division, Paul Kuiper, described Middleton as a womanizer and a drinker with a pattern

---

[2] Frank Armstrong contributed to this story and his name is used with permission.

of erratic, sexually deviant behavior that continued in a downward spiral.[3] Ironically, Paul Kuiper was still in the unit when detectives were sent to bring Middleton back to Miami on a fugitive from justice warrant a few short years after they originally became partners. The arrest was for another microcosmic event in the big scheme of things, but an enormously devastating event in the life of a sixteen-year-old female referred to in court documents as A.C.[4]

Middleton was a detective and worked his primary assignments in plain clothes. At times, detectives work overtime assignments and wear uniforms. It seems Middleton had a habit of putting on his uniform and going out at night, telling his wife he was working overtime. In actuality, he would check out his unmarked police car and cruise the streets looking for prostitutes. When he found one, he would offer a deal to not arrest the prostitute in return for her providing sex acts for him.

Middleton was engaged in such activities on Saturday, September 29, 1989, when he came upon a young girl walking the streets in the area of the downtown courthouse building. Middleton was off-duty but in uniform and driving his unmarked police car. He made his standard offer to exchange a get-out-of-jail-free card for sex acts, but this time, the girl turned out not to be a prostitute. She was a sixteen-year-old whose only crime was being out past curfew. Instead of taking her home or calling her parents, Middleton handcuffed her, drove her to a dark field, and sexually assaulted her in the backseat of his police car. This crime will be further referenced later in this book. Still, it subsequently ended up being the end of Middleton's police career, the reason for his arrest and imprisonment, and the external force that caused Middleton to change directions and move further into his criminal career.

Middleton's sixteen-year-old victim testified in court, and he subsequently went to prison for his crimes. For every action, there is an equal and opposite reaction. The victim's actions of testifying put Middleton in prison and ended his "good life" as he knew it. His reaction to this action was to never again allow a victim to live to testify. His Florida rape victim suffers from a psychological disease called "survivor's guilt," and she will carry it with her forever. She blames herself for every victim

---

[3] Paul Kuiper was consulted for this book and verified information contained in this book that had been source referenced though news articles and police reports. His name is used with his permission.

[4] A.C. was identified and interviewed for this book. She gave permission for her name to be used, but to respect her privacy, a pseudonym will be used throughout this book.

Middleton killed after he got out of jail because, in her mind, she was the force that caused him to move in this new direction.

Many more microcosmic events occurred related to Middleton's Florida arrest that contributed to the whole of the more significant events that led him to kill in Colorado, Nevada, and possibly other unknown places along the way. An attempt to avoid bad publicity in the Miami case and a trial judge, who himself was arrested on bribery charges the morning Middleton was to be sentenced on his kidnap and sexual assault charges, contributed to him receiving a much lighter prison sentence than he should have.

He did three years and was released. Had the Florida case been properly prosecuted in 1990, Middleton would have gotten at least ten years in prison and would not have made it to Montrose, CO. to kill in 1993, or Reno, NV. to kill his victims there in 1995. He would have still been in prison in Florida, and how different would life have been today for his victims and their families.

It's a big world, but small things can change it, and they do...

Chapter 2:
Dumpster Divers

The radio call sending Reno Police Officer Pat Dreelan to check a report of a dead body found in a dumpster didn't evoke much of a reaction from him when he received it at 9:50 P.M. on Saturday, February 11, 1995. Radio calls rarely seemed to be what they actually were when initial information was given. The last time he'd checked a supposed body in a dumpster, it turned out to be the remains of a dead deer a poaching hunter had disposed of. He hoped this call was bogus because standing in the cold at a crime scene wasn't quite as appealing as the warm restaurant he was headed to for his dinner break when the call came out.

The information given to Officer Dreelan was vague. The witness who phoned it in said he was told by a transient leaving the area to call the police because he discovered a body wrapped in a sleeping bag inside an apartment complex dumpster while searching for discarded aluminum cans. The apartment complex in the southeast section of Reno was in a predominantly Hispanic area, and a gang calling themselves CVC claimed it as their territory. Since the possibility of a gang-related crime existed, Officer Dreelan's awareness was heightened as he pulled into the area.

The Southwest Village Apartments were located at 2450 Lymberry Street in Reno, Nevada. This was an older section of the city, and the sprawling apartment complex had become quite rundown over the years. The property managers tried their best to spruce things up, but every time they painted a wall or fence, it would be covered by gang graffiti the next day.

Officer Dreelan located the dumpster in question in the southeast parking lot of the complex. The sector sergeant was already on the scene talking to a witness when Officer Dreelan parked his black and white next to the rusting hulk of a Chevy Impala propped up on cinder blocks. The witness lived in the apartments and had been taking his trash to the dumpster when he encountered the harried homeless person who told him about the dead body. The transient left before the police arrived, but he had told the apartment dweller the sight of the body scared him so badly that he wasn't even going back in to retrieve the full pack of cigarettes he dropped while trying to climb out of the dumpster.

The large yellow dumpster was about six feet in height and covered in blue spray-painted graffiti like everything else in the area. The witness who waited for the police didn't actually see the body, so the inside of the dumpster still had to be checked. Officer Dreelan climbed up the metal ladder attached to the side of the dumpster and peered inside. He could see a brown sleeping bag wrapped in heavy yellow plastic bound in rope lying on top of the trash on the opposite end of the dumpster. Even when he illuminated it with his flashlight, he couldn't tell if it was a body or not.

Someone needed to actually get inside the dumpster and check for a body in the sleeping bag. Officer Dreelan was a weightlifter, and hoisting his large frame encumbered by an additional forty pounds of police gear over the side of the dumpster would be no easy feat. Since rank does carry some privileges, there was no discussion about which officer would be going in.

When relating this story ten years later, Officer Dreelan still remembers it like it was yesterday. "It was Monday, so my uniform just came out of the cleaners that day. Nobody wants to jump into a dumpster in the first place, but doing it in your Monday uniform really sucks. It was darker than hell inside that dumpster, but I couldn't use my flashlight when I was jumping in because I needed both hands to boost myself over the side. The dumpster was half full, and I slipped when I landed inside on top of all that garbage. I came down on top of somebody's half-eaten Big Mac and got ketchup all over my pants.

I was crawling through that dumpster on my hands and knees, holding my mini-flashlight in my mouth so I could see where I was going. I tried to remember all the stuff from the academy about crime scene preservation, but all I could think about was a rat the size of Chuck E. Cheese jumping out of the trash at me. That dumpster was only about six feet across, but it seemed like a mile because I had to move so slowly. I kept sinking in the garbage and didn't even want to think about what was getting all over me.

When I finally got to the sleeping bag, the zipper on it was opened a little bit. I shined my light inside and saw what looked like pink skin, but I couldn't tell if it was a body or not. I opened the bag a little further to get a better look, and when I did, I saw a pair of little pink hands tied together with rope. I shined my light up a little higher, and that's when I saw this big friggin dead eye staring back at me. Right then, I didn't care about garbage or Chuck the rat anymore. I just wanted to get the hell out of that dumpster. I reached inside the sleeping bag and grabbed one of the exposed wrists to check for a pulse, but the body was colder than the chills running down my spine. Kneeling there in the dark with mystery meat and ketchup sinking through my pants, holding hands with a corpse, is still the freakiest thing I've ever had to do. All I could think about was taking the next sergeant's test so I'd be the one on the outside of the dumpster from now on."

Pat Dreelan was visibly shaken when he crawled out of that dumpster and reported what he saw to his sergeant. He forgot about his ruined Monday uniform and even tuned out the jokes the other cops made about him smelling like the alley behind a Chinese restaurant. He busied himself by stringing crime scene tape and wanted nothing more than to finish his shift and try to drown out the experience with some cold ones.

One of the transients watching the scene gave Officer Dreelan some advice that evening. He said never to go into the *big* dumpsters the night before trash pick-up because even aluminum cans weren't worth the risk of drowning in a five-foot pile of trash. That tidbit of dumpster-diver wisdom would be passed on several times before the night was over.

Chapter 3:
Wheel Of Fortune

The call-out rotation for detectives is known as "the wheel" in police jargon. Detectives Dave Jenkins and John Douglas from the department's Major Crime Unit were at the top of the wheel on the night the body was found in the dumpster, and that was the first stroke of luck in the investigation.

As in most modern departments, the detective position in the Reno Police Department was temporary. Officers were generally assigned to a detective slot for a period of four years and then rotated back to uniform patrol. This was done to provide as many officers as possible with investigative training and eventually filter that experience back to the street where it could do the most good.

The elite Major Crime Unit was the exception to this process. Detectives assigned there remained as long as they wanted—or until they pissed off the wrong person, as some insiders said. The lead investigators on anything but a "smoking gun" homicide came from the Major Crime Unit, and detectives from other units would assist with ancillary investigative tasks. Jenkins and Douglas had both been around the block a couple of times, and they swam in the deep end of the pool of experience that existed in the Major Crime Unit.

Jenkins was the most seasoned investigator in the department, and there was nobody better to have on a who-done-it homicide. Douglas had a quick-witted sense of humor and an easy style of talking to people that made them want to cooperate with the law even if they were guilty. Their investigative skills complimented each other—right down to their nicknames. Jenkins was known as D.J., and Douglas was known as J.D. However, since Jenkins was very white and Douglas was very black, and cops sometimes have *very* sick senses of humor, they were better known in the Detective Division as Ebony and Ivory.

Jenkins received the homicide notification at 10:10 P.M. on Saturday, February 11, 1995, twenty minutes after the original radio dispatch call. Like most nights, he was at home with his wife and two children when he got the call. Being a devoted family man, Jenkins was the type of detective his boss never had to worry about chasing down when he needed him. He was an eighteen-year veteran cop the night of the murder, and his wife,

Terri, had been with him since the day he graduated from the academy. She was a veteran cop-wife, so even though she hated the late-night call-outs, she knew there was nobody better responding to a murder than her husband.

Douglas was also at home when he received the phone call describing the homicide scene, but his evening was not quite as relaxing as his partner's. He was in the midst of a quiet romantic soirée with his soon-to-be next wife, and the call came at a particularly inconvenient time. After hanging up the phone and muttering a few expletives, he got out of bed and got dressed.

When his fiancée asked him why he was dressing in old work clothes instead of a suit like he normally would wear to a crime scene, he answered her in his usual stand-up comedic style, "The man just told me there is a dead woman's body inside of a dumpster. I can't even get *live* women to do what I want, so I seriously doubt this one is gonna come out and talk to me if I tell her to."

Jenkins and Douglas arrived at the crime scene almost simultaneously, twenty minutes after the notification. They parked their department-issued cars well away from the yellow crime scene tape, hung their gold badges around their necks, and headed toward the scene together. The parking lot was full of parked cars, and a crowd of onlookers had already begun to gather. Jenkins made a mental note that the first thing he would need to do was expand the crime scene so the plates on all cars could be run for owner information before they were allowed to be moved. This would be just one of many mundane tasks that needed to be done, and he hoped his boss had called in enough help.

Jenkins believed a homicide investigator should always dress the part regardless of the circumstances. Tonight, he wore a dark woolen overcoat over a grey suit, a crisp white shirt, and a blue tie. Were it not for the fact his neatly cut brown hair was matted down in the back, one might have thought he had just left his office instead of his warm bed. At thirty-eight years old, Jenkins still had the short, powerful frame of a powerlifter, but eighteen years in police work—most of them spent as a "corpse cop"— was beginning to take its toll on him. Too many nights spent at crime scenes and too much time spent behind a desk doing follow-up investigations were starting to make him a little soft around the edges. The yellow pallor of his skin and dark circles under his eyes attested to the fact that on those nights, he was not pulled from his bed for a homicide call out; perhaps ghosts from past investigations came to visit him.

A stark contrast to Jenkins, Douglas was dressed in faded blue jeans, scuffed Nike high-tops, a black hooded sweatshirt, and an old olive-drab Air Force field jacket. He looked younger than his forty years and still moved with an athletic grace that made him look like he'd be more at home on the blacktop basketball court across the street than involved in a homicide investigation. He was a Master Sergeant with the Nevada Air National Guard and looked well-rested since he just returned from fulfilling his two-week yearly obligation. His smooth, dark skin was tanned to an even darker shade, attesting to the fact he'd spent the time in a much more exotic climate than Reno. His military buzz cut had already begun growing back to the short afro he normally wore, and the hint of grey beginning to show in his jet-black hair was the only thing that hinted at his age.

The local news stations had picked up the call on their scanners, and the sector sergeant was busy giving an initial sound bite to a couple of reporters on the outskirts of the crime scene. Officer Dreelan walked over to the detectives and gave them the initial briefing on what he found inside the dumpster. When he told them about the warning the transient gave him about dumpster diving the night before trash pick-up, both detectives exchanged knowing glances and headed toward the twenty-cubic-foot yellow metal casket.

Since Officer Dreelan already determined the victim was deceased, there was no need for them to enter the dumpster until the proper resources arrived. They took turns climbing the metal ladder and illuminating the sleeping bag-entombed body with the beams of their flashlights. After seeing enough, they walked to a quiet corner of the lot to compare initial impressions.

Jenkins was the more scholarly of the team and pulled a pen and notebook out of his coat pocket to record their observations. Douglas pulled a pack of gum out of his and put three sticks into his mouth, hoping to cover up any trace of odor from the bottle of merlot he had shared with his fiancée over dinner.

The first thing they both noted was there was very little garbage on top of the body, meaning it had been placed into the dumpster fairly recently. They also agreed the fact that the dumpster was due to be emptied in the morning was probably not a coincidence. There are no coincidences in police work—especially in homicide. Whoever put the body in the dumpster more than likely knew that if it wasn't discovered before morning, it would be buried in a landfill forever. They filed that piece of information away in hopes it would help them cull a future list of suspects.

After completing a list of things that needed to be done, they headed back to the group of officers standing at the edge of the crime scene, waiting for their assignments. The entire apartment complex would have to be canvassed, and they'd use the uniformed cops for that. Every scrap of garbage in and around the dumpster would also have to be checked, but the most important pieces of evidence would be on top of or directly underneath the body. They were anxious to get into the dumpster to see exactly what they had, but unfortunately, they had to wait for the arrival of the C.S.I. techs before that could be done. The first twenty-four hours of any homicide investigation were the most important, and the clock was ticking.

During the downtime, Jenkins headed off to interview the reporting person while Douglas remained at the crime scene to direct the activity. The reporting party was a Mr. James Jansen*, who lived in the apartment complex. He was a thirty-eight-year-old single father who lived in an apartment with his two sons, ages ten and twelve. Jansen's statement that he left the apartment only long enough to take out the trash was confirmed by both of his sons. He was visibly shaken and Jenkins viewed his statement as credible.

The transient who had told Jansen about the body was no longer on the scene, so he immediately became a person of interest. Jenkins put out an A.P.B. for the man based on the description given to him by Jansen, but unfortunately, a dirty-looking homeless white male in his mid-twenties wearing a tattered coat fit the description of a large percentage of Reno's population, so he held little hope of finding him.

The C.S.I. truck was pulling into the lot, and the temperature steadily dropped when Jenkins got back to the dumpster. He hoped they would find some clues when they removed the body from the dumpster, but the sinking feeling he had in his stomach led him to believe they were in for a long night.

Chapter 4:
Death Whispers

It was certainly not a corpse cop who coined the phrase "dead men tell no tales." Any experienced homicide detective knows the evidence recovered from a dead body can be the most significant gathered in the case. That is why the more difficult murders to solve and prosecute are those where the body is never found.

When it came time for someone to crawl back inside the filthy dumpster and perform the initial examination of the body, there was no question who it would be. Dave Jenkins was a highly religious man who believed in God—not spirits or witchcraft. He also believed he needed to spend time alone with the body of a murder victim in order to let his initial impressions sink in. It was almost like the victim was whispering to him from beyond, and if there were any distractions, he might miss a clue that could shape the entire investigation.

Deputy Chuck Lowe from the Forensic Division of the Washoe County Sheriff's Office responded to the scene. After he had taken photographs of the outside of the dumpster and the surrounding area, it was time for Jenkins to go inside and check the body. He removed his overcoat and suit jacket and then donned a white Tyvek jumpsuit, blue paper booties, and white latex gloves. Stopping outside the dumpster, he spoke into a mini-cassette recorder in his shirt pocket to record his initial observations.

The large yellow dumpster measured twenty cubic yards, and the sides were approximately six feet tall. Jenkins carefully read each letter from the graffiti painted on the dumpster into the recorder so the transcriber would have the proper spelling. He then climbed the metal rungs of the ladder and paused at the top before going over the side.

The inside of the dumpster was now illuminated by the bright Klieg lights hooked up to the generator on the crime scene truck, so Jenkins could not use his flashlight. He could see the trail through the garbage used by Officer Dreelan to get to the body and decided to try and stay as close as possible to that route in order to avoid unnecessary disturbance to the scene. Since both of his hands were free, Jenkins lowered himself into the dumpster slowly and landed on top of the piles of garbage without the messy impact experienced by Officer Dreelan.

Once inside the dumpster, Jenkins slowly crawled toward the body, stopping twice to record names and addresses from discarded mail on top of the trash heap. In a homicide investigation, one never knew when a scrap of information might be important. Jenkins stopped when he got to the body and knelt in silence on top of the garbage next to it. Douglas and Deputy Lowe watched from above, standing on a pair of ladders they had removed from the crime scene truck and set up at the end of the dumpster closest to the body. They were ready to jump in and assist Jenkins if requested, but they quietly watched as the detective performed the ritual they'd witnessed many times before.

Jenkins spoke briefly in hushed tones into his recorder and then quietly knelt motionless next to the body. After a few minutes, he slowly nodded and began moving the trash from on top of the body while Deputy Lowe took photographs of his perch above. The dumpster was about one-third filled, but only a cardboard box and a few small plastic bags of household trash were on top of the sleeping bag. Once they were moved, Jenkins was able to get his first clear view of the body contained inside.

The sleeping bag had been wrapped inside of a large semi-transparent yellow plastic bag. This plastic outer covering had been partially pulled away to expose the top part of the sleeping bag, which was unzipped just enough to show a portion of the victim's body. Jenkins surmised the transient who initially found the body had begun removing the plastic covering in order to see what treasures awaited him inside. White-colored rope, approximately one-half inch in diameter, was tied around the outside of the yellow plastic bag and had been fashioned into a makeshift handle. Jenkins carefully pulled the rope and outer plastic away enough to allow him to better see the inside of the sleeping bag.

A small portion of the right side of the victim's torso, as well as one eye, could be seen through the partially-opened zipper. Jenkins slowly unzipped the sleeping bag further, all the time speaking into his recorder while he worked. The victim's head, neck, and shoulders were partially covered by a dark green kitchen-type plastic bag that had apparently been placed over her head, but enough of the face was showing for Jenkins to be able to tell he was dealing with a white female adult.

Bright red discoloration could be seen on the victim's right side, which, to the untrained eye, might appear as bruising. It was actually liver mortis, also referred to as lividity, caused by gravity pulling blood to the lowest parts of the body after death. In and of itself, this is not much use in determining the time of death, but Jenkins knew he could use it in conjunction with other clues being whispered to him to provide valuable information.

He reached in with a gloved finger and pushed hard against a patch of the victim's reddened skin. If the liver mortis showed a change in color, referred to as *blanching*, it would mean the victim had been dead for less than eight hours. There was no blanching, so he knew the liver mortis was *fixed* and the victim had been dead for at least eight hours or longer. The victim was lying on her left side, but the liver mortis was on her right. The fact the blood had not drained to the victim's left side told Jenkins she had been positioned on her right side for at least twelve hours after death before being moved to the dumpster. After that amount of time, the blood remains where it is, regardless of how often a body is moved.

Jenkins grabbed the exposed fingers of the victim's right hand and checked for rigor mortis, another phenomenon that occurs after death caused by the buildup of lactic acid in the musculature of the decedent. It results in stiffening of the body and sets in within six hours of death. What most people don't realize is rigor mortis only lasts twenty-four to thirty-six hours from its onset. After that, the muscles begin to degenerate, and the rigor mortis completely disappears.

Using the exposed portion of his wrist above the rubber glove, Jenkins felt the victim's skin. It was cold to the touch, but all that told him was the body hadn't been indoors recently. Body temperature drops about three degrees per hour after death, but the cold winter air and the even colder temperature inside the steel dumpster would accelerate that process.

The fact there was fixed liver mortis in the victim told him rigor mortis had already come and gone. That information, taken in conjunction with the fact there was not yet any visible decomposition in the victim, put his educated guess at the time of death to be in the area of forty-eight hours. A more precise time of death would be established by the coroner during the autopsy, but the victim had given Jenkins a ballpark figure to work with.

The last thing Jenkins did was shine his flashlight inside the sleeping bag in order to get a good look at the body, but he saw nothing to indicate an obvious cause of death. The victim was naked, with the exception of a sleeveless black shirt pulled up around her neck and a pair of dark blue socks. The same white rope wrapped around the outside of the sleeping bag had been used to bind the victim. Her hands were tied tightly in front

14

of her, and the rope continued between her legs. It was then wrapped around her ankles, and the loose end was looped around her neck and cinched tightly so that her feet and legs could be pulled behind her. The victim had ended her life the same way it began—naked and in the fetal position. But the look of terror frozen on her face in death attested to the fact something had gone horribly wrong upon her exit into the afterlife.

Chapter 5:
Kathy

It was just after midnight when the investigator from the Coroner's office arrived on the scene. By that time, the sergeant and an additional detective team from the Major Crimes Unit were there to assist. They decided to take the entire body, wrapped just as it was found inside the dumpster, and zip it into a black plastic body bag. This way, they could move it to the controlled environment of the Coroner's examining room without losing any trace evidence.

After several attempts and a few choice words, Jenkins and Douglas were able to lift the body bag out of the dumpster and hand it to the other two detectives standing at the top of the ladder. The victim later weighed one hundred thirty pounds, but lifting *dead weight* over their heads while standing in two feet of loose garbage was no easy job. Both detectives were exhausted and filthy when they climbed out of the dumpster, but they still had work to do.

Since Jenkins and Douglas were the lead detectives on the case, they would follow the body to the Coroner's office and try to get an identity. One of the other detectives would supervise the removal of the dumpster to a secured evidence yard so it could be searched properly in the morning. This job was assigned to Detective Ed Dixon, also known as "Evidence Eddie." He wasn't the sharpest investigator in the unit, but there was no job he wouldn't do and no scrap of evidence that would get by him in an investigation. Dixon's partner would remain on the scene to supervise the area canvass, and a third two-man team would meet Jenkins and Douglas at the Coroner's office to get their assignments.

It was now two in the morning, but one thing a homicide detective cares nothing about is waking people up in the middle of the night. Jenkins called Detective Wood at home and learned the name of the missing person from the case he was working on. It was Katherine Powell, a forty-five-year-old elementary school teacher who had been missing for eight days.

The adrenal buzz from the possible break in the case helped them overcome the fatigue Jenkins and Douglas were starting to feel. They drove the few short blocks to the main police station where the Detective Division was housed and retrieved the missing person case from Detective Wood's desk. Stapled to the inside flap of the file was a photo of Kathy

Powell taken in much happier surroundings than the Polaroid photos Jenkins had just taken of her. Although official identification would have to wait until morning, both detectives were certain the body from the dumpster and the missing school teacher were one and the same.

Looking through the file, they learned Ms. Powell had last been seen at 3:00 P.M. on Friday, February 3, 1995, when she was leaving her teaching job at Sun Valley Elementary School north of Reno. She was not reported missing until the following Monday when she didn't show up for work, which the report said was out of character for her. The school itself was in the jurisdiction of the Washoe County Sheriff's Office, but Reno P.D. got the call since Powell lived in the city.

Once the body was at the Coroner's office, Jenkins pulled back the plastic bag covering the victim's head so he could take Polaroid photographs of her face for identification purposes. The body itself would not be removed from the sleeping bag until a morning autopsy. One of the robbery homicide detectives who responded to the Coroner's office to assist with the investigation walked in while Jenkins was taking photographs. He immediately noted a similarity between this victim and a photograph he had seen earlier in the day while reading a missing person case assigned to another detective. He could not recall the name of the missing person, but he knew Detective Dave Wood had the case.

Officers got no answer at Powell's northeast Reno apartment when they checked it after the initial report. The doors were locked from the inside, but based on the circumstances, they forced entry into the apartment to check for her. She was not inside, and there were no obvious signs of a struggle, but a friend was able to tell police some items were missing from the apartment. Among these were a laptop computer, a fax machine, and a computer printer. The missing items and the no-call-no-show for work raised the investigating officer's suspicions enough to have Powell listed as a missing person.

This was the next stroke of fortune in the investigation because the quick victim identification would keep the fledgling homicide investigation moving forward. Douglas poured two cups of oily-looking black coffee from the coffeemaker in the squad room and brought them back to the desk where Jenkins was busy making a to-do list. The report listed Powell as divorced and living alone in the apartment. A former spouse is always a suspect in a murder investigation until proven otherwise, so one of the first things they needed to do was interview Kathy

Powell's ex-husband and get a feel for his involvement. Jenkins and Douglas would take that interview themselves.

Powell's apartment would also need to be thoroughly searched, but since there was no longer an exigency, they would need a search warrant before going back inside. They decided to wait until morning instead of waking up a judge at this late hour to sign the search warrant, so Douglas called Detective Dixon and asked him to go by the apartment and seal it until they obtained the search warrant. Dixon said not only would he do that, but he'd arrange for a patrol car to be stationed out front and personally obtain and execute the search warrant first thing in the morning. Evidence Eddie was on the job.

Powell's apartment complex would have to be canvassed, all of her co-workers and friends would need to be interviewed, and the person who reported her missing in the first place would have to be re-interviewed now that it was a homicide investigation. There is a fine line between people thinking of themselves as a witness or a suspect; waking someone up at 2:30 in the morning to talk could make them think they were on the wrong side of that line. The two detectives were convinced that whatever happened to Kathy Powell occurred at least two days ago, so waiting until the morning in order to get better cooperation from witnesses wouldn't hinder the investigation.

Jenkins called his boss, who was still out at the original crime scene and filled him in on the latest details. Reno didn't have the backlog of dead bodies that plague some larger cities, so the Coroner's Office would give this case priority and call someone into work on Sunday to perform the autopsy. It was scheduled for 9:30 the next morning, so Jenkins suggested everyone assigned to the case head home for a couple of hours of sleep and meet back at the office at 8:00 A.M. They were on a roll, but a little sleep and some clean clothes would be a good start to what would assuredly be a long day.

Chapter 6:
Beginnings

The two hours of sleep Jenkins got after returning home from the station actually consisted of a series of several ten-minute naps. Thoughts of the ensuing investigation were churning in his head, and any semblance of a restful night's sleep was impossible. By 7:00 A.M., he was headed out of his door, showered and shaved, wearing a clean black suit and carrying a travel mug containing his third cup of coffee of that morning.

Another Sunday family day had been interrupted, but at least he'd had time to have breakfast with his wife and kids before leaving. His daughter, Ali, was eleven, and his son, Adam, was nine. It seemed like yesterday they were both babies, and sometimes he thought family time for homicide investigators should be measured in dog years. His family was his support system, and they understood the importance of his job. Somebody needed to speak for the dead, and that's what he hoped to do today.

Jenkins started a pot of coffee when he arrived at the Detective Division and then sat down at his desk to go over the original missing person report taken on Kathy Powell. There were five detectives and one sergeant in the Major Crime Unit. Each man had a standard gunmetal-gray desk in the small cubicle that separated the unit from the other detectives in the division. The cubicle itself was made of gray six-foot tall portable partitions placed next to each other to form a square. It did little to keep out noise or provide privacy, so Jenkins was thankful for the quiet time the early hour and off-day afforded him as he started reading the report.

Officer Bob Bennett initially responded to the missing person's call and did an excellent job of writing a detailed report of his preliminary investigation. Powell was a third-grade school teacher and left work at 3:15 in the afternoon on Friday, February 3, 1995. Not only did she fail to show up for work the following Monday morning, she did not call and arrange to have a substitute teacher take her place. Powell was described as a dependable and caring teacher who would drag herself out of a sickbed rather than leave her students without a teacher. It was this uncharacteristic behavior that caused the school principal to be concerned enough to call the police.

Powell's townhouse apartment was located at 3484 Terrace Knolls Court, and Officer Bennett was met there by the school janitor at 10:30 in the morning on Monday, February 6, 1995. The janitor, Stephen Mizzen, said he was not only a co-worker of Ms. Powell's but also a friend of hers. He said he had been an invited guest in Powell's home on prior occasions and that he knew her well enough to be certain she would never miss work under these conditions unless something was wrong.

The only entrances leading into the apartment were the front door and the overhead garage door. Both were locked, but Officer Bennett could see inside the apartment through a partially opened curtain on the front window. There did not appear to be any sign of a struggle, and two rolled-up newspapers were on the kitchen counter. Additionally, there were two newspapers delivered that morning still in the driveway, as well as mail in the mailbox and a note from T.C.I. Cable Company on the door. The note indicated a repairman had been there at 1:30, but there was no date. Officer Bennett surmised this would have been 1:30 the previous Friday since cable company repairmen routinely don't work on weekends.

After knocking on the door several times, Officer Bennett contacted his sergeant and requested permission to force entry into the apartment to check for Powell. Powell drove a small pickup truck, which was not in the driveway. Since her car was not there, the sergeant denied the request for forced entry and told Officer Bennett to have Mizzen go to the police station to make a missing person report if Powell did not show up for work by the next morning.

Jenkins had been around long enough to be able to read between the lines in a police report, but Officer Bennett was obviously not happy with the sergeant's response. In his report, he wrote that he told his sergeant he could not be sure Powell's car was not there because he could not see into the garage. The sergeant again denied the request for forced entry, but fortunately, Bennett took good notes on his initial response and even performed a brief canvass of the neighboring apartments.

Jenkins sipped coffee and silently wondered if Kathy Powell had still been alive during this encounter and if so, would things have turned out differently for her if Officer Bennett had been allowed to listen to his cop instincts. Forced entry into the apartment would entail the sergeant writing a report to detail the event. He despised sloppy police work and hoped it was more than avoidance of paperwork that influenced the sergeant's decision.

Reading on, Jenkins saw that Officer Bennett contacted three of Kathy Powell's neighbors before leaving the apartment complex. None of them knew her well, nor did they remember seeing her over the weekend. One of the neighbors did recall seeing an older model car parked in front of Powell's apartment early Saturday morning, but she did not remember anything about it except that it was a *beater*.

The next morning, Tuesday, February 7, 1995, the police were summoned again when Powell did not show up for school. Officer Bennett responded to the school and took the missing person report from the school principal. The school nurse, Grace Johns, was a friend of Powell's and accompanied Officer Bennett back to Powell's apartment. The apartment looked the same as it had the day before, with the exception of another newspaper in the driveway and more mail in the mailbox.

Officer Bennett's sergeant showed up at the apartment, and this time they *did* force entry in order to get inside. Ms. Powell was not there, and there were no obvious signs of foul play. Her pickup truck *was* located inside the closed garage. Ms. Johns had been to the apartment several times before and looked around to see if there was anything amiss. It was she who noticed the laptop, printer, and combination fax/answering machine were missing. In addition, Powell's backpack-style purse was on her desk in her bedroom. Ms. Johns said Powell never went anywhere without it and that she rarely accepted rides from anyone. The fact that her car and purse were there, but she wasn't, was even more of a cause for concern than her absence from work.

Ms. Johns said she was aware Powell had suffered bouts of depression in the past, most recently over her deteriorating relationship with a boyfriend who had moved to Pittsburg, Pennsylvania. She said she knew Powell had a prescription for lithium but did not think she was currently taking the drug and did not consider her to be suicidal. She based that opinion on her personal *and* professional knowledge of Powell.

Officer Bennett found a note next to the two rolled-up newspapers on the kitchen counter. The note read, "Kathy, I came by to get the pets but you weren't here. I let myself in and locked up behind me. Thanks for watching them and call me when you get home."

The note was dated Sunday, February 5, 1995, and signed by a man named Jerry Brown. Ms. Johns said she knew Brown was a friend of Powell's, and she had been looking after his pets for him while he was out of town. Officer Bennett found Powell's phone book in her purse, which contained both Brown's home and work numbers. Using his cell phone to avoid disturbing any potential evidence in the apartment, he located Brown at his office.

The last page of the report said Brown stated he had returned from a two-week business trip in Arizona on Sunday, February 5th, and went straight to Powell's apartment from the airport to pick up his pets. Powell had been caring for his dog and ferret for him while he was away, and she had informed him she would be home grading papers on Sunday upon his return. He said he was surprised upon arriving at Powell's apartment and finding her not there, but used a key she had given him to retrieve his pets. He found his dog in the garage, and judging from the mess, it didn't look like he'd been let outside for a while. Powell had mentioned she had plans to go skiing the day before, so he assumed she must have spent the night away from home.

The follow-up reports from Detective Wood were next in the file. He was assigned the case in the late afternoon of Tuesday, February 7th. The first thing he did was re-interview Jerry Brown since he had been inside the apartment over the weekend. Brown showed Detective Wood his airline ticket receipt, proving he had returned to Reno from Phoenix at 5:50 P.M. on Sunday, February 5th. He explained that upon arriving at Powell's apartment, he found newspapers from Saturday and Sunday in the driveway. He picked them up and brought them inside. That accounted for the two rolled-up newspapers Officer Bennett had found on Powell's kitchen counter.

Brown said he had a key to Powell's apartment because he would take care of her plants when she traveled. Brown had known Powell for about five years and their relationship was friendly but not of a romantic nature. He said he found it odd that Powell was not home when he went to her apartment, and it was completely out of character for her to miss work. The only other detail of interest Jenkins found in Brown's statement was that he mentioned Powell always went in and out of the apartment through the garage door and used her electronic door opener to open and close the overhead door. However, the opener was not found in her truck in the garage, and Detective Wood did not locate it inside her apartment during a later search.

Detective Wood conducted telephone interviews with Powell's mother and brother, who lived in Southern California. Neither of them had heard from her in the past week. Powell's ex-husband, Roy Robbins, lived roughly five miles from the school where she taught. Robbins hadn't spoken to Powell all weekend and he also remarked that it wasn't like her to miss work. He was able to supply the name of Powell's cousin in San Francisco, who she was supposed to meet for a ski outing in Lake Tahoe on Saturday, February 4th. The man's name was listed as Russ Davis and although he had not been formally interviewed yet, he did tell Detective Wood during a phone call that Powell did not show up for the trip as planned.

A phone call to Powell's boyfriend in Pittsburg, Pennsylvania, also yielded no valuable information. Mr. Don Barley told Detective Wood he could account for his whereabouts in Pennsylvania all weekend. He said although his relationship with Powell is long-distance, they still remained close and spoke by phone every night. He last spoke to her on the evening of Friday, February 3rd, and tried to call her several times thereafter but got no answer. He did say he found it strange that Powell's answering machine did not pick up, as she always kept it turned on.

Jenkins had four pages of notes scribbled on a yellow legal pad by the time the rest of the detectives arrived at 8:00 A.M. He tore the pages from the pad and placed them, along with the copy of the missing person report, into a brand new black three-ring binder, now the official murder book. Over the years, Jenkins had initiated more than his share of murder books, and his handwritten notes were just the beginning of the story of Kathy Powell's death. It was now up to him and the other detectives assigned to the case to make sure the story had a proper ending.

Chapter 7:
In Dubio

Latin phraseology is heavily used in the medical and legal fields, and forensic science is no exception. The word "forensics" itself is derived from the Latin "*forēnsis,*" which means public knowledge. In 1100 A.D., the King of England commissioned doctors to examine the dead, and they became known as *Crowners* since they answered to the crowned heads. The Latin word for crown is "*corona,*" and over the years, the examiners of the dead became known in the English language as Coroners.

In the state of Nevada, any suspicious or non-clinical deaths are investigated by a coroner. Therefore, the autopsy of Kathy Powell would be conducted by the Washoe County Coroner's Office. It is the job of the coroner to establish not only the *cause* of death but the *mechanism* and *manner* of death as well. The difference between these terms is widely misunderstood by the general public.

The cause of death is simply the reason why a person died. Some argue the cause of every death is same – stoppage of the heart. The mechanism of death is the actual physiological change or variation in the body's inner workings that causes the cessation of life. For example, a heart attack and a bullet will both cause the heart to stop functioning, but the evidence to tell the difference can only be obtained through an autopsy.

Perhaps the most important evidence discovered through autopsy, from an investigative viewpoint, is the manner of death. The four main manners of death are natural, accidental, suicidal, and homicidal. The Latin term for the fifth and less often used category is "*in dubio,*" which translates to "*undetermined.*" This is used when the coroner cannot accurately determine the appropriate manner of death. Since homicides are deaths that occur by the hand of someone other than the deceased, a finding of an undetermined manner of death is the one most feared by a homicide detective.

The task of attending the autopsy of Kathy Powell fell to Jenkins and Douglas, as they were the lead detectives on the case. The other three Major Crimes Unit detectives, with the assistance of Detective Wood, were already busy working on other aspects of the investigation when Jenkins and Douglas arrived at the coroner's office at 9:00 A.M.

Deputy Chuck Lowe was waiting for them in the dressing area outside of the autopsy room. Since he performed the initial crime scene investigation, it was his job to follow through with evidence collection at the autopsy and to fingerprint the victim for positive identification. The mood was somber in the room as the three men exchanged greetings. Some cops used *black humor* to mask the atrocities they witnessed on a daily basis, but not these cops. Working homicides taught them respect for the dead, and none of them looked forward to the task ahead. Witnessing the autopsy was a necessity, but a cop who claimed to enjoy it was someone they preferred to keep at a distance.

The three men pulled on green surgical scrubs, complete with booties, caps, and masks over their clothing. In most medical procedures, protective garments are worn to shield the patient from germs, but the opposite is true in an autopsy. All autopsies are considered potentially infectious, so universal precautions are required before entering the examining room. The last thing they did was pull on white latex gloves before pushing through the door to Autopsy Room One.

The room was large and well-ventilated. Seeing the doctor and his assistant pulling the body bag containing the remains of Kathy Powell off the large scale in the corner and onto a stainless steel cadaver table gave Jenkins a chill that added to the cool air temperature in the room. The stark walls, light-colored floor tiles, and bright white overhead florescent lighting made the room seem even colder. The interior smelled slightly antiseptic, but even the scent of Pine-Sol couldn't cover the smell of death that had seeped into the walls over the years.

Dr. Roger Ritzlin would be performing the autopsy. Jenkins hadn't had any bad experiences with him, but he hadn't had any really good ones either. The only cases he'd worked with the man so far had obvious causes of death, and judging from what Jenkins saw during his initial inspection of Powell, this one might be a bit different. Corpse cops always shared autopsy horror stories when they got together, and as Jenkins watched the doctor wheel the table with Powell's body on it toward the center of the room, two of these came to mind.

Both autopsies were from the Las Vegas Coroner's Office, and the doctor who had performed them was fortunately no longer with the Coroner's Office. In the first case, the doctor would not rule a homicide in a death where the victim was shot in the heart with an arrow from a crossbow, even though the weapon was never found. His reason was that the victim might have accidentally discharged the arrow while loading the crossbow, and vandals might have stolen the weapon before the body was discovered.

In the second case, the victim was bludgeoned to death with a ball-peen hammer. The victim had been despondent over a divorce, and the coroner ruled the death a suicide. Even though the man had been struck in the head six times, only one of the blows was severe enough to cause death. The coroner said the first five blows must have been hesitation strikes since the victim's fingerprints were among those found on the hammer. The fact that his wife's fingerprints were also found on the hammer didn't play into his decision because the hammer was taken from the garage, so they both would have had access to it over time.

Both of these cases were eventually cleared by arrest as homicides, but the investigation and prosecution were made much more difficult due to the reluctance of the coroner to make a firm decision as to the manner of death. Jenkins and Douglas exchanged sideways glances over their surgical masks as they watched Dr. Ritzlin arrange his instruments, both silently hoping for the same thing. Some cops loved to clear their caseload in any way possible, but not these ones. The old adage says if it looks like a duck, walks like a duck, and quacks like a duck—it's probably a duck. The same could be said for a homicide, and both felt that was exactly what they were dealing with. All they needed now was for the man unzipping the body bag to confirm their gut feelings.

Chapter 8:
Warp

Once the body was removed from the body bag, the black bag itself was folded and sealed inside a clear plastic bag to be examined by the crime lab later. The body was still enclosed in the sleeping bag and yellow plastic bag, just as it was when removed from the dumpster. It was the outer plastic bag that drew their attention now that they could see it much clearer under the bright lights. The two homicide detectives, along with the crime scene detective and corpse doctor, agreed on one thing: none of them had ever seen a plastic bag quite like this one.

The doctor carefully removed the bag, and Deputy Lowe stretched it out on a work table. The bag was bright yellow and a heavy enough grade of plastic to hold the body without tearing. It measured sixty inches by one-hundred-eight inches, making it much larger than the standard thirty-three-gallon trash bag covering Powell's head. After the bag was photographed, Lowe left it stretched out on the table so the remaining condensation on it could dry before he packaged it. They then turned their attention back to the cadaver table.

The sleeping bag had been hand-sewn closed at the top with black thread. The stitching was sloppy, making it appear that whoever did it was in a hurry. Dr. Ritzlin was able to unzip the bag and pull it away from the body without cutting the threads in case they had evidentiary value. Once the sleeping bag was removed from the body, it was photographed, folded toward the inside to preserve any potential evidence, and sealed in plastic by Deputy Lowe.

Dr. Ritzlin next removed the black plastic bag that was partially covering the victim's head and handed it to Deputy Lowe for processing. The victim's eyes appeared to be ready to bulge out of her head, and her tongue was protruding from her mouth. Dr. Ritzlin explained this was the result of bacteria in the decomposing body creating gasses that were trying to escape. He then pointed to an olive-green-colored patch of skin on the right side of the victim's lower belly and said that was a further sign that internal decomposition had begun. His educated guess was the victim had been dead for at least five days, but he'd be able to narrow that down after a complete examination.

The knots in the rope binding the victim's body were tight, but the ropes themselves were loose enough to allow Deputy Lowe to move the right hand in order to obtain fingerprints freely. He inked each finger and rolled the prints onto a white laminated fingerprint card. He then stepped over to a lighted table and used a magnifying glass to compare the victim's prints to Kathy Powell's fingerprints on the card Jenkins had brought with him. After a minute, he returned to the cadaver table and informed the rest of the group that the prints matched. Additional DNA and dental record comparisons would be made at a later time, but the photograph and fingerprint match would be enough for the coroner to say this victim was definitely Kathy Powell.

Dr. Ritzlin began carefully cutting the ropes off of Powell's body under the watchful eyes of both detectives—cutting between the knots so they could be preserved. As each section of rope was removed, it was picked up and packaged separately by Deputy Lowe. The manner in which the killer had looped the rope from Powell's ankles around her neck would have caused the rope to tighten if she tried moving her legs too much. It appeared to the detectives that Powell's death had resulted from ligature strangulation caused by the rope, so they were shocked when Dr. Ritzlin voiced his disagreement with their observations.

When the last piece of rope was removed from Powell's neck, Dr. Ritzlin pointed out that although the rope had left a mark on the skin, it wasn't deep enough to have been caused by the force necessary for strangulation. He also pointed out the absence of petechiae—small red conjunctival dots—in the whites of Powell's eyes. Dr. Ritzlin said it was his belief that petechiae are present in all deaths related to strangulation or asphyxiation. Jenkins knew from his research on the subject that Dr. Ritzlin's opinion on this was not accurate, but he decided not to voice his opinion until all the facts of the autopsy were in. Nevertheless, his opinion of Dr. Ritzlin had been formed.

Powell's body was stretched out on the table, and the autopsy room attendant flipped a wall switch to turn on the overhead fan so the escaping gasses could be ventilated. This was one of the parts of the procedure that sometimes caused onlookers to vomit, but the men in the room continued working without making mention of the odors of death. Dr. Ritzlin removed Powell's black tank top and blue socks from her body and handed them to Deputy Lowe. He then performed a visual examination of the body.

There was heavy bruising on Powell's knees and elbows. After examining them, Dr. Ritzlin determined they had been caused ante-mortem. There was also a discernable human bite mark on Powell's left breast, which was likewise caused while she was still alive. Using a special blue light to examine the body, a semen stain was found on Powell's right thigh. Deputy Lowe gathered evidence from the bite mark and semen stain, and then Dr. Ritzlin continued his examination.

Rolling the body over on its side, Dr. Ritzlin pointed out the absence of fecal staining, which would also be present along with the petechiae if the death resulted from strangulation or asphyxiation. He did see enough tearing and discoloration to lead him to believe Powell had been engaged in vaginal and anal sex shortly before her death—possibly not as a willing participant.

When Dr. Ritzlin began cutting into Powell's body to examine her organs, Douglas walked over to the table where Deputy Lowe had laid out the evidence gathered so far. He knew the drill well enough by now. Each organ would be taken out of the body, examined and weighed, and then placed back inside of the body before the doctor sewed it back up. It wasn't squeamishness that caused him to step away from the cadaver table, but the yellow plastic bag that caught his eye.

Using a gloved hand, he lifted the bag and examined the writing etched into the lower corner of it. There were a series of numbers, and underneath them, in large letters, was the word "WARP." Douglas smiled his toothy grin under his surgical mask as he transcribed the letters and numbers the manufacturer had put on the bag into his notes. Every detective loved clues, and he'd just found his first.

Chapter 9:
Old School

Signs of frustration were evident on the faces of Jenkins and Douglas as they entered the Detective Division at 1:00 that afternoon. The other detectives assigned to the case were at their desks, and the unit's sergeant was on the phone inside of his glass-walled cubicle. They all looked up when Douglas loudly said, "Man, that was bullshit!"

Sergeant Matt Toliver hurriedly finished his conversation and hung up his phone. He was fifty-five years old, a twenty-five-year veteran, and it was rumored he was only in the Detective Division to pad his salary with overtime to boost his retirement rate. Since his retirement was close at hand, he rarely left the safe confines of his office. The detectives said it had been so long since he'd been outside during daylight he was paler than Count Dracula jonesing for a blood fix.

Toliver stepped out of his office and said, "Does that mean things didn't go well at the autopsy?"

Douglas said, "The autopsy was *perfect,* but that lame-dick doctor is gonna say the death could have been an accident."

Jenkins cleared his throat and said, "What my esteemed partner is trying to say is the doctor performed professionally, but in his opinion, he is not entirely certain this death occurred at the hands of another person."

Douglas gave a sideways glance and added, "No, what I meant was that lame-dick doctor is gonna say the death could have been an accident."

"How could it be an accidental death?" Toliver asked. "She was tied up and dumped into a trash dumpster!"

Jenkins briefed them on the ante-mortem injuries, the bite marks, and the semen stain found on her thigh. He then looked at his notes and said, "Preliminary lab tests show a non-toxic amount of lithium in the victim's blood. This isn't out of the ordinary because the initial police report shows a prescription for lithium was found inside Ms. Powell's apartment. The lithium *could* have caused some judgmental problems or slowing of other bodily functions."

Toliver asked, "So if the lithium was in a non-lethal dose, what does it have to do with the cause of death?"

"The doctor is basing his entire theory on the lack of petechial, which he says is present in all deaths related to strangulation or forced asphyxiation. This is where he and I disagree, but he's the doctor, and I'm just a homicide detective."

"He located some fibrosis and acute cell death in the left ventricle of the victim's heart. It appears the cell death occurred a couple of days before her death. Naturally, the cause of death, in this case, is the stoppage of the heart. The doctor is not prepared to say the circumstances causing the heart to stop fit the description of a homicide since other contributing factors are not present. There is evidence of sexual activity shortly before death, albeit rather rough sexual activity. It is the doctor's opinion the victim *might* have had a heart attack during some type of auto-erotic sexual encounter. The lithium might have masked the symptoms of a possible heart attack until it was too late for the victim to do anything about it."

Douglas remarked, "The way he's describing it is worse than the old joke about having a heart attack during a game of charades. You're writhing in pain, and the other people think you're just really getting into the game."

"So, the ruling from the coroner is accidental death?" Toliver asked.

"No," Jenkins answered. "There were enough inconsistencies with what we found on the body to keep the coroner from saying it was definitely accidental. I got him to commit to the fact there was no way she could have tied herself up like that without help, and there were a couple of other things that looked out of place. The one visible bite mark on the victim's breast occurred before death, and it was so deep it most assuredly would have been very painful. There were also blue fibers and trace amounts of some type of metal—probably aluminum—located around the victim's neck. We got a ruling of *undetermined* cause of death, but we're still investigating it as a homicide until we rule out foul play."

"Accidental death would be a lot easier," Toliver said.

In an annoyed voice, Jenkins said, "If you want a quick-fix to this you're going to have to assign it elsewhere."

"Relax," Toliver cautioned. "You know I want this thing investigated properly. I'm just saying don't rule out the accidental thing all the way yet. For now, I'll leave the whole team assigned to this, but if you don't get some evidence pointing away from what the coroner said, I might have to pull some manpower off of it. Things are slow right now, so let's just see what happens."

"Fair enough," Jenkins said. "What did the rest of you come up with?"

"We finished the search of the condo," Detective Dixon replied. "The friend of Ms. Powell's who reported her missing met us there to see if she could help identify the missing items. So far, we know the missing items are a Brother brand combination fax and answering machine, a Sony cordless phone, a Texas Instrument computer printer, and a Macintosh laptop computer. I got the brand names and serial numbers from a file I found on Ms. Powell's desk.

"We combed the place pretty well, and the evidence tech took a ton of fingerprints, but she said almost all of them match, so they're probably from the victim herself. I did find a rolled-up ball of used duct tape and two unopened packages of Trojan condoms behind the garbage can under the kitchen sink. It looks like somebody tried to throw them in the garbage can but missed, so that's why the cops didn't see them when they originally went through the place. The lab says it's kind of tough to get DNA off of tape, but they'll see what they can do. When they unrolled the tape, it was a single strip just about big enough to be used as a gag, too."

Jenkins nodded and commented, "An excellent job, as usual, Eddie. Who's next?"

Detective Joe Dypsynski had assisted Dixon in the search. He replied, "I found Powell's banking and credit card records on her desk. She banks at First Interstate Bank and only has one credit card issued through Chemical Bank MasterCard. Banking information is tough to get on a Sunday, but the head of F.I.B. security is an ex-cop buddy of mine. I called in some favors and found out the only banking activity done on Powell's account was a check she cashed at their Sun Valley branch at 3:15 P.M. the Friday she was last seen. The check was only for sixty dollars, and her account has been dormant since."

"Well, that begins to establish her movements after she left school that day," Jenkins said. "Are they able to retrieve any video of the transaction so we can be sure it was actually her that cashed the check?"

"Yeah, but we're gonna have to wait till tomorrow to look at them. I need to get a subpoena for the video so my guy doesn't get his ass in a jam for releasing the information, but he's already gone to the bank and looked at them. I faxed him a photo of Powell, and he says it's definitely her who cashed the check. Woody has the credit card information from his original case, so I'll let him cover that."

Detective Wood looked at his notes and said, "I just pulled this stuff up on Friday and haven't really had a chance to get into it because I was on my days off. Kathy Powell's credit card was used for a telephone purchase from the Good Guys Electronics Store at 2:36 P.M. on Sunday, February 5th. That was two days after she was last seen, but it was also two days *before* she was reported missing, so it didn't raise any red flags at the time."

"I called down there and talked to the guy who took the order." Wood stopped to flip through his notes and then added, "Here it is. His name is Gary Cable, and he was just about to get off work when I called. He said a person identifying herself as Kathy Powell called the store and placed an order for a Yamaha stereo amplifier valued at about two thousand dollars. The caller said it was going to be a gift and that it would be picked up the next day. The charge went through OK, so the sale was approved."

"The same person called Cable the next morning and said a courier service would be by in the afternoon to pick up the stereo equipment. Later that afternoon, a white female with blonde hair wearing a yellow windbreaker with some type of logo on it came to the store and picked up the merchandise. Cable didn't actually help the lady, but he remembers her because he said she was wearing so much makeup that she looked like a clown. He also said the person who called the store saying they were Kathy Powell sounded like a man trying to disguise his voice to sound like a woman."

Jenkins asked, "Did this guy get a look at the logo on the courier's jacket or the car she was driving?"

"Nah, but he said the kid who helped her must have. I was planning on talking to him on Monday, but I can call down there today to see if he's working."

Toliver said, "Well, if he's not, find out where he is and get his ass down here for a statement. It might be nothing, but he also might have dealt with our killer. Didn't you think that lead would be worth following up on when you got it? Powell had been missing for at least five days by then!"

"Of course I did," Wood replied disgustedly. "Like I said, it was Friday afternoon, and I was about to get off duty for the weekend. The lieutenant wouldn't approve the overtime, so my boss told me to follow it up on Monday. I didn't like it, but I can't overrule the lieutenant."

Detective Bruce Hunt had been quietly listening to this exchange. The square-jawed former Army Ranger didn't speak often, but when he did, people usually listened. At this moment, he spoke up, using the term of endearment he reserved for people who irked him. "The lieutenant's a fuckin *clam*! We could've had a lead on the suspect last night if we had that information."

Toliver said, "Give the guy a break. The lieutenant has to answer to the Deputy Chief if his O.T. budget goes overboard, so he has to be careful with it."

Hunt's face was red with anger when he said, "The Deputy Chief is an even *bigger* clam than the lieutenant. You don't solve murders worrying about budgets. Anyway, me and Woody will head over to the Good Guys as soon as we finish up with this other interview we have scheduled."

"What interview is that?" Jenkins asked.

Hunt looked at his notes and said, "According to Powell's date planner she was supposed to meet a friend of hers for coffee right after school the Friday she was last seen. The guy's name is Royal Alexander, and he lives up in north Reno. What kind of clam names their kid *Royal*? Anyway, I called him, and he said Powell and he had coffee at that French place *Deux Gros Nez* on Friday evening at about 5:30.

"So this guy Alexander is the last person we know of right now who saw Powell alive. He's meeting us here at 2:00 for an interview, but he doesn't feel right to be a suspect. He's been in San Francisco all week on business, and from the sound of his voice, he doesn't seem like the type to be too interested in kinky sex with a woman. I guess you predestine a kid to go that way when you name him Royal."

Jenkins said, "Your powers of perception never fail to amaze me. John and I stayed at the Coroner's office while they made the death notifications to the next of kin. Powell's mother and brother are driving up from California in the morning, and they asked that the ex-husband be notified since he and Powell were still quite close. I made that call myself, and he sounded legitimately upset. We're heading up to his house as soon as we break here to interview him, but my gut feeling says he's not going to be a suspect. When we finish with him, we're going to stop by the evidence yard to complete the search of the dumpster. Who said homicide work isn't glamorous?"

Dixon said, "Joe and I are heading back to Powell's complex to re-interview the neighbors. We'll swing by the evidence yard and meet you when we're done. There was a lot of garbage in that dumpster, so it'll go faster with four of us working on it."

Douglas had been working on his computer throughout the meeting. He sat back and exclaimed, "I found it! Our mystery yellow plastic bag is called a Warp's Brothers Banana Bag and they're manufactured in Chicago. They only list two local outlets here in Reno. One is up in the north valley and the other one is downtown. The number on the bag is a tracking number, so we should be able to tell which store sold it."

"That's *if* our suspect is a local," Toliver said.

"He's a local," Douglas said. "I checked with the trash company, and they said the apartment manager pays extra for the additional Sunday pickup at that complex because of the rat problem they get if the garbage piles up too high. I think whoever dumped Powell knew the trash schedule and picked that place so her body would end up in the landfill while they had a skeleton crew working there."

"I concur," said Jenkins.

Douglas stood up and said, "Then let's get off our asses and start knocking on doors. It's old school, but it has always worked for Joe Friday on Dragnet."

Chapter 10:
Omicron

The buzzing noises made by the overhead fluorescent lights were the only sounds in the detective's conference room as Jenkins sat alone, going through his notes. The main squad room was empty at 10:00 on a Sunday night, but the private conference room shielded him from the occasional inquisitive uniformed officer who wandered into the detective division to see what was going on.

The other detectives had completed follow-up reports on their activities before heading home for some well-deserved sleep an hour earlier. Jenkins decided to stay after they were gone so he could review all the reports before their morning briefing. Deciding to save his own notes till last, he pushed them to the side and grabbed the top report off of the pile stacked next to him.

It was Detective Hunt's report detailing his interview with Royal Alexander. Mr. Alexander described himself as a close friend of Powell's but not in a dating capacity. He said he had met Powell for coffee at the *Deux Gros Nez* restaurant on California St. in Reno at 5:30 P.M. on Friday, February 3rd.

Powell told Alexander she was planning to go on a ski trip the following day and had just cashed a check at her bank to cover the expenses for it. He was certain she had her backpack-style purse and her checkbook with her because she had written him a check for some business products she had purchased from him. She left in her truck at about 6:30 P.M., and Alexander said this was the last he saw her as he left for San Francisco later that night. He still had Powell's check with him and gave it to Detective Hunt to be placed into evidence.

Detective Hunt's case notes said he had ruled Alexander out as a suspect based on his alibi for his whereabouts during the days following his meeting with Powell, as well as "other contributing factors." Jenkins knew they were Hunt's gut feeling that Alexander wasn't the type to engage in sexual activity with Powell, but that isn't the kind of thing a detective writes into his police report.

The second report was written by Detective Douglas. It was short and to the point but did little to describe the agonizing hours four detectives had spent wading through trash in the police evidence yard. The last line of the report read, "Nothing of evidentiary value was discovered, but a good time was had by all."

The next report was six pages long and listed the names and addresses of everyone Detectives Dixon and Dypsynski had spoken to in Powell's apartment complex. Two of her neighbors had seen an older model pickup truck parked in front of Powell's condo when they came home at about 4:00 A.M. on Saturday, February 4th.

The truck stood out because it had household belongings in the back. It was dark outside, but they both described the truck as being faded red with a light-colored license plate on the back. They didn't notice what state the license plate was from, but both were certain it wasn't Nevada. Neither neighbor knew Powell well, but they said she often had visitors, so they didn't think anything was amiss when they saw the truck. Their description of the truck seen outside Powell's apartment made the next report seem even more important.

This one detailed the interviews Detectives Hunt and Wood conducted with the employees at the Good Guys electronics store. Two employees spoke to the person identifying herself as Kathy Powell on the phone, and they both described the caller's voice as deep and husky. They were almost certain the caller was a male, but since Reno has a large transsexual population, neither of them gave this much thought.

The caller told the store manager they were buying the stereo equipment as a gift for a family member in Lake Tahoe. They also said arrangements had been made with a local courier service to pick up the equipment at the store and deliver it to Lake Tahoe. The Lake Tahoe connection wasn't given when Detective Wood first contacted the store. Since he'd already confirmed Powell had no relatives in the area, this might have made the transaction seem more suspicious if he'd had the information two days earlier.

The courier arrived at the Good Guys store at 2:45 P.M. on Monday, February 6th. She was assisted by a store clerk named Mike Sarratea, and Detectives Hunt and Wood took a detailed statement from him. Sarratea described the courier as a heavyset white woman in her mid-forties with frizzy blonde hair. He said her face was heavily made up, and she was wearing a yellow windbreaker with some type of logo on it. He couldn't remember the exact logo, but he did remember it was a company name with the word "Messenger" in it.

Sarratea said the woman had a clipboard with papers on it and the proper customer ID number with her for the order placed by the caller. She loaded the stereo receiver onto a red hand truck she brought with her and wheeled the merchandise out to her truck, which was parked in the customer loading zone. Sarratea helped her load the large box into the bed of the truck, and she left after he gave her a receipt for the merchandise. She was not required to sign anything, and the copy of the receipt included with the report had the words "phone order" handwritten on the signature line.

Sarratea said the courier's voice was neither deep nor husky as the caller's voice was described. When Hunt asked him to describe the courier's vehicle, Sarratea said it was an early 70s model International Harvester open-bed pickup truck, faded orange in color, with plywood covering the bed and a green and white license plate. When Hunt asked him how he could be certain the truck was an International Harvester, Sarratea told him he was helping his father restore the exact type of truck. He said he might be off by a year in either direction, but it was definitely in the right time frame because that style of truck was only used between 1970 and 1975.

Jenkins smiled when he read the last paragraph, thinking about this next stroke of luck in the investigation. Since the witness had personal experience with the exact brand of the truck the courier was driving, his statement was credible enough to use on a nationwide law enforcement B.O.L.O. to try and locate it.

There were five courier services with the word "Messenger" in their names listed in the phone book, and he was reasonably certain none of them would be using an early 70s International Harvester truck. He'd have to wait till morning to check with them to be certain though. It would be an incredibly stupid move for the suspect to use a distinctive vehicle like that if it was actually theirs, but Jenkins' instincts told him the two crimes were related.

The last report Jenkins read was the one he had written describing the interview he and Douglas had done with Kathy Powell's ex-husband, Rick Hughes. Jenkins eliminated Hughes as a suspect not more than a minute into his conversation with him. It wasn't what Hughes said; it was how he said it that gave both Jenkins and Douglas the gut feeling they were dealing with an honest man.

Hughes was a fifty-one-year-old electrician. He was a big man, bulked up like a construction worker, not like a weightlifter. When he met the detectives at the door to his house, his eyes were red-rimmed, and the telltale salt stains from tears streaked his face. With a meaty paw, he shook hands with both detectives and invited them into his home.

They sat at the kitchen table, and Hughes poured them coffee from a glass coffeemaker on the counter. Next to the coffeemaker was a mason jar filled with Tennessee Moonshine, homebrewed by relatives of Hughes' current wife. He said he held off on opening the white lightning as a show of respect for the detectives, but he intended to put a dent in it as soon as they left.

Hughes had been a cop in a central California city for twelve years when he met Kathy Powell. By that time, he was frustrated with the trials and tribulations of police work. He said Kathy brought out the good in him and turned his life around. He got out of law enforcement, married Kathy, and moved to Reno to be with her. Hughes described Powell as a good and trusting person, but it was her trust in people that brought about their divorce in 1989.

Shortly after they were married, Powell became involved in a cultish-style set of beliefs called the Trust Theory, also known as *omicron* for the Greek letter *o,* which signifies unity. Hughes explained that people involved in the Trust Theory were called *seekers,* believing there was good inside of everyone if you looked hard enough. She once told him even a genocidal butcher like Hitler had a kernel of sweetness at his core—it was just never brought out into plain sight.

Eventually, trust became the driving force behind Kathy's thinking. She disdained monogamy and promoted openness and experimentation in everything — including sexual relations. Her credo became, "Life is short, and death is long, so why not be passionate and see the potential in everyone."

The last statement Hughes made in his interview was that he never stopped loving his ex-wife—he just couldn't live that type of life with her. His cop senses made him too cynical to trust people, and he told Kathy that someday her beliefs would get her hurt. His tears flowed freely as he wondered out loud if that had been a self-fulfilling prophecy, and the detectives set the jar of white lightning on the table in front of him before they silently let themselves out of his house.

Chapter 11:
Calls Unanswered

The detectives were back at it by 7:00 A.M. Monday morning, and the day brought with it a flurry of activity for them. At their morning briefing each man was given a list of persons to contact. By 4:00 in the afternoon, they were back in the Detective Division, seated around the oval conference room table, comparing notes on their progress.

The conference room had become the temporary headquarters for the ad hoc task force, and a timeline based on what they knew so far was written in black marker on the white dry-erase board at the front of the room. The timeline was sparse, but enough room had been left between entries to add on as more information was obtained.

Jenkins started the afternoon meeting by going over what he'd learned about Kathy Powell thus far. Besides the interview with her ex-husband, Jenkins and Douglas also spoke to several of Kathy Powell's co-workers in addition to her brother and mother, who were now in town. They all painted the same picture of Kathy Powell—a caring and trusting person who looked for good in everyone.

The Trust Theory was continually mentioned as a rudder that Kathy Powell used to guide her life, so Jenkins researched the philosophical belief and learned it had quite a large following. The Trust Theory was started in San Diego in the early 1970s by a psychologist named Jack R. Gibb. Interestingly enough, Powell's brother told the detectives Kathy had actually taken Gibb into her home for a short time and cared for him until he succumbed to terminal cancer just a month before her own death. The two deaths appeared unrelated, but the fact she brought the man into her home went along with everything they heard about Kathy Powell. She took in strays that had nowhere to go and tried her best to make life comfortable for them.

Kathy Powell had no serious medical problems other than having had a hysterectomy at an early age. Perhaps the fact she couldn't have children of her own was the reason she was so loved by the underprivileged children she taught. Her co-workers said she was the students' favorite teacher and that she allowed them to call her Kathy instead of Ms. Powell. She cited developing trust within her students as the reason for the lack of formality.

Trust is also what brought Kathy Powell into her long-distance relationship with her fiancé, Pittsburg attorney Don Barley. She met Barley at a Trust Theory meeting six years earlier while she was still married to Hughes, and the two started a relationship almost immediately. Powell's brother said she dove headfirst into a fascination with everything about Pittsburg, from its sports teams to its history, and she planned to move there to be with Barley after she retired from teaching.

Powell's family never approved of her relationship with Barley and suggested this might be a good place for detectives to focus their investigation. It seems she spent five weeks with him in Pittsburg a year earlier while he was recovering from an aneurysm. While she was there, he made her the sole beneficiary of his will. In turn, she did the same with him. Powell's assets included her condo, a modest life insurance policy, and a small savings account. Everything combined equaled just under $100,000, which was not a staggering figure, but Jenkins had seen murders committed for far less monetary gain.

Jenkins and Douglas had done a taped telephone interview with Barley earlier in the day, and he seemed legitimately upset by Powell's death. Barley was fifteen years older than Powell, but he said their mutual beliefs in the Trust Theory gave them something in common and kept them together. He said they visited as often as possible, given the distance between them, but when they were not together, they spoke by phone nightly.

Barley said the last time Powell called him was at about 7:30 P.M. P.S.T., and they spoke for about thirty minutes. He knew about her ski trip the following day but became concerned when he did not hear from her the following night. He made several calls to her apartment over the next two days, but they all went unanswered. He found it strange that her answering machine did not pick up his calls since she religiously kept the machine turned on and checked her messages frequently. After Detective Wood had contacted Barley during the initial missing person investigation, he stopped trying to call Powell. He said he and Powell shared a mental connection and, deep inside, knew something had happened to her.

Barley was able to substantiate the fact he had not left the Pittsburg area during the time frame of Powell's disappearance. Even though murder for hire was always a possibility, Jenkins and Douglas ruled him out as a suspect. They made their living listening to their instincts and decided to focus their efforts locally.

A detailed telephone interview was also conducted with Russ Davis, Kathy Powell's cousin, with whom she was supposed to ski on Saturday, February 4th. Davis said he was supposed to meet Powell in Truckee, California, thirty miles west of Reno, and drive from there to a Lake Tahoe ski resort. He got a late start leaving his San Francisco area home and began calling Powell from his car phone at about 6:30 A.M. to let her know. He made several calls to her home over the next couple of hours, but they all went unanswered. He made the same statements as Barley about it being out of the ordinary for Powell not to have her answering machine on.

Powell was not at their pre-arranged meeting place when Davis arrived in Truckee. He waited for a short while and then drove to the ski area in case she had gone there without him. He did not find her there, and Powell did not have a cell phone on which he could call her. He spent part of the day skiing and then drove back to the Bay Area without having contact with her. He had his punched ski pass to confirm his story, and his whereabouts before and after skiing could be confirmed by family members.

The detectives had also contacted every courier service in the Reno-Lake Tahoe area—even those without the words "Messenger" in their names. None of them used a 70s model International Harvester pickup truck for deliveries, so the truck was now listed as used by a person of interest in the case. A nationwide teletype was sent out, and the information was passed on to all local departments.

Several sightings of similar vehicles had already come in locally. Detectives went to Good Guys and picked up Mike Sarratea to look at two possible matches. A 1972 model parked on a street in south Reno was an exact match for the style, but Sarratea said it looked too clean and did not have the plywood in the truck bed. Regardless of the false sightings, the detectives were certain the truck was one of their best clues.

The other solid clue was the Warp's Brothers Banana Bag, and Douglas spent a better part of the day tracking that down. Using the tracking number, he was able to determine the bag had been purchased at the Commercial Hardware Store in downtown Reno at 3:32 P.M. on Thursday, February 8, 1995. When Douglas went to the store, he learned they had a copy of the receipt for the sale on file, but no one remembered who made the purchase, and there was no video of the sale. The $9.36

transaction had been done in cash, so there was no credit card paper trail to chase, and the ten-dollar bill used for the purchase was long gone.

According to the receipt, a fifteen-count box of heavy-duty 33-gallon black plastic garbage bags had also been purchased at the same time as the four-bag package of Warp's Brothers Banana Bags. Douglas purchased these two exact items from the store in order to compare them with the bags taken from Kathy Powell's discarded body. The black plastic bags and the Banana Bags both matched exactly in brand, color, and size. Since coincidences rarely exist in police work, Douglas' theory about the killer being local was bolstered by this discovery.

Jenkins used a black marker to update the timeline with the new information from this afternoon's discussion. He then picked up a red marker and drew brackets around the time frame between Powell's last call to Barley at 7:30 P.M. Friday, February 3rd and Russ Davis's first call to her at 6:30 A.M. Saturday, February 4th. Whatever hell Kathy Powell had gone through had already begun before that unanswered phone call because whoever took her also took her telephone answering machine.

There was only one entry between the two times bracketed on the timeline chart. It read, "Feb. 4, 1995, 0400 hours: Faded red beater pickup truck seen in front of victim's condo." Their investigation now had a focus.

Chapter 12:
The Cable Guy

During the next morning's briefing, it was decided that the Good Guys transaction would become the focus of the investigation as this was by far the most active lead in the case. The department's civilian statistical analyst was brought on board and tasked with compiling a list from Department of Motor Vehicle records of trucks matching the description of the one used by the courier at Good Guys. They would start with Nevada-registered vehicles and branch out to other states from there as needed.

The registered owners of each matching vehicle would have to be checked for criminal history and the likelihood they might have crossed paths with Kathy Powell. This would be a time-consuming job, and their resources had already begun to dwindle. Since the official Coroner's ruling on the cause of death was now "undetermined," the division lieutenant decided to lessen the priority of the case and moved Detective Wood back to his unit. He also said further manpower would be removed from the case if progress wasn't shown in the near future. This decision brought on one of Detective Hunt's infamous tirades, which of course ended in the words *"that fuckin clam!"*

A computerized database was created, and Toliver was able to get two clerical employees to assist with logging vehicle and owner information into it. This alleviated some of the workload on the detectives, but there was still a lot to be done. In addition to looking for the vehicle through records and putting the word out to patrol, they decided to go public with the information and put out a press release with the description of the truck and the courier from Good Guy's. This would generate a lot of tips — mostly false — but everyone would need to be checked.

By the end of the day, sightings of matching vehicles had already started coming in from law enforcement agencies, one of them from as far away as Navajo County, Arizona. They were all logged into the data bank, but it would take time to run checks on the registered owners. Eventually, none of these initial sightings proved useful to the investigation.

The detectives also had a chance to review the video surveillance tapes from the F.I.B Bank. Not only did they confirm it was Powell who cashed the check on the date she was last seen, but that she was also wearing the same black shirt that was found on her body when she was discarded in the dumpster. In addition, she had her backpack purse, and the outside camera captured her coming and going alone in her pickup truck. Besides adding credibility to Royal Alexander's story, this also told the detectives they were working within the right timeframe. Kathy Powell went home that evening, but she never had the chance to change out of the clothes she was wearing the last time she was seen alive.

The first twenty-four to forty-eight hours in a homicide case are the most important; after that, incoming information starts to fade. Unfortunately, the investigation into Kathy Powell's death was no different. Within days, the detectives were at a virtual standstill, and all of them except Jenkins and Douglas were assigned to different cases. The command center set up in the detective's conference room was disassembled, and the timeframe once written on the large whiteboard was now condensed to a page on a yellow legal pad.

On Wednesday, February 22, 1995, Jenkins and Douglas decided to go back to square one in the investigation and pore over everything they had accumulated. They both had the nagging feeling they'd missed something and even the most minute, overlooked detail might give them the direction they needed. They were slogging through their notes when the phone on Jenkins's desk rang at 10:40 in the morning.

A young patrol officer named Reed Thomas had located an International Harvester pickup truck matching the description put out by Jenkins. The truck was parked in the employee parking lot of the T.C.I. Cable Company on Vassar Street in south Reno. The officer was watching the truck from a distance and didn't want to get too close to it in his black-and-white in case it belonged to the suspect, so he was requesting detectives come to his location to check it out.

Jenkins hung up the phone and told his partner about the truck. Douglas asked, "Didn't we have something about T.C.I. Cable in the reports somewhere?"

"I think you're right," Jenkins said. Flipping the murder book open, he said, "Here it is. The original missing person report from Bob Bennett says there was a note from T.C.I. Cable on Powell's front door saying an installer had been there, but she wasn't home."

Douglas said, "That's it! We assumed since the note was still on the front door, that it was left there after Powell went M.I.A. Because she would have taken it off the door if it had been left there before. That's why we never followed up on it! But remember what the dude with the ferret told us about Powell never using the front door?"

Jenkins excitedly paged through the murder book until he found the statement given by Powell's friend, Jerry Brown. "I've got it," he said. "It says here that Powell always used the garage entry to go in and out of her house. That note could have been on the front door for a while, and she never would have seen it."

"Bingo!" exclaimed Douglas. "So, we've got a note from T.C.I. Cable Company at the front door, and a Beater International pickup is in their employee parking lot. There ain't any coincidences in this job, baby! You get down to T.C.I., and I'll get over to Good Guys to pick up the witness and see if it's the right truck."

Before heading out of the office, Jenkins stopped by Detective Ed Dixon's desk and asked for some unofficial help. Powell's records were in a box underneath Jenkins' desk. Somebody needed to go through them to see if she was a customer of T.C.I. Cable Company, and if so, make a discreet inquiry about the service call to her condo. Even though he'd been pulled off the case, there was nobody better suited for the job than Evidence Eddie.

Jenkins met Officer Thomas across the street from the lot where the truck was parked. The young officer had been keeping a vigil on the truck, and Jenkins had borrowed his binoculars to look at it. The truck was parked with its rear end facing the street and Jenkins' heart began beating faster with excitement when he looked at it.

There was no tailgate on the truck, so Jenkins could see into the bed even from this distance. It matched the description given by the witness right down to the plywood and spare tire in the truck bed. The green and white license plate was from Colorado, and Jenkins wrote the plate number 7861-WC into his notebook. Officer Thomas had already run the plate and found out the truck was registered to a David Middleton with a listed address in Montrose, Colorado.

Witness Mike Sarratea wasn't working when Douglas got to the Good Guys store, but the other employee who had assisted the courier with the transaction was. Douglas brought him to look at the truck in the T.C.I. lot, but he hadn't gotten as good of a look at it as Sarratea had. The witness said he was almost certain it was the same truck, and almost certain was more than they'd gotten so far.

Since the truck was parked in the secure employee lot at the cable company, Jenkins wasn't concerned about leaving anyone to watch it. If it was there today, it would be there again tomorrow, so he pulled Officer Thomas off the surveillance and headed back to the station to run a background check on David Middleton. Douglas said he would meet him back there to help after he dropped the witness off at Good Guys.

Ed Dixon was at his desk talking on the phone and taking notes when Jenkins walked into the Detective Division. Jenkins heard him say, "So your technician Dave made the service call on January 28th at 3:30 in the afternoon, and his last name is spelled M-I-D-D-L-E-T-O-N? Thank you very much. You've been a big help."

Jenkins was smiling when Dixon hung up his phone. He said, "Eddie, if you weren't so big and ugly, I'd hug you."

Dixon said, "Then I'm glad I'm big and ugly because you're not my type. Does that mean I'm back on the case?"

Chapter 13:
Sympathy For The Devil

The detectives were like sharks on the scent of fresh blood after discovering Middleton's link to the case, except it was information feeding their frenzy. All five Major Crimes detectives were back on the case, and by 8:00 that night, they had compiled enough information to convince them Middleton was involved with the disappearance and murder of Kathy Powell. What they had on Middleton thus far was only the tip of the iceberg, but that wasn't the part that had sunk the Titanic. The detectives now needed to see what lurked below the waterline in David Middleton's life.

The only thing the Reno P.D. had on file for Middleton was a burglary report he'd filed when his truck had been broken into in front of his apartment in November of 1994, but this was enough for a start. In the report, he listed his address as 1425 Carlin St. in northeast Reno, his place of employment as T.C.I. Cable Company and the red International Harvester pickup as his vehicle that had been burglarized. Besides giving the detectives points of reference, this also established Middleton as a Nevada resident since he'd been living in the state for longer than sixty days. His truck registration and driver's license were both still from Colorado, so this would give them built-in probable cause if they needed leverage to stop and detain him at a later time.

The other interesting information gleaned from the report was a statement taken from Middleton's live-in girlfriend, Evonne Haley. She'd also had property taken in the burglary and said she often drove Middleton's truck with his permission. Haley's photo was on file with the Reno P.D. Records section since she had a work card for employment at a local casino. When the detectives looked at the photo, they agreed her heavily made-up face actually *did* make her look like a clown, and they'd have to write a thank you note to the Good Guys employees for their accurate description if they ever made a case on her.

Since all of Middleton's personal information was listed on the police report, the detectives didn't have to risk tipping their hands by going through the personnel department at T.C.I. Cable Company to start their investigation on him. When the records clerk who was helping them ran Middleton through the National Crime Information Center's computer program, she got an instant hit. Jenkins and Douglas huddled around the computer and read Middleton's arrest record over the clerk's shoulder.

David Stephen Middleton was a convicted sex offender—arrested and convicted in Miami, Florida, in 1990. His original charges were kidnap and sexual assault, and the arrest date was November 19, 1989. According to the N.C.I.C. readout, he was convicted on the charges of false imprisonment and aggravated battery in June of 1990. He was sentenced to two concurrent five-year prison terms but was released in 1993 after serving a little more than two years of this sentence.

Middleton was no longer on parole, but since he was an ex-felon, he still needed to register his local address with the police department within forty-eight hours of moving. It was a misdemeanor crime for him not to do so, but they needed to be careful about arresting him prematurely.

The best way to interview Middleton about the Kathy Powell case was to do it while he was not in custody. This way, they would avoid any Miranda issues regarding the right to an attorney during custodial interrogations because those rights only kicked in after he was under arrest. If they had a valid charge for him being an ex-felon who failed to register, then his attorney could later argue the only reason they didn't arrest him was to deny him his rights. They decided to wait until after they talked to Middleton to contact the Records section of the Miami Police Department to confirm his ex-felon status. This way, they could say, in all honesty, they didn't have probable cause for an arrest when they talked to him. The Miranda decision has been around since 1963, and both sides of the law have been trying to figure out how to use it to their advantage ever since.

Detectives equate building a case against a suspect to erecting a brick wall. You start with a strong foundation and work your way up from there. Middleton's obvious involvement in the fraudulent use of Kathy Powell's credit card was their foundation. The connection with his installing her cable and now the fact he was a convicted sex offender were the first two bricks in the wall.

The records clerk pointed out something else interesting on Middleton's rap sheet. Included in the N.C.I.C. information bank is a program called Criminal Justice Information Services, or C.J.I.S. More secure information was contained in this program, and Middleton's records had a C.J.I.S. number attached to them. The clerk could not access the information without security clearance, but all Major Crimes detectives were issued control numbers to access secure files. Jenkins typed his security number into the computer program, and he and Douglas stared at the screen in disbelief when the following information popped up:

MIDDLETON, DAVID STEPHEN: B/M/A D.O.B. 25 JUNE 1961

P.O.B.: BOSTON, MASS.

LAW ENFORCEMENT AFFILIATION:

    1)   BOSTON POLICE DEPT:

01/15/80-01/20/82 RANK: POLICE CADET

STATUS: RESIGNED

    2)   MIAMI METRO-DADE POLICE:

01/25/82-12/12/90 RANK: OFFICER

STATUS: RESIGNED

It didn't take them long to notice the sequence of dates contained in the printout. Middleton had been a cop with the Miami Police Department for eight years when he was arrested for kidnap and rape in Florida. His arrest date was in November 1989, but his date of resignation from the department was December 12, 1990. That meant he was still actively employed as a cop when he'd committed the crimes he'd been convicted of. Based on what they knew about cops who are convicted of sex crimes—two years in prison seemed light.

The fact that his employment status read *resigned* instead of *terminated* was important, too. Police departments—their own included—were notorious for cutting deals to avoid embarrassing publicity. Officers were sometimes allowed to resign in lieu of termination if they promised to go away quietly. This way, they could save some of their benefits and employment prospects while the department avoided public scandal. It was a win-win situation—except for the public they were sworn to protect. If one deal had been involved when Middleton was arrested in Miami, then there was a possibility there would be others, too. It rankled the detectives when the other anomaly in the dates on the computer printout jumped out at them. If Middleton was still serving time for his Miami crimes, could Kathy Powell still be alive?

With copies of the computer printouts in hand, Jenkins and Douglas headed back to the conference room to share the news with the other detectives that their main murder suspect was an ex-cop. One of a cop's worst nightmares is investigating another cop. One reason is the suspect's knowledge of police procedures can severely limit the investigative tools used against them. The bigger rationale is that cops are idealistic, and none of them like to face the reality that there are bad members in the brotherhood of the badge.

A fraud detective working late had a stereo on his desk tuned to a classic rock station, and the Rolling Stones *Sympathy for the Devil* was playing. Mick Jagger belted out the line, "Every cop is a criminal, and all the sinners are saints," just as Jenkins and Douglas walked into the Detective Division office. The déjà vu experience caused them to stop and exchange wide-eyed looks because neither one of them liked the direction the investigation had just taken on.

Chapter 14:
Stupid Crook Tricks

After a roundtable discussion, the detectives unanimously agreed to keep their cards close to their chests for now when it came to Middleton's involvement in the case. The Miami connection needed to be checked, but there was no way to know if Middleton still had friends in the department there. Cops were notorious gossipers, and if word got out that Middleton was being investigated in Reno, it could get back to him. He'd only been out of the department for five years, so there was a good chance he still spoke to people there.

The arrest of a cop usually generates publicity, so they booted up the computer in the conference room and logged into the archives of the *Miami Herald*. Jenkins typed the words "arrest of David Middleton" into the archive search box and hit the enter button. Six articles popped up, which didn't seem like a lot for a case that sent a cop to prison. They were dealing with Miami, though, so events like that were a bit more commonplace than in a small town like Reno. Jenkins used the cursor to scroll through the articles while the other detectives pulled up chairs to see what he came up with.

The first article they looked at was dated October 12, 1990, and the bold-face title jumped out at them from the computer screen. It read:

METRO COP CHARGED WITH RAPING TEEN ELUDES ARREST

Carlos Harrison Herald Staff Writer

A Miami Police detective was charged Thursday night with kidnapping and raping a 16-year-old girl handcuffed inside of his unmarked police car-but officers who went to arrest him at his home found he had vanished. Metro detective David Middleton, 29, a seven-year member of the department's Warrants section, had been absent without leave since he found out that investigators suspected him of sexually assaulting the girl, sources in the department said.

Police went to arrest Middleton at his home Thursday evening after a warrant was issued but couldn't find him.

The girl was raped Saturday, September 29, 1990, between 1:30 and 4:30 A.M., detective Lizette Williams said.

Investigators said Middleton allegedly found the unidentified girl wandering near the Metro Justice Building. Middleton was off-duty but dressed in his police uniform and driving his unmarked car at the time of the incident. Williams said Middleton questioned the girl, who said she was waiting for a friend, then ordered her into his unmarked car.

He told her he was taking her to Juvenile Hall but then drove her to a South Dade parking lot, where he handcuffed her and raped her. Then he drove to North Dade, where he dropped her off.

Police sources say the victim picked Middleton out of a lineup as her rapist. Middleton's unmarked police car was impounded after the incident, sources said, presumably so investigators could check the car for evidence. The Dade State Attorney's Office declined to comment. "I just can't comment at all," said Chief Assistant Attorney John Hogan.

Jenkins pushed his chair back and said, "I don't want to read too much into this because we all know newspapers can sometimes be slightly jaded in their publications. But if this article is even half true, what does it tell us?"

Dixon answered, "It tells us we were right about him still being a cop when he committed the crime."

"Right," Jenkins said. "But look at the part where the article says he was off-duty but in uniform. He was a detective, so what's he doing out on the street in uniform at four in the morning?"

Dixon shrugged and replied, "Maybe he was working some O.T."

"Or maybe he's out trolling the streets like Jack the Ripper," Dypsynski said.

"I like that idea better," said Douglas. "And the article says he was gone when the cops got to his house, so that means the brother runs when he gets spooked."

Hunt shook his head and said, "And *that* tells me I'm being discriminated against. If I use the words 'run,' 'brother,' and 'spook' in the same sentence when I'm talking about a black suspect, I'll be up in front of some clam in I.A. for making racial statements."

Douglas smiled and said, "And don't you forget it either. But it still means we've got to be careful about him bolting if he finds out we're looking into him. The fact that he split before the cops got to him also means he probably got tipped off from the inside, so I say we stay clear of Metro P.D. till we get our shit together. Bring up the next article so we can decide what we're gonna do with this dude. My ass is dragging so bad even this plastic chair is starting to feel good on it."

The next article was dated November 21, 1990, almost one month after the first one. It read:

FUGITIVE COP IN RAPE CASE FOUND IN MISSISSIPPI

David Hancock Herald Staff Writer

A Miami Police officer who disappeared after he was charged with raping a 16-year-old girl in his police car was returned to Miami Tuesday night, a month after he fled to a small city in western Mississippi. Metro-Dade officer David Middleton, 29, was arrested Monday morning at his new apartment in Greenville, Miss., population 50,000. He had been laying low with his two children and his common-law wife, Evonne Haley, who joined him after he fled Miami last month, police said.

Middleton, an eight-year veteran of the department, was arrested without incident when Metro-Dade and Greenville police knocked on the door to his apartment. Greenville Police Chief Ken Winter said, "He was somewhat surprised."

Winter also said that after being tipped off that Middleton was in Greenville, police were able to locate his apartment. Middleton is black, and his wife is white. "That drew attention to them in these parts," Winter said. Middleton's wife was not arrested.

Middleton is accused of picking up a 16-year-old girl in Northwest Dade County on September 29, 1989. He told her he was taking her to Juvenile Hall but instead handcuffed her and allegedly raped her in the front seat of his unmarked police car. Middleton, who worked in Metro's Warrants section, called in sick for three days before officers went to his home to arrest him and discovered he had left.

Winter said Middleton and his wife didn't explain why they stopped in Greenville after being arrested. "We asked why they came to Greenville, and they said they didn't know," Winter said. "They would've fit in a lot better in some other places I can think of if they were trying to lay low."

Middleton faces charges of kidnapping and sexual assault. He waived his right to fight extradition and was flown to Miami on Tuesday.

Douglas whistled and said, "Too bad homeboy wasn't being tried in Greenville instead of Miami, cause a brother ain't getting a *fair* trial in that town. I'm picturing that cop Buford Justice from those old *Smoky and the Bandit* movies giving that interview while banjo music is playing in the background. You just *know* there's a pillow case with some eye holes in it and a rope noose hanging in that dude's locker next to his deputy chief uniform."

When the laughter subsided, Jenkins said, "So, our girl Evonne was with Middleton way back then. That means she waited for him to get out of prison on top of running away with him when he was trying to avoid arrest. It also means she must have been with him if he was living in Colorado before he got to Reno, too. It's interesting the article refers to her as his *common law wife.* Maybe there's more to our prom queen than meets the eye."

"Her meeting my eyes isn't something I'm looking forward to," Douglas said. "Read on."

Jenkins said, "I looked ahead while you were making your astute observations about our esteemed law enforcement colleague in Mississippi. You're gonna love this one because it proves the theory that if crooks were smart, we'd probably never catch them."

The next article was dated March 14, 1991, and it read:

OFFICERS USE OF TOLL CARD LEADS TO HIS ARREST

Don Van Natta Jr. Herald Staff Writer

Police may never have pinned kidnapping and rape charges on a former Metro-Dade detective if he had paid his own way at a toll booth on State Road 874. Instead, then-cop David Middleton charged the fare to Dade County by handing the attendant a county-issued credit card.

The toll was 25 cents.

"If it wasn't for that toll, we never would have traced the car and found our suspect," Assistant State Attorney Kathleen Hoague said Wednesday.

The victim told detectives she saw the police officer who had just raped her hand a credit card to a toll-taker. The girl remembered the card was cracked and "the toll booth lady put tape on it."

That night, only two unmarked Metro patrol cars used county-issued cards at the Southwest Dade toll plaza. Only one matched the victim's description of the officer's car: a 1988 grey Dodge Aries, vehicle number 10871.

And only one of four officers with keys to car 10871 matched the description of her attacker: a black male, around 30, over six feet tall, heavyset, with a distinctive underbite. That description fits David Middleton, 29, an eight-year veteran in Metro's Warrants section.

"The toll booth record was good luck for us and bad luck for him," Hoague said.

The next three articles covered the court proceedings against Middleton.

Victim testimony—often described as tearful—was given by the 16-year-old female referred to in the papers as "A.C." This was damning testimony because she said the only reason she willingly went along with Middleton was because he was a police officer, so she *trusted* him.

Middleton never took the stand in his defense, but twenty-three witnesses testified throughout the court proceedings. Some defense witnesses testified that Middleton was an excellent and respected officer who would never break the law, but this was overshadowed by a personnel record that showed him being disciplined for charges of consorting with known criminals.

At the end of the trial, the sequestered jury deadlocked after twelve hours of deliberation. They agreed to find Middleton guilty of the amended charges of false imprisonment and sexual battery. Since the most serious charges had been dropped, so was the cap for prison sentencing. Instead of life in prison, he was now facing a maximum of five years on each charge.

The prosecutor was quoted as being disappointed with the verdict and pointed to the fact that the trial judge, Philip Davis, was forced to drop out of the case during deliberations because he was being investigated for bribery charges. She said this very well might have contributed to the hasty verdict, but there were no plans for re-filing.

Jenkins rubbed his eyes with the back of his hands. He said, "Something's not right here, but I'm too tired to see it. What are we missing?"

They were all silent in thought, and then Douglas snapped his fingers and exclaimed, "Rodney King! That's what we're missing!"

"What in the hell are you talking about?" asked Hunt. "Every case involving a black crook don't have to be racial."

"I ain't talking about the black crook; I'm talking about the white cops. When the State jury came back with the not-guilty verdict on the cops involved in the Rodney King thing, the prosecution went federal with it. They charged the cops under the Oppression under Color of Authority statutes, and they all got federal jail time for violating King's rights while they were on duty."

"I'm with you," Jenkins said excitedly. "Even though Middleton was off duty when he snatched that girl, he was in uniform and driving a police car. That puts him *on* duty when he committed the crime, no matter how you look at it."

Douglas stood up and said, "Exactly! And you can't violate a person's rights much more than committing sexual battery on them while you've got them falsely imprisoned. So why didn't the Florida people file federally after Middleton got his charges reduced?"

"That ain't our investigation," Hunt said. "Who the hell knows what goes on in places like Miami?"

"Well, somebody has to ask that question," Jenkins said. "John raises a legitimate point. If you put a cop in front of a federal jury, they're going to find him guilty of *something*. And in a case like this, it would be a slam-dunk. Double jeopardy doesn't come into play because the oppression charge is completely separate from the other charges. Middleton would have gotten at *least* ten years federal time if they would have pushed this."

"And ten years federal is ten *real* years," Douglas added. "There ain't no early release program in Club Fed, so Middleton would have been off the street till about the year 2000 if they'd have done things properly!"

"We can't go back and undo what's been done," Jenkins said. "The ball is in our court now, so what are we going to do with it?"

"I say we pick this clam up and sweat him on the Good Guys case," Hunt said. "At least that way, we can get him off the street for a while till we look into the murder."

"That's plausible," Jenkins said. "I'd like to give some thought to how we go about picking him up, though."

Dixon said, "It should be easy getting to this guy. First, he uses his city credit card while he's kidnapping a girl, and then he sends his girlfriend down to pick up a stereo charged on a dead lady's credit card using his own truck, which is so distinctive looking even *we* found it. My son watches some T.V. show called Stupid Pet Tricks. Maybe we should make a show called Stupid Crook Tricks and feature our guy Middleton on it."

"I'm not seeing stupidity here, Eddie," Jenkins said. "I'm seeing complacency, and that only shows in crooks who have done things so many times they feel confident they will never get caught. Unfortunately, it's my opinion the 16-year-old girl Middleton got caught raping in Florida was not his first victim. That's why he was comfortable enough to use his city credit card. It was just business as usual. Do you know what that means?"

"Yeah," answered Dixon. "He was complacent after Kathy Powell, too, so she's probably not his first. I gotta get out of here and get some sleep. This investigation is getting way too complicated for my simple mind."

Everyone stood up to leave, but Jenkins continued, "There is a link at the bottom of the Miami Herald page saying to go to the archives of the Rocky Mountain Press for additional information on Middleton. Let's see what they've got to say about our friend."

Jenkins used the computer mouse to click on the link. After a few seconds, an article from the Colorado paper filled the screen. Douglas summed it up in two words. "Holy shit!"

"I couldn't have said it better," said Jenkins. "Sit down, gentlemen. We've got work to do."

Chapter 15:
Buffy

Five bleary-eyed detectives read the article from the *Rocky Mountain News* describing the disappearance of 18-year-old Buffy Rice Donohue from Montrose, Colorado, on November 21, 1993. The article was dated December 24, 1993, and the title read:

DISAPPEARANCE DARKENS CHRISTMAS; MONTROSE MAN TELLS STORY IN DENVER IN HOPES OF FINDING HIS DAUGHTER

Robert Jackson, Rocky Mountain News Staff Writer

The story was an interview of Walt Rice—the father of the missing girl. Buffy Rice had married her high school sweetheart Mason Donohue five months before her disappearance. Walt Rice and his wife Bonnie were letting the couple live at their Montrose, Colorado home until they raised enough money to rent a place of their own. Buffy worked at a local Sizzler Restaurant, and her husband worked in construction.

Buffy was last seen when she left the family home at 1:30 in the afternoon to get her car washed and go to a Walmart two miles away. Her husband and father went out looking for her when she did not return home four hours later. They found her car in the Walmart parking lot with the doors locked and her wallet inside. There were no keys, and Buffy was nowhere to be found.

Montrose is not a big town, so Rice and Donohue started checking to see if anyone had seen Buffy. They located two of Buffy's friends who had seen her getting into a red Mazda RX-7 in the Walmart parking lot at about 2:30 that afternoon. The car was driven by one of Buffy's co-workers at Sizzler, Evonne Haley. The witnesses knew the car was owned by Haley's boyfriend, David Middleton.

Both Rice and Donohue were familiar with Haley and Middleton. Middleton was employed by an aluminum siding contractor, and Donohue had befriended him after meeting him at a job site. Buffy worked with Haley at Sizzler, and the two couples had socialized on several occasions. Their friendship deteriorated after Buffy admitted to her husband and father that she had started experimenting with cocaine and that Middleton was her supplier. Buffy told her husband she wanted to get away from the drugs and that being around Middleton scared her. They decided to stay away from Middleton from that point forward.

Middleton and Haley had moved to Montrose about six months earlier, and Walt Rice was familiar with them. He knew Middleton was an ex-cop from Florida who had done some prison time, and Haley was an ex-stripper. When Buffy confessed her drug use to him, Walt went to the Colorado Bureau of Investigations with the information to ask agents if they could do something about it. He told reporters he felt that because of the drug connection, Montrose Police didn't take the investigation of his missing daughter seriously when he and Donohue reported it the night of November 21, 1993.

Rice and Donohue had gone to the apartment Middleton and Haley shared to check for Buffy before calling police. The RX-7 was gone and they were told by Haley's daughter that Buffy had been there, but Middleton left to take her home. Haley was not at the apartment either and this did not make sense to them since the car was a two-seater. If they had both left with Buffy, where would she sit in the car? It was this inconsistency that caused them to go to the police.

The police took the report from Rice and Donohue but said since Buffy was over 18 years–old, an active investigation could not be done until she was missing for over twenty-four hours. Even though she was last seen getting into a car with Haley, she did so of her own free will. They were told if she was still with Middleton and Haley, it would most probably be by choice, so officers would not go out to the residence to speak with them until the twenty-four-hour time frame had elapsed.

The frustration Rice and Donohue felt that night was compounded the next day when a friend of Buffy's who works at a convenience store directly across from Middleton's apartment called to tell them she had seen suspicious activity the night before. She had a clear view of Middleton's apartment through the plate glass store window, and around midnight, she saw Middleton and Haley loading plastic bags into the trunk of Haley's car. She said Middleton was struggling with one of the bags because of its weight, and he needed to wrap both of his arms around it in order to carry it. She said the bag was easily big enough to conceal a body.

The friend was aware of Buffy's disappearance and Middleton's involvement, so she telephoned the police with the information. She was told by the dispatcher that the police were not taking calls on that case for at least twenty-four hours. Two days later, the police finally contacted Middleton and Haley, and Buffy was nowhere to be found.

Rice said the reason he'd come to Denver from Montrose was to try and generate public interest in the case and to put pressure on the Montrose Police Department to investigate Buffy's disappearance more aggressively. Buffy had never left home for an extended period of time before and there was no reason to believe she had left of her own volition this time. Rice was certain David Middleton was responsible for his daughter's disappearance, but so far, the Montrose Police were treating Rice himself as more of a suspect than Middleton.

The last line of the article was a quote from Walt Rice: "We will have no Christmas this year. Christmas was Buffy's favorite part of the year, and we won't have another one until Buffy returns home."

All five detectives reading the article had children of their own. It was silent in the room for a moment before Douglas said, "That poor bastard. His daughter ain't coming home."

"I'm afraid you're right," commented Jenkins. "Look at this other article from the *Colorado Springs Gazette* a month later. It says Buffy's not the first girl to go missing from that area. There was a 14-year-old girl named Cindy Booth who disappeared from a town called Delta, about twenty miles from Montrose. She was last seen riding her bicycle on August 4, 1993.

"The reporter draws a very interesting timeline here. Middleton moved to Montrose on June 25, 1993, just after he got out of prison. Haley was already living there because she had relatives in Grand Junction, Colorado, so Middleton moved in with her and her two kids. The 14-year-old girl disappeared on August 4, 1993—just a little over a month after Middleton got to town. Then Buffy Rice went missing on November 21, 1993. The reporter says that the area didn't have a suspicious missing female case for ten years before Middleton arrived and there hasn't been one since he left. And my guess is they won't have another one because their nightmare is now ours."

Chapter 16:
Montrose

As Jenkins scrolled down the screen, Douglas said, "Some of those articles are pretty recent, so I'm guessing Buffy's never been found. Judging from the titles of the news stories, it looks to me like her family has gone on a press campaign against the police department, too. Click on the article that says charges were brought against her parents. I wonder what in the hell that's about."

The detectives took their time reading the *Denver Post* article because none of them could actually believe what had been written. The article began with an incident on November 27, 1993, six days after Buffy disappeared. Walt Rice had received a tip that Middleton and Haley might be holding his daughter in a cabin in an area called Waterdog Mountain. He gave this information to a Lieutenant Chinn at Montrose P.D., but since this was out of their jurisdiction, Rice was told the police would not investigate the tip.

The distraught father and husband took it upon themselves to check the information. Rice, Mason Donohue, and two friends went to the Waterdog Mountain cabin at 11:00 P.M. that night to see if there was any sign of Buffy. A blacked-out truck was driving down the dirt road leading away from the cabin in question when they got there. When the driver spotted the four men, he attempted to make a U-turn but got stuck in a ditch. The men surrounded the truck, but it turned out to be a hunter poaching game after hours. Rice and his friends detained the driver until they were satisfied he wasn't involved in Buffy's disappearance. They left the area after finding no trace of her.

In January of 1994, Walt and Bonnie Rice were told by someone within the Montrose Police Department that investigators had found a roll of undeveloped film while searching the trailer Buffy and her husband lived in just after they were married. The investigators developed the film and found that it contained nude photographs of Buffy that her husband took on their honeymoon. The police source told the Rices he had walked by Lieutenant Chinn's office, and the nude photos of Buffy were spread out on his desk. Chinn and several officers were laughing and making crude comments about the photos. The officer came forward with the information because he thought the conduct was inappropriate.

When Walt Rice began checking the information, he discovered a female employee at the local Sheriff's Department had also seen the photographs of Buffy. She told Walt that two Montrose P.D. officers had come to the Sheriff's Department to see a co-worker of hers, and they had nude photographs of Buffy with them. She said they showed the photographs to several male officers like they were pornography and made disparaging remarks about Buffy's character.

Walt Rice was incensed and went to Lieutenant Chinn to ask about the photographs. Chinn said they did, in fact, have nude photographs of Buffy and they were part of the investigation. He could not offer a reason why these photographs were important to the investigation or why they were not placed into evidence. He refused to give the photographs to Rice, who left after threatening to sue the department over this incident and their inept investigation. [5]

Shortly after this confrontation, charges of felony menacing and false imprisonment resulting from the Waterdog Mountain incident were filed against Walt Rice and Mason Donohue.

One week after Walt Rice was criminally charged, Bonnie Rice also had a run-in with the Montrose P.D. She and a male friend went to Haley's apartment on February 21, 1994, to confront her about Buffy's disappearance. While Bonnie and her friend stood outside Haley's doorway in a heated discussion, David Middleton came out of the apartment and threatened them with what Bonnie described as a 12-gauge shotgun.

The police were summoned, but by the time they got there, Middleton had put the shotgun inside the house. Instead of investigating Middleton for being an ex-felon in possession of a firearm, the police cited Bonnie Rice for trespassing. Only *she* was cited, even though the friend who accompanied her had been standing right next to her during the confrontation.

David Middleton and Evonne Haley left Montrose in April of 1994. Bonnie Rice told reporters that Haley said the Montrose Police had advised Middleton that leaving town might be a good idea because they were

---

[5] This incident was included in the lawsuit Donohue v. Hoey and is further referenced in Chapter 69 of this book.

getting public pressure to arrest him for Buffy's disappearance. A police spokesperson would neither confirm nor deny that allegation.

In May of 1994 the charges of trespass were dismissed against Bonnie Rice. Walt Rice and Mason Donohue pled no contest during that same month to the charges against them stemming from the Waterdog Mountain incident.

The article ended by saying the animosity between the Rices and the Montrose Police Department continued even after Middleton and Haley moved from this sleepy bedroom community of 12,000. The Rices are preparing a lawsuit naming Montrose Police Chief Gerald Hoey and Lieutenant Thomas Chinn as principles.

The Rices also filed charges against a Colorado State patrolman for calling their home and making threats. They recorded the conversation unbeknownst to the caller, identified as Patrolman Jack Charlton. During the phone call, the officer expressed his displeasure with the Rices' criticism of the local police, and is heard saying, "You're a dead S.O.B." Charlton pleaded no contest to the charges.

After reading the article, Hunt remarked, "What kind of bullshit is this? Instead of jamming this guy up on the missing girl, these fucking yahoos tell him to get out of Dodge? First Florida gives him the boot, then Colorado throws him out of their state, and now we're stuck with him in our backyard."

"Let's remember we're only dealing with news articles here," Jenkins said. "We won't be able to sort out the mistakes in the investigation from journalistic sensationalism until we talk to the cops themselves. There is a much shorter article here where the police say they gave Middleton a polygraph test before they allowed him to leave their jurisdiction. The results were inconclusive, which really doesn't mean anything, but I'm sure they still felt confident they didn't have anything to hold him on."

"Any cop who's been around a polygraph can beat the test," Dypsynski said. "Especially one who is a sociopath, and that's what this guy sounds like."

Douglas shook his head and asked, "The local cops can't nail Middleton, so they figure they'll go out and arrest the victim's parents instead? That's always good for P.R. The mother said Middleton pulled a gauge on her. An ex-felon in possession of a firearm is a felony in all 50 states, so they could have at least held him on that. I've only been reading about this guy for two hours, but I've already seen about a half dozen times he could have been stopped before getting to Reno. If he really *is* our killer, then I'm gonna be asking some questions."

"All I know is we've got to do something with this asshole quick," exclaimed Hunt. "If he gets away, there's gonna be a bunch of slob cops like us in another city sitting around bashing us the way we're bashing these other guys."

'You're right," said Jenkins. "We don't have nearly enough for an arrest, but based on the truck and Haley's physical match of the courier at Good Guys, we certainly have enough to pick him up and question him about that case. I'm sure I can get search warrants for his truck and apartment too, especially if I bring copies of these articles to show the D.A. There's no exigency for a nighttime search warrant though, so I'd like to set up surveillance on Middleton at his apartment right now and stay on him until we have the search warrants in hand. I'll call Toliver at home and see if he can get some people from the Street Crimes Unit to help out with that so we can get some sleep."

"Sleep's highly overrated," Hunt said. "I'll head out there now and get an eyeball on Middleton's place while you're setting things up with Toliver."

"I'll go with you," said Dixon. "But you might want to show this to the D.A. too. I scratched out some notes on the physical descriptions the news articles gave of the victims we think are related to Middleton so far. They are all petite in height and weight, they're all white, and they all have long hair. Kathy Powell fits into that category, too. Middleton's driver's license information puts him at six-two and two hundred and forty pounds, so that all matches the profile of a dominant sociopath who is into kidnap and bondage."

Douglas smiled and exclaimed, "I'll be damned! And here I thought you were just another pretty face, Eddie. That's one more brick in the wall.

Chapter 17:
The Prince Of Darkness

Within an hour a five-man team of undercover detectives from the department's Repeat Offender Unit were set up on Middleton and Haley's apartment to assist Hunt and Dixon with the surveillance. Middleton's International Harvester truck was parked in the lot in front of his apartment building. An older model red Mazda RX-7 with Colorado license plate UUB811 was parked in the space next to the truck. This car was registered to Middleton and Haley and the detectives recognized the description from the article they had read about the disappearance of Buffy Rice Donohue.

Jenkins, Douglas, and Depsynski had initially remained at the station to prepare the search warrant affidavits, but by 1:00 A.M., they joined the other detectives watching Middleton's apartment. Accompanying them was Detective Sergeant *Steve Burns, who had taken over the supervision of the investigation. Toliver was preparing to leave for a vacation, so he asked Burns to take over for him. Burns was a hard charger and well-liked by the detectives so they welcomed the change in supervision.

After a brief strategy session held in a darkened grocery store parking lot it was decided the Major Crimes detectives would turn the surveillance over to the undercover cops so they could get some rest. Jenkins planned to meet with the on-call Assistant District Attorney at 8:00 in the morning to review the search warrant affidavit, so there was not much to do until then. If Middleton made any suspicious moves before that, the surveillance teams would detain him for the driver's license and vehicle registration violations until the detectives could respond. One of the benefits of dealing with a hardcore criminal was there was usually *something* they could be held on.

By 9:00 the next morning, Thursday, February 23, 1995, Jenkins had search warrants for Middleton's apartment and truck signed by Washoe County Justice of the Peace Fidel Salcedo. The warrants covered only evidence related to the crimes stemming from the Good Guys' case. Since there was nothing yet to tie Middleton or Haley to the murder of Kathy Powell, the warrant would not cover a search for evidence related to that crime. But if the cops discovered something linking Middleton or Haley to the death of Kathy Powell while searching for credit cards or stereo equipment, it was fair game.

The surveillance teams followed Middleton to work at T.C.I. Cable Company at 8:00 that morning. He drove his International Harvester truck to work and parked it in the employee lot. A short time later, he emerged from the building and began loading equipment into a T.C.I. Cable Company truck. When he was through, he drove out of the lot in the company truck, and the surveillance team followed him to his first service call of the day.

Since Jenkins had a court appearance on another case scheduled that morning, he gave the search warrants to Douglas to execute. Detectives Douglas, Depsynski, and Dixon went to Middleton's apartment to serve the search warrant. They borrowed Detective Mike Whan from another unit to watch the outside of the apartment while they were searching since Detective Hunt had gone to T.C.I. Cable Company to photograph and search Middleton's truck.

Evonne Haley was at the apartment when detectives arrived to execute the search warrant. After they advised her of the reason for the search, she denied any knowledge of the crime or possession of any new stereo equipment. She also said she never heard of Kathy Powell and had never seen her credit card. Haley remained at the apartment while detectives searched and she was less than cooperative. She made a phone call and they assumed it was to Middleton as the surveillance team had him moving immediately after the call.

Fifteen minutes after they started searching the apartment one of the detectives following Middleton called Douglas to tell him he was pulling into the area of the apartment in his T.C.I. truck. Douglas went outside and, with the assistance of Detective Whan, intercepted Middleton before he got to the apartment. The detectives advised Middleton of the reason they were searching his apartment and also told him Detective Hunt was in the process of searching his truck at T.C.I. Cable Company. They told him about the Good Guys' case but made no mention of Kathy Powell's death. When they were through explaining, Middleton agreed to accompany the detectives to the station for an interview. He rode to the station with Douglas and Whan and left his T.C.I. truck parked at the apartment.

When they got to the station Detective Hunt called in to advise he had photographed and searched Middleton's truck, but no evidence relating to the Good Guys' case was found. He did note the inside of the truck had recently been cleaned. The truck was left at T.C.I. Cable

Company and Hunt said he was going to track down Powell's two neighbors who saw the truck outside of her apartment to show them the photos. One detective from the surveillance team was left with the truck in case Middleton or Haley went to get it.

When Jenkins returned from court, Middleton was in an interview room being watched by Detective Whan. They had decided Jenkins would handle the initial interview of Middleton, and Douglas would watch over closed circuit T.V. from an adjacent room. This way if something started going wrong in the interview or if the chemistry was wrong between Jenkins and Middleton, Douglas could come in and take over the interview from a different angle without being tainted by whatever went wrong with Jenkins. Detective Whan would act only as a witness to the interview and would not ask any questions.

Jenkins started the interview at 11:00 A.M. by first obtaining basic personal information from Middleton and then telling him the interview would be recorded. The next thing he did was tell Middleton he was not under arrest and that he was free to get up and leave at any time. Jenkins was the most skilled interviewer in the department and, in fact, taught interview techniques to other departments. Just from what he'd read thus far about Middleton he knew he was the type of person who would welcome the interview—not walk away from it. A sociopath always thought he could lie his way out of a situation, and Jenkins knew he was looking into the eyes of a true sociopath as he stared at the man across the table from him.

True to form, Middleton consented to stay for the interview, so Jenkins told him he first wanted to talk to him about a cable installation he did at 3484 Terrace Knolls Court in Reno. Jenkins did not initially mention Kathy Powell's name, but Middleton said he remembered the installation. He said he had given the female resident a cable converter box, and she had also asked him to install an additional two outlets in her home.

Jenkins then asked Middleton if the resident's name was Kathy Powell. After a brief hesitation, Middleton said that name did sound familiar. Jenkins next told Middleton that Kathy Powell had recently been found dead, and her credit card had been used for a telephone transaction at the Good Guys store. He then told Middleton that he strongly believed his International Harvester pickup truck had been used to collect the stereo equipment purchased with Kathy Powell's credit card.

Middleton denied any knowledge of the credit card transaction or of Kathy Powell's death. He said his girlfriend often uses his truck when he is at work, and perhaps she had been at Good Guys when the person had picked up the stereo equipment. That could have caused confusion among the salespeople who saw the truck.

When Jenkins asked Middleton if he had ever been to the Southwest Village Apartments, Middleton said the apartment complex is on his route, and he responds there often for service calls. When Middleton asked why Jenkins wanted to know about the Southwest Village complex, Jenkins let the question hang in the air unanswered while he pretended to be studying his notes.

Middleton appeared to be very nervous and apprehensive during these beginning stages of the interview, so Jenkins asked him about this instead of answering his question. Middleton said he was nervous because the other detectives told him they were in the process of searching his apartment. He said his wife had a small amount of methamphetamine in the apartment, and he was afraid she would get in trouble if they found it. Middleton admitted to using methamphetamine on a recreational basis but said he hadn't used any in a couple of days.

Jenkins asked Middleton if he and Haley were legally married, and Middleton said she was his common-law wife. Jenkins told him Nevada didn't recognize common-law marriages, so for the purpose of the interview, he would refer to Haley as his girlfriend. He then asked Middleton if it was possible Haley might have picked up the stereo equipment from Good Guys, to which Middleton said if she did then it was without his knowledge.

Jenkins then switched the line of questioning to the Commercial Hardware store. Middleton initially denied knowing where the store was but then said he had been in there a few times to buy tools and drill bits. He said he had no checking account or credit cards and always paid cash for purchases. Jenkins asked him specifically if he had gone to the Commercial Hardware store on February 8, 1995, and bought some 33-gallon plastic trash bags and some plastic wrap. Middleton said he had definitely not made those purchases.

Middleton's key ring was on the table in front of him and Jenkins noted there were several smaller keys on it. He asked Middleton to describe what each key was for. Middleton identified his truck key, the key for the Mazda RX-7, and his house key. He said the other keys were just for miscellaneous locks. Jenkins thought one of the keys looked like the type for security padlocks like those utilized in storage sheds. He asked Middleton if he had a storage shed and Middleton replied he did not.

Throughout the interview, Middleton mentioned several times that he used to be a cop and he wanted to help the detectives any way he could because he was *one of them*. Jenkins asked him if he would voluntarily supply samples of his blood and fingerprints if he really did want to help. It was at that point Middleton said he wanted to consult with an attorney before doing that or going any further with the investigation. Jenkins terminated the interview at that time but asked Middleton if he would remain at the station for a couple of minutes while he cleared up some minor details. Middleton agreed, and Jenkins left the room to confer with the other detectives.

Douglas had the same gut feeling as Jenkins that Middleton was lying and trying to ingratiate himself with them by continually saying he was *one of them*. They decided right then that Middleton might himself be a skilled interviewer, so they would have to incorporate a system of checks and balances for themselves into any further interviews. A skilled crook could turn an interviewer into an interviewee without the cop even realizing it if he wasn't careful.

While Jenkins was interviewing Middleton, Detective Hunt had returned from showing the Polaroid photos of Middleton's truck to Kathy Powell's neighbors. One of them said the truck looked about right, and the other said she was almost positive it was the same truck. It wasn't a positive identification, but it was another brick in the wall.

At the same time Detective Dixon had been on the phone with the Records section of the Miami Police Department. He'd confirmed that Middleton was an ex-felon out of their jurisdiction, so now the detectives knew he met the criteria for registration with the Reno Police Department. Part of that registration process was fingerprinting, and he had no right to consult an attorney prior to doing it.

Jenkins went back into the interview room and asked Middleton if he had registered with the Reno Police Department as a convicted person. Middleton said he was not aware of the requirement so he had never registered. Jenkins told Middleton since he had been so cooperative with the investigation, he would help Middleton register so he wouldn't get into any trouble. Jenkins then made arrangements for a clerk to meet them in the Records room during the time it was closed to the public for lunch so

Middleton could complete the registration process in private and avoid embarrassment—since he was *one of them.*

The idle conversation is not considered questioning, so even though Middleton invoked his right to an attorney, Jenkins kept talking to him as they made their way to the Records division. He told Middleton that he realized he was afraid, but all the detectives were interested in was getting to the truth. He also said he was aware there could be circumstances involved in Kathy Powell's death that might make it something other than a murder. Jenkins said if it was not a murder, then he didn't want Middleton held for such a crime. He mentioned nothing about what they knew of Middleton's criminal involvement in Florida and Colorado.

Jenkins then threw out the bait. He said, "I can tell you were a good cop at one time, and you know how cops work off of their instincts. I don't have all the answers, but I know in my heart you were associated with Kathy Powell's death. You were *one of us,* so you know what I'm talking about."

Middleton took the bait, and Jenkins silently cursed himself for leaving his cassette recorder in the interview room. Middleton stopped and said, "Well…it's not a murder, but I think I need to talk with an attorney before I tell you anything else about it."

Jenkins considered that statement to be an admission by Middleton that he was somehow involved in Kathy Powell's death, but there were no witnesses, and it was not recorded. When Douglas joined them after the ex-felon registration process was completed, Jenkins tried to get Middleton to repeat the statement. Middleton denied making any statement and said even if he had, it would be inadmissible because he'd already asked for an attorney.

Middleton smiled and said, "So am I free to go now, detective? If so, then I'd appreciate a ride back to my truck. I don't want to keep my other customers waiting too long."

An equally disingenuous smile spread across Jenkins face as he tried his best to hide his anger. He said, "Not recording your statement was a mistake on my part, David. It won't be the last mistake I make in my life, but I guarantee it will be the last one I make as far as you're concerned. Now, by all means, let's get you back to your truck. I said you were free to go, and I'm a man of my word. Remember that."

Douglas drove the unmarked detective car with Jenkins in the front passenger seat and Middleton in the back as they made their way to Middleton's apartment. A cassette recorder hidden under a newspaper was running throughout the ride, but Middleton only made small talk about police work and the difference in crime rates between Miami and Reno. When they got to his apartment, he thanked them for the ride, got out of their car, and drove away in his T.C.I. Cable truck without going into the apartment. Two unmarked surveillance cars followed him from a safe distance. Jenkins was reasonably certain the key on Middleton's ring was to a storage shed and he hoped he'd lead the surveillance team to it.

When they were alone in the detective's car, Jenkins asked, "So what do you think?"

Douglas shook his head and replied, "If I didn't know better, I'd think we were talking to another cop when we were with that guy—*most* of the time. He seems like a regular guy and looks like he used to be an athlete, but then when he gave you that wicked grin in the hallway after he said you couldn't use his statement, it was like I saw little horns sprout out of the front of his head. I had to check his nametag to make sure it didn't change from Dave to *Lucifer*! That dude's evil man—I can feel it!"

Jenkins said, "I get the same vibes from him—and we can't both be wrong. He played us this time, but that won't happen again. Let's go check with the boys in the apartment and see what they came up with inside the Prince of Darkness's lair."

Chapter 18:
The Truth Will Set You Free

Evonne Haley was seated on the living room couch when Douglas and Jenkins walked into the apartment. This was their first exposure to her, and she silently glared at the two detectives when they introduced themselves. Dixon was kneeling next to the couch, looking through some drawers in an end table. He said, "Ms. Haley isn't very happy with us at the moment."

Detective Depsynski called Jenkins into the kitchen and showed him a black plastic garbage can liner he'd found in the kitchen cabinet. It was a 33-gallon size with the same grey block-lettered suffocation warning label printed in the corner as the bag used to cover Kathy Powell's head had borne on it. This bag was distinctively different from the variety of trash bags routinely sold in grocery stores. The only place he'd seen this type of bag other than on Kathy Powell was at the Commercial Hardware store when he and Douglas had purchased a box of them.

The four detectives gathered in the kitchen for a brief conference. They now had Middleton's statement to Jenkins about having knowledge of the murder, his recorded statement that there might be drugs in the apartment, and the garbage bag that was possible evidence linking him to Powell's death. They could also now bring in what they knew about Middleton's past criminal history. It wasn't nearly enough to arrest him, but it was certainly enough to go back to the judge and request the scope of their search warrant be widened to include evidence linked to the murder and narcotics activity. That would virtually open up every inch of the apartment and the couple's two vehicles to their search.

When Jenkins told Haley they would be remaining at the apartment while he met with the judge to get a new search warrant, she flew off the couch and unleashed a stream of profanities at him. It was then he noticed the telltale signs of methamphetamine use on her. After calming her down somewhat, he asked her about the drugs Middleton said might be in the apartment and if she had been using them. She admitted using methamphetamine just before the detectives got to the apartment that morning and said there was none left in the apartment.

The next decision was a no-brainer. Detective Whan had just pulled up in front of the apartment, and Jenkins told him to take Haley up to the

County Jail, have a drug recognition test done on her, and then book her for being under the influence of methamphetamine. Haley struggled with the detectives at first but then became somewhat cooperative when they said she could call some friends and arrange to have her twelve-year-old daughter picked up from school before they took her to jail.

Arresting Haley would benefit them in three ways. First, it would get her out of the way while they completed their search of the apartment. Second, it would get her on file, and they would now have her fingerprints and photo to use to further their investigation. And third, it would show both Haley *and* Middleton the investigation was about more than just credit card fraud.

After Haley was gone Jenkins and Douglas drove to the District Attorney's office to get help with updating the search warrant. The attorney who worked on the original warrant with Jenkins was busy, but a young attorney named Thomas Viloria volunteered to assist them.

The thirty-year-old prosecutor was fairly new to the Washoe County District Attorney's office, but he'd already earned the reputation of having a bulldog mentality and the tenaciousness of a pit bull when he was prosecuting a case he believed in. Vilonia's handsome Mediterranean features, coupled with the build of a middleweight boxer, earned him the nickname Italian Stallion since his co-workers said his courtroom demeanor mimicked Sylvester Stallone's character Rocky Balboa in the ring.

After Jenkins laid the case out for him, Viloria was fascinated by it. Not only did he help update the search warrant, he cornered Judge Salcedo, who had signed the original warrant, and had him personally read and sign this one. Before they left the courthouse Viloria told the detectives he would like to stay involved in the case and for them to call him if they ever needed further assistance. The young bulldog attorney had no idea at the time how drastically that one statement would change his career *and* his life.

At 3:30 in the afternoon, Jenkins radioed Depsynski and told him he and Douglas were on their way back to the apartment with an updated and signed search warrant. The scope of this new warrant expanded their search to any items associated with Kathy Powell's body as well as evidence of narcotics possession. The warrant covered Middleton's truck and the red RX-7 in addition to the apartment. They would have to call in a crime scene team to collect trace and fingerprint evidence, but Jenkins gave the go-ahead for Depsynski and Dixon to start the search in the interim.

Thirty minutes later, Jenkins and Douglas walked into Middleton's apartment and found two smiling detectives standing in the dining room. Depsynski and Dixon were both wearing white latex gloves, and lying on the table in front of them was a Remington 870 Wingmaster .12-gauge pump shotgun. This is the kind of shotgun used by most police departments, but it was also exactly like the one Bonnie Rice said Middleton pointed at her the night she went to confront Haley about her missing daughter in Montrose, Colorado. Although this brand of shotgun is mass-produced and a big seller amongst gun enthusiasts, the old adage about there not being any coincidences in police work ran through all the detective's minds.

Depsynski had discovered the shotgun hidden under the covers of the bed Middleton shared with Evonne Haley. Since the gun was in that close proximity to Middleton's everyday living area, there was no way he could deny knowledge of its presence in the apartment. The law said as long as they could show that a convicted ex-felon had that knowledge, they did not have to prove actual ownership of the gun.

The discovery of the shotgun gave validity to the Montrose news article, and they were now more convinced than ever that Middleton was involved in Kathy Powell's murder. Unfortunately, they could not arrest him based on their gut instincts, but they now had a valid felony charge to arrest him on if they chose to do so.

The state of Nevada took the crime of ex-felon in possession of a firearm seriously. A high bail was set for persons arrested for the charge, and a minimum mandatory sentence of one year in prison was given if convicted of it. The next decision was another no-brainer for the detectives. They would take the extra step the Montrose cops didn't and remove David Middleton from society while they continued their investigation into Kathy Powell's murder. With Middleton in jail, at least they could be sure he wouldn't rack up any more victims while they put their case together against him.

A slamming car door got their attention, and when they looked out the front window, they saw Middleton walking toward the front door from his International Harvester pickup truck. Jenkins and Douglas met him outside of the front door, and this time, the smiles on their faces were anything *but* disingenuous.

Jenkins explained the updated search warrant and the discovery of the shotgun to Middleton. He looked almost relieved, saying the shotgun actually belonged to Haley and that it couldn't be fired since it was unloaded. For those two reasons, he said the detectives couldn't arrest him for possessing the shotgun.

Jenkins said, "That may be true to a jailhouse lawyer, but let me explain the way the law really works. The statute says 'possession of a firearm—constructive or physical—by a convicted felon is a felony and shall be punished by a minimum of one year in a State institution.' You see, David, there are no exceptions in the law based on whose side of the bed the gun was on or whether you loaded it before you went to sleep last night."

Douglas said, "And like my grandma used to say, '*once burnt, twice learnt.*' I think she used to say *boy* first, too, but that was socially acceptable back in those days."

"What my partner is trying to say in his own way," Jenkins added, "is you are under arrest for being an ex-felon in possession of a firearm."

"No, I *said* what I was trying to say," Douglas said. "You burned the cops once with that gauge, and you *ain't* gonna do it again. Now put your hands behind your back so I can put these nice silver bracelets on you."

Jenkins searched Middleton after he was handcuffed and removed the large key ring he'd seen earlier at the police station from his pants pocket. He said, "We'll need your keys, David. We're going to be towing your truck to the crime lab for processing, and it will be much easier for the driver to hook it up if he can back it out onto the street. We also need to search the RX-7 and I'd like to have a key to the house so we can lock up when we're through here. It seems Evonne won't be back for a few hours."

After Jenkins explained Haley's arrest, Middleton said, "You can take the ignition key for the truck off the ring, but I want the rest of the keys kept with me in my property. The RX-7 is unlocked, and you can use the handle lock on the front door to lock up the apartment when you leave."

The keys felt like they were on fire as Jenkins held them in his hand. He knew in his heart they were somehow involved in the case, but as hard as he tried, he couldn't think of a reason to put them into evidence. If he kept the keys without cause and they later proved pertinent to the case, anything he discovered by using them would be thrown out of court as fruits of the poisonous tree since Middleton was specifically asking that they be returned to him.

Jenkins took the truck key off the ring and put the remaining keys back into Middleton's pocket. He said, "As you wish, David. I'll know where to find them if I need them. I'm going to drive you to jail myself, and I'd like you to remember something. From this day forward, if there is anything at all you want to discuss with us, we're always available."

Douglas added, "All we're after is the truth, and like my grandma *also* used to say—' *the truth will set you free.* '"

Jenkins gave a tug on the handcuff chains and said, "Of course, his grandma spoke in metaphorical terms. Let's go."

Chapter 19:
Dead Ends

Nothing was found during the search of Middleton's apartment and vehicles to tie him or Haley to the Good Guys' case or to Kathy Powell's murder. As a matter of fact, with the exception of some drug paraphernalia and the shotgun, nothing was found to tie them to *any* type of criminal behavior. This made the detectives even more certain Middleton had a storage shed somewhere because, as Douglas put it, "nobody *that* dirty can be *that* clean."

Evonne Haley was released from jail on her own recognizance later that evening. The detectives did not charge her with anything related to the Good Guys crime because they felt they didn't have enough yet. All they had was the fact she matched the description of the courier and Middleton owned a truck matching the one used to pick up the stereo equipment.

There were several sightings of similar trucks since the start of the investigation, and Reno had more than its share of overweight blondes who wore too much makeup. To say Haley was the courier and Middleton's truck was the same as the one used at Good Guys wouldn't hold up in court without additional evidence. They didn't want to do a photo lineup to see if the witnesses from Good Guys could pick out Haley since if even one of them didn't pick her out, it would ruin the chance of filing charges against her later. Even if they *did* identify her, they wouldn't be able to prove she knew she was picking up merchandise that had been fraudulently obtained. They needed to keep building their wall, but at least Middleton was off the street while they were doing it.

By Friday, February 24^{th,} the investigation appeared to be once again coming to a standstill. It had been thirteen days since Kathy Powell's body was discovered, and although they had zeroed in on a suspect, they weren't even close to making a case against him. The motive was a key clue in any homicide investigation, but they had none. They didn't even have a viable cause of death to work with, and the only evidence they did have was circumstantial at best. Without any new leads, overtime to work the case over the weekend certainly would not be approved, and everyone but Jenkins and Douglas were pulled from the case to help with the mounting caseload.

The detectives were still convinced Middleton had a storage shed, and finding it would give the investigation the boost it needed. They began calling storage facilities and, by noon, had contacted everyone in a fifty-mile radius. None of them had a storage unit rented to Middleton or Haley, and they all said they required identification from their renters. It looked like another dead end, so they treated themselves to a sit-down lunch and spent the rest of the day organizing their case notes.

Jenkins made a phone call to Montrose, Colorado, that day and spoke with Lieutenant Chinn from the Montrose P.D. As they suspected, Buffy Rice Donohue still had not been found—dead *or* alive. The case was still listed as open, and both Middleton and Haley were persons of interest in Buffy's disappearance.

When Jenkins told Chinn about Middleton's arrest for being an ex-felon in possession of a firearm, he was told a story that may have contributed to the reason the same thing wasn't done in Colorado. Most people in Montrose didn't know Middleton was an ex-felon, and that may also have been true of the officers who had responded to the disturbance. Middleton told people that he was an ex-cop from Miami and had been put in prison as part of an undercover sting operation targeting drug dealers. He alluded to the fact that he ended up in Montrose as some type of Witness Protection Program.

Shortly before Buffy's disappearance, she told her parents she found out Middleton had actually been in prison as a prisoner and not as an undercover cop. Walt Rice came forward with that information after Buffy's disappearance. Nobody believed it at first because by then, Middleton had a lot of friends in the community—local cops included. As a routine part of the investigation Chinn ran Middleton's criminal history a few days after the missing person report was filed. He learned Middleton was, in fact, an ex-felon, but he wasn't certain if that information ever filtered down to the rank-and-file officers.

Jenkins had researched the Montrose Police Department through their website before making the call and learned it was a forty-three-man department with a five-man detective division. How information that important could not *filter down* in a department that small was beyond him, but it was not his job to second guess, so he kept quiet. He also didn't ask whether the officers who responded to Middleton's apartment during the shotgun incident were among the group he had befriended. He could picture Middleton standing on the steps of his apartment, saying, "Come on, I was *one of you* once. I'd never pull a gun on a lady."

Chinn did not know how Buffy had learned Middleton was an ex-felon, and he would not be able to ask Walt or Bonnie Rice about it. Due to the hostility between Rice and the police department, the City's attorney had advised against any unsupervised contact between the two parties. Jenkins again kept silent about his knowledge of the pending lawsuit and the allegations of misconduct regarding the nude photos of Buffy.

Chinn surprised Jenkins when he told him he had traveled to Reno in October of 1994 to interview Middleton about the Buffy Rice case. He said he notified Reno P.D. that he was in town to interview Middleton, but when questioned about the notification, he said he called police dispatch and advised them. The fact this information never made its way to the Detective Division did not surprise Jenkins. The Dispatch Center was sometimes referred to as the "Black Hole," among other things. Sometimes, information went in there and just never came out. It was water under the bridge now, but it would have been nice to have Middleton on their radar screen five months before Kathy Powell was killed.

After Jenkins got off the phone he discussed the conversation with Douglas. His handwritten notes confirmed most of what they'd read in the newspaper articles, and it seemed to them like Middleton did, in fact, slip through some very large cracks in order to get to Reno. They decided right then and there that the focus of their investigation would remain on what Middleton did in Reno—not what could have been done to prevent him from getting to Reno in the first place. Their job was to bring to justice the murderer of Kathy Powell, and dragging investigations from other jurisdictions into their investigation would only muddy the waters. If mistakes were made, the people they were made by would have to live with them.

Before leaving for the day, Jenkins made one more telephone call. This one went to Assistant District Tom Viloria who Jenkins had called earlier to ask assistance in getting Middleton's bail amount raised. Viloria talked to the judge, and Middleton's bail was raised from $25,000 to $750,000 cash-only based on his flight from justice when he was a fugitive in Florida. Jenkins thanked him and smiled as he hung up the phone.

Middleton did not even have a checking account, and his most valuable possession was the 1972 International Harvester pickup truck, which was still in police custody. There was no way he could raise

$75—never mind $750,000. They decided to let him sit in jail over the weekend and try an interview with him on Monday. A few days in jail might jar his memory, and two days away from the investigation might help them blast through their dead ends.

Chapter 20:
A New Day

Monday morning came around all too soon for Jenkins. He managed to spend a rare two-day weekend devoid of any detective callouts, but his days off still flew by. He was able to spend some quality time with his family, hit the gym twice, and sip some good red wine for the purpose of relaxation instead of memory obliteration for a change. But the weekend was over, and he had his game face on when he walked into the Major Crimes Unit office at 7:00 in the morning on February 27, 1995.

It had now been sixteen days since the discovery of Kathy Powell's body. Even though he had time for relaxation over the weekend, his mind often drifted back to the investigation and how to get things moving. He was convinced they were focused on the right suspect, but getting to David Middleton was now the problem.

The new day brought with it one of the Sierra Nevada's biggest winter storms of the year. Although large accumulations of snow usually fell only in the high mountains surrounding Reno, this storm threatened to dump six inches in the valley before it moved on. As a result of the storm, the morning commuter traffic was a nightmare. There was a pink telephone message slip on Jenkins' desk when he got to it informing him Douglas would be late. He lived in a community thirty-five miles east of Reno and a wreck on I-80 currently had the road closed. The message said he'd catch up with him when he got there.

Crime had been relatively slow in Reno over the weekend, so the Kathy Powell case was all that was discussed in the morning detective staff meeting. Even though they were convinced that they already had their suspect identified, other leads had to be followed up on and eliminated. It was a common defense technique for an attorney to go in front of a jury and say the police focused only on their client from the beginning of the investigation, so the *real* killer went free. This was especially true when the suspect was black, the victim was white, and there were other possible suspects who also happened to be white that were not properly eliminated as suspects.

Sergeant Burns dedicated the rest of the unit to the case to help Jenkins and Douglas as long as things remained slow. Follow up interviews needed to be done with everyone involved, but especially with

Powell's boyfriend in Pittsburg. He would be the one a defense attorney would focus on since he stood to gain monetarily from Powell's death. Depsynski volunteered to interview Don Barley and said he hoped he could nail everything down over the phone. If somebody had to fly to Pittsburg in the winter for a face-to-face interview, he would not be volunteering.

Other interviews and tasks were assigned, but Jenkins said his first stop was going to be 911 Parr Boulevard—the Washoe County Jail. He'd given a lot of thought over the weekend as to how he was going to handle Middleton, and it was time to play his first card. Since Douglas hadn't arrived yet, Hunt volunteered to accompany Jenkins. Keeping Douglas out of the interview process while it was still in its infancy was also still a good ploy because he could always come in and play the good cop if things went bad with Jenkins.

The Washoe County Jail complex was located in the foothills overlooking north Reno. The Sheriff's Department, crime lab, and jail intake were housed in the main building, and the inmate facilities were located in pods that extended from that building-like fingers from a hand. The section of the complex that faced the main road consisted of modern-looking buildings constructed of clean white brick and an abundance of tinted glass. At first glance one would think it was a modern office complex—until they drove to the rear of the building. Located, there was the telltale ten-foot chain link fence topped by concertina wire that surrounded every jail in America. It was *this* section of the complex that the detectives entered when they arrived.

It was 8:35 in the morning by the time they got to the jail, and all of the inmate interview rooms were already filled. Mornings were the busiest times at the jail, and they'd wanted to arrive earlier, but the drive took them twice the usual time because of the inclement weather. After a brief conversation with the jail intake personnel Jenkins got approval for Middleton to be brought out to the jail corridor for a short conversation. Since Middleton had already invoked his right to an attorney the detectives would not be able to ask him any questions, but that wasn't the purpose of this meeting.

Middleton was brought out into the jail corridor wearing a jail garb consisting of an orange jumpsuit and blue plastic sandals over white socks. The outfit made him appear smaller than he did in his civilian clothing. He also appeared less confident than he had during their last meeting. The dejected look on his face reminded Jenkins of a dog who had just been disciplined with a rolled-up newspaper.

Jenkins introduced Middleton to Detective Hunt and told him they were just stopping by to see how he was doing. He told Middleton that since he was an ex-cop, they were worried about his physical and mental well-being now that he was behind bars again. When asked if he'd like to be placed into protective custody Middleton replied he was fine for the time being. Jenkins was trying to establish some type of rapport with Middleton, and it seemed to be working.

Middleton told the detectives he wanted to speak to them and tell them what happened, but before he did that he wanted to talk to an attorney to ask a couple of legal questions. He said no matter what his attorney told him, he would still speak to the detectives—he just wanted to make sure he had the right understanding of the law before he did.

Middleton said he knew the detectives weren't there to talk about the gun charge, so that's why he wanted to talk to an attorney first. He said he'd called Haley over the weekend and she said she'd called a local attorney for him, but he hadn't been contacted by anyone yet. Middleton said as soon as the attorney contacted him, he'd have the jail deputies call the detectives to set up an interview.

Jenkins told Middleton he was eligible for representation by the Public Defender's office and to send him a "kite" if he would like that arranged. A "kite" is jailhouse language for a written note inmates can send through the interdepartmental mail inside the jail. Middleton thanked Jenkins for the offer and said he'd be in touch. He was then led back inside the jail by his escort deputy.

Before leaving the jail, the detectives stopped at the intake desk and checked Middleton's property and visitor log sheet. He'd had no visitors since he was booked, but he had released his cash and key ring to Evonne Haley. Jenkins was now more certain than ever that the keys were somehow related to Kathy Powell's murder.

Detective Depsynski called Jenkins as he and Hunt were leaving the jail. An operator from T.C.I. Cable Company had heard about Middleton's arrest and contacted the police with some information she thought might be pertinent. The operator had received a call two weeks ago from a female who identified herself only as Suzy. The female said she had been getting threatening phone calls from Middleton's girlfriend, and she wanted it to stop. The caller said Middleton's girlfriend was calling her place of employment to make the threats, and she was about to get fired over it. She said she wanted T.C.I. Cable to put pressure on Middleton for this to stop.

Jenkins looked up Evonne Haley's phone number from his notes and called her to see if she would speak to him. He didn't tell her the exact reason, and she said the detectives could come to her apartment to talk to her. The weather and the roads had begun to clear, so thirty minutes later, Hunt was pulling the unmarked detective car into the spot Middleton's truck usually occupied.

Haley looked disheveled and exhausted when she let the detectives into her apartment. The inside was in the same state of disarray as they had left it after their search, and traces of black fingerprint powder could still be seen on the white paint on the door jambs around the front door. She apologized for the appearance of the apartment but said she felt as if her whole world was crashing down around her since Middleton's arrest. She said even though she worked at a local casino, Middleton's check paid for most of their living expenses, and now she was afraid he'd lose his job. She then quickly switched gears and asked if what she'd heard on the news was true—that the police thought Middleton killed Kathy Powell.

Jenkins' tone of voice was sympathetic when he explained that the police were looking at Middleton as being involved, but they hadn't narrowed their investigation into Kathy Powell's death to any one suspect. He told her that, of course, the police needed to look into Middleton's possible involvement since his truck had been identified as being used in the fraudulent use of the deceased woman's credit card. He then told her they were somewhat familiar with Middleton's problems in Colorado and Florida, so it was only natural the police needed to look into his possible involvement in Kathy Powell's death.

Haley crossed her arms in front of her chest and stepped away from the detectives when Jenkins mentioned Colorado and Florida. There was so much Jenkins wanted to ask her, but based on her body language, he decided to keep this interview focused on the present. There would be time for the other questions later.

Jenkins moved the conversation to Haley's daughter and asked if she had been picked up from school alright the day she was arrested. Haley seemed to calm down at the mention of her daughter and said she had been taken care of. She then thanked Jenkins for allowing her to make those arrangements before going to jail.

Haley sat down on the living room couch, and Jenkins took a seat on a worn-out armchair across from her. Hunt remained standing by the door since they'd already decided Jenkins would take the lead on the interview. Now that the mood was more amicable, Jenkins asked Haley about the female caller to T.C.I. Cable.

Haley's face blushed, and she wrung her hands together as she spoke. She said she knew Middleton cheated on her with other women over the years, but she loved him and didn't want to leave him. She said she was an extremely jealous person, and when she found Suzy's phone number in the pocket of Middleton's work pants, she became incensed. She began calling the woman and making threats to hurt her if she didn't stay away from Middleton, and even confronted her in person one night as she was leaving the bar she worked at.

Jenkins asked Haley the name of the bar, and she said it was The Brew Pub on Victorian Square in Sparks. He then asked Haley to describe Suzy, and the description she gave caused the two detectives to exchange quizzical looks while Haley was staring down at the table in front of her. With the exception of the weight, Suzy's description closely matched the description of the courier seen at Good Guys. This threw their investigation into that crime in an unexpected direction.

Jenkins changed the subject and asked Haley if she had retained an attorney for Middleton. She said she had left a message for one, but he hadn't gotten back to her yet. Jenkins told her that if he didn't hear from her by the end of the day, he would contact the Public Defender's office and arrange representation for Middleton. She thanked him, and he stood to leave.

As an afterthought, he asked her about Middleton's keys. She said Middleton got a message to her through the deputies as she was being discharged from jail and asked her to take his keys and cash out of his property. She said she needed the cash, and figured he wanted her to have the extra house and car keys with her.

Jenkins asked if she would mind giving him the keys in case they could somehow help in the investigation. Haley's mind seemed to be in another place, but she took the key ring out of her purse and handed it to Jenkins without questioning his reason for wanting it. Jenkins looked at the key ring and saw it was the one he had seen Middleton with. He now had legal possession of the keys and slipped them into his coat pocket without making further mention of them.

When they were back in the car, Hunt said, "That's just great. If you shave forty pounds off that broad, she could have been describing herself instead of that bartender. Do you think there really *is* a bartender, or do you think she's blowing smoke to throw us off?"

"I don't think she's smart enough to throw up that kind of smokescreen," Jenkins replied. "We've got the phone number and name of the bar, so tracking the girl down can't be too difficult for a couple of super sleuths like us. You're right about this other girl matching the description of the courier, but there is one other troubling possibility."

"What's that?"

Jenkins turned in his seat and said, "If you shave forty pounds off of Evonne Haley, she would be about the same height and weight as Kathy Powell. That means this bartender, Suzy, fits into the same list that Eddie put together of the physical characteristics of Middleton's known victims. When we find her, we might just be looking at Middleton's next victim. That is, *if* we don't do our jobs before he does his."

Chapter 21:
Stalker

By 3:00 that afternoon, the detectives had Suzy identified as forty-two-year-old Suzanne Atkinson*. Jenkins and Douglas had gone to The Brew Pub and spoken to the owners who supplied them with Atkinson's information. She no longer worked at the bar, as the owners fired her just after the first of the year. They said the reason they fired her was that a person named Evonne had been constantly calling the bar and making disturbing threats toward her. They also heard rumors that Atkinson was selling methamphetamine to bar patrons.

The mention of methamphetamine sales interested the detectives, and they began thinking maybe it *was* her instead of Haley who had been involved in the Good Guys crime. They went to Atkinson's Sparks apartment, and when she answered the door, the detectives were surprised by her appearance. Jenkins was right—she looked like Evonne Haley with forty pounds shaved off.

When Jenkins told Atkinson they were there to ask her questions about David Middleton, she said, "That creep?"

She then invited them into her apartment but told them she had to leave for work shortly. Since being fired from The Brew Pub, she had taken a job tending bar at one of the local casinos, and she was currently working the night shift.

When Jenkins asked how she knew Middleton she said she first met him about three months ago in a Sparks' bar called Sierra Stix. She had gone there with friends one night and noticed Middleton sitting at the bar by himself. She sat down next to him and struck up a conversation. She told him he looked athletic, at which point he told her he used to play football for the Washington Redskins until an injury ended his career.

At some point in the evening, Atkinson invited Middleton to go into the lady's room with her and do some methamphetamine. Atkinson said the methamphetamine was hers, and while they were doing the drugs, Middleton told her he used to be a Miami cop. She said she was about to run from the ladies' room because she thought he was going to arrest her, but then he assured her he was no longer in police work.

He told her he worked for T.C.I. Cable Company, and later that night, he asked her if she would be interested in getting cable installed in her apartment for free. She said she would like that and gave Middleton her address and phone number. She also told him the name of the bar where she worked and said she would buy him drinks there if he ever did install the free cable.

Atkinson said she left the bar with her friends and had no further contact with Middleton that night. About two weeks later, she came home and found a note from T.C.I. Cable Company on her front door saying cable had been installed in her apartment. The note was not signed, but since she never ordered the cable service and never received a bill, she knew it was Middleton who hooked it up.

A couple of days later, Middleton began coming into her bar, and she would buy him drinks each time. He asked her out several times, but she continually declined his offers. She said there was something about him that gave her an odd feeling, but she couldn't say exactly what it was. Middleton eventually stopped coming into the bar, and shortly after that, Atkinson began receiving threatening and obscene phone calls at her home and work. The caller identified herself as Middleton's wife and told Atkinson to stay away from Middleton. She described the woman who eventually confronted her at the bar, and the description matched Evonne Haley. It was right after that incident that Atkinson got fired from the bar.

Jenkins asked Atkinson when the last time she saw Middleton was, and she said this whole thing happened in late December 1994, right before Christmas. She said the calls from Middleton's wife stopped right after she complained to T.C.I. Cable Company, and she hadn't seen Middleton or his wife since.

When questioned about Middleton's truck, she said she had no idea what type of vehicle he drove. When asked about her whereabouts on Monday, February 6th—the date of the Good Guys transaction—Atkinson consulted her date planner and said she had worked a day shift at her new job on that date. She gave the detectives the name of her boss, who could confirm her whereabouts, but they both already knew what they'd be told when they called him.

As the detectives were leaving, Atkinson said, "You know, I've been in this business a long time, so I'm a pretty good judge of character. I can tell a stalker a mile away, and that guy Dave is stalker material."

As Jenkins started the car, he said, "When Hunt and I left Haley's apartment I told him when we found Suzy we would probably be looking at Middleton's next intended victim. I was wrong. He moved from her to Kathy Powell, and Suzy Atkinson will never know how lucky she was."

Douglas said, "Kathy Powell might still be alive too if she got into a cult run by a bartender instead of a psychologist. Bartenders and cops are a lot alike. We don't *trust* nobody."

"And I believe they call that a blessing and a curse," Jenkins said. "Let's round up the rest of the cynics and compare notes before we call it a day."

The detectives met in their conference room at 4:30 in the afternoon and Douglas briefed the rest of the unit about their interview with Suzanne Atkinson. After he was through, Depsynski told them another female had called the detective squad earlier in the afternoon to recount her experiences with David Middleton.

A forty-year-old female named Tina Bronson*, who lived in the Smithridge Condominiums was referred to detectives when she called in information to T.C.I. Cable Company. Her condominium complex was about two miles from where Kathy Powell's body was discovered and was on Middleton's route. Ms. Bronson told Depsynski that Middleton installed cable service in her condominium in early November 1994 and made arrangements to return after hours to provide additional service at no cost.

In addition to the cable services, Middleton spent the night at Bronson's condominium to provide services of a different sort. Bronson said she and Middleton engaged in consensual sex that evening, and he left early in the morning. He told her he was divorced and lived alone on Carlin Street in Reno but had to leave in order to get to work in the morning. She had since spoken to him on the phone several times and always called him at T.C.I. Cable since he told her he did not have a home phone. They had planned to get together again but never did due to scheduling conflicts. Bronson said she became concerned for her safety after seeing the news story about Middleton's arrest, and that is why she called T.C.I. Cable Company.

Bronson said there was nothing unusual about her sexual activities with Middleton in the way of violence or bondage, but one thing did stand out in her mind as being out of the ordinary. After they had begun getting romantic, Bronson told Middleton she would like him to use a condom. She offered him one from a box she had on her nightstand, but he refused, saying it was not his brand. He got dressed and went to his truck to retrieve a condom, telling her he preferred Trojan condoms because of a reaction he had to some of the other brands on the market. Bronson described herself as five-three and one-hundred-fifteen pounds with shoulder-length brown hair.

They now had an established pattern of behavior relating to Middleton becoming involved in romantic encounters with female customers, his interest in another female fitting the victim profile, and Middleton stating his preference for condoms was the same brand found in Kathy Powell's apartment. The wall was becoming taller, and it was time to find Middleton, a lawyer.

Chapter 22:
A Pig In A Poke

Jenkins received a phone call from the Public Defender's office at 10:30 in the morning on Wednesday, March 1, 1995. The head Public Defender, Michael Specchio, had gone to the jail the day before to interview Middleton since all of his deputies were busy with other cases.

Mr. Specchio stated he didn't believe police had the elements necessary for a murder investigation. He had advised Middleton not to discuss the case with them, but Middleton insisted on doing so.

The attorney ended the conversation by saying, "I guess he's all yours."

As soon as Jenkins hung up the phone, he and Douglas drove to the County Jail to do a second interview with Middleton. They secured an interview room in the Sheriff's Detective Division and Dixon set up in the adjacent room to record the proceedings.

The first thing Middleton did when he was brought into the room was that he complained that one of the detectives involved in the case had told his twelve-year-old step-daughter that he was a rapist and a murderer and would be going to the electric chair. Because of that, he now had doubts about whether or not he wanted to cooperate with the police.

Jenkins smoothed things over by telling Middleton none of the detectives had yet spoken to the child, and perhaps she had misinterpreted something she heard on one of the news stories about his arrest. The department had not put out any press release regarding his possible involvement in Kathy Powell's death. Still, some parts of the investigation, such as the search warrant affidavits, were public information routinely examined by the press. This seemed to placate Middleton, and he agreed to talk to the detectives without his attorney present.

In answer to Middleton's concern about the death penalty, Jenkins explained to him that it was only an option in first-degree murder cases. He told him about his conversation with Mr. Specchio and that the attorney represented it was his opinion that there was not a murder involved in Kathy Powell's death. Jenkins told Middleton Kathy Powell's death was shrouded in unanswered questions, and the only promise he would make was to fairly and accurately record what he said in an effort to determine the truth about what happened.

Middleton told the detectives he wanted to negotiate some type of cap on his prison sentence in exchange for giving his statement. He said he could provide information on his drug use, involvement with the fraudulent use of Kathy Powell's credit card, grand larceny, and unlawful disposal of human remains.

Both detectives perked up when Middleton mentioned the disposal of human remains but tried not to show their excitement. It appeared Middleton was getting ready to talk about what happened to Kathy Powell and they did not want to shut him down by appearing overanxious. Jenkins informed Middleton that he couldn't discuss any potential sentencing deals, but he promised to contact the District Attorney for help. Jenkins and Douglas stepped out of the room to make the call and strategize their next steps. Washoe County District Attorney Richard Gammick had been voted into office in January of 1995. Because this had the potential of being the first major case prosecuted by his office since he took control, the District Attorney personally responded to Jenkins' request for assistance with Middleton.

Gammick was a short, wiry, bald man in his fifties who had been a prosecutor with the D.A.'s office for ten years before being elected to the top job. His country drawl and the cowboy boots he routinely wore with his business suits were remnants of his upbringing in Elko, Nevada. Since Gammick had been a Reno cop before becoming an attorney, he was familiar with both Jenkins and Douglas. He listened intently as they briefed him on the case before going into the interview room to speak to Middleton.

After making sure Middleton understood his rights and the information his attorney discussed with him, Gammick let Middleton talk. Much to the detective's disappointment, Middleton made no concrete statements regarding Kathy Powell's death while he spoke to Gammick. He reiterated that this was not a murder and said he would give detailed accounts of the entire incident if they could reach an agreement.

What Middleton wanted in return was a promise of a limited amount of jail time based on the property crimes he was willing to admit to. He would name the crimes he thought he was guilty of and wanted to know how much time each carried as a penalty before he admitted to them.

Gammick was a hardnosed prosecutor, and he listened patiently as Middleton described the deal he wanted. When he was talking, Gammick said, "So what you're asking me to do here, Mr. Middleton, is buy a pig in a poke. Well, I don't buy pigs in pokes because that's just plain stupid. The deal I have for you is that you admit to everything you've done in this case, and then we'll discuss the penalties. If this investigation determines you've only been involved in property crimes, then I'm sure there'll be room for negotiation between your attorney and my office."

After Gammick left the room, Middleton gave Douglas a quizzical look and asked him what buying a pig had to do with anything. Since Douglas grew up in an inner city, he had no idea what the saying meant either. Not wanting to appear uninformed in front of the prisoner, he said, "Everybody knows what that pig in a poke thing means. Tell him, Dave."

Being astute in the old English language, Jenkins knew exactly where the phrase came from. A burlap sack was referred to as a poke in the English countryside in the 1800s, and it eventually evolved into the word pocket in the modern language. The advice from one farmer to another was never to buy a pig concealed in a burlap sack because you just didn't know what you were getting. This sound advice was the segue into our modern saying, "let the buyer beware."

Knowing that the history lesson would be lost on Middleton, Jenkins said, "It's like the reason dope dealers wrap rock cocaine up in cellophane instead of aluminum foil. There is so much bunk out there that the person buying it wants to see he's getting the real thing before he closes the deal. Mr. Gammick just wants a little transparency to your deal before he commits to anything."

This seemed to make perfect sense to Middleton. He said, "Come back to see me in twenty-four hours. I need time to think about what I'm gonna say."

Chapter 23:
Marathon

On Thursday, March 2, 1995, at 3:00 in the afternoon, Jenkins and Douglas drove to the Washoe County Jail. They had Middleton released into their custody so they could take him to the Reno Police Detective Division to complete their third interview with him. They wanted him on their turf in order to demonstrate to him who was in control of the interview.

After they arrived at the police station, Middleton was placed in an unoccupied office and allowed to use the telephone to contact his attorney, Mr. Specchio. The two detectives waited outside the closed office, and after twenty minutes, Middleton opened the door and told them he was through. He was then moved to an interview room where Jenkins and Douglas read him his Miranda rights and had him sign the waiver agreeing to talk to them. Dixon was recording the interview from the video surveillance room.

What followed next was certainly not the longest police interview in the history of law enforcement—but it was the longest any of the three men seated in the interrogation room had ever been through. In later appeals, Middleton's attorney would refer to it as the *Marathon Interrogation* and seek to have statements made by Middleton quashed because of the duration. Since Middleton was treated humanely, and he never actually *asked* to leave, what was said over the next nine and a half hours would remain on record.

The interview started at 4:45 in the afternoon with Middleton making statements about his relationship with Kathy Powell. He said he first met Kathy Powell when he made a cable service call to her apartment on January 28, 1995. He said he installed a cable converter box for her, and afterward, she requested he provide two additional cable outlets in the apartment. He told her he could not do that at the time and then heard her on the phone with the cable company setting up an appointment to get the additional work done.

Middleton struck up a conversation with Powell and told her it would be much easier and cheaper for her if he came back after hours and did the additional work. She agreed to this and gave him her phone number so he could contact her when he had time to do the work.

Middleton said he next went to Kathy Powell's apartment on Wednesday, February 1, 1995. He went there at her invitation and performed the additional cable service for her. He said he spent a couple of hours with Kathy Powell, and the two of them conversed at length. He said it was during that conversation that the two of them discussed beginning a sexual relationship. He claimed Kathy Powell told him she had a serious love relationship in Pittsburgh, and she planned to eventually marry that person. According to Middleton, she then told him she was open to sexual experimentation but had no interest in anything other than that with him. He left that evening without having any type of relationship with her, but they agreed to get together again soon.

Middleton said he next saw Kathy Powell on Friday, February 3, 1995, when he once again was a guest at her apartment. Middleton also said he drove to Powell's apartment in his International Harvester pickup truck and parked on the street in front of her building. This was consistent with Powell's neighbors' recollection of seeing his truck parked there.

According to Middleton, he and Kathy Powell spent at least two hours after his arrival talking and drinking vodka. He said they then engaged in consensual sex in her bedroom. He described the sex as normal and in the missionary position. The detectives asked Middleton no questions, electing to let him tell the story in his own words and get it on record without interruption. Middleton stopped at this point and drank half of the bottle of water on the table in front of him before continuing.

When Middleton continued, he told the detectives that after he and Powell were through having sex, he got dressed and went out to the store to get them more vodka. He said when he returned from the store approximately one hour later, he found Kathy Powell had died while he was gone.

At this point, Jenkins sat forward and asked Middleton how Kathy Powell had come to be bound in rope. Middleton calmly said that she was into some different kinds of sex and had apparently bound herself while he was gone. He said the rope was hers, and she must have died while she was waiting for him to get back to her apartment. He said he panicked when he found her dead and disposed of her body.

Jenkins pressed Middleton for more details on the claimed sexual activity and to explain how Kathy Powell's property had come to be missing from her apartment. Middleton maintained his calm façade and steadfastly declined to provide any further information. The detectives spent the next several hours trying to pick apart Middleton's story without giving up what information they had, but Middleton stuck to his story. The only thing he did do was ask for something to eat at 8:00 P.M.

Jenkins and Douglas huddled in the outer office to discuss Middleton's statement while Dixon went out to get pizzas and sodas. The most glaring inconsistencies were the time of death, the date Powell had been placed into the dumpster, and the fact the Warp's Brothers Banana Bags were not purchased until February 8th—five full days after Middleton said Kathy Powell had died. There was also the fact that the coroner's report said Powell had been brutally raped prior to her death.

In spite of all that, both detectives agreed on one thing. David Middleton was good at holding his own in an interview—perhaps the best either one of them had come up against. They said he was the master of the Jedi mind trick, and they both felt him getting inside their heads during the interview. There were times *they* even began doubting the evidence they possessed and began imagining Kathy Powell wrapping herself up in rope while poor David Middleton was out fetching more booze. The frequent breaks they took during the interview were used to get their heads straight—not to try and figure out how to get inside Middleton's.

So, there they sat at a crossroads in the investigation. They were now more convinced than ever that Middleton was a textbook sociopath. One of the qualities possessed by a sociopath is an above-average intellect, and Middleton certainly had that. He had just laid the groundwork for his defense, and when the detectives tried to pick apart his story, they could see how it could actually work in court.

Since Middleton admitted being inside Kathy Powell's apartment lawfully on at least three occasions, any fingerprint or trace evidence associated with him found inside the apartment could be explained away. Likewise, any DNA evidence resulting from the consensual sex he admitted to having with Powell could not be used against him.

He admitted to disposing of her body after finding her dead but would not commit to where or when he did so. Even though Powell's body had not been in the dumpster for longer than a day, the possibility that someone other than Middleton had placed her in there, not knowing the bags contained a body, could be raised in court. The bags bought on February 8th could not actually be traced to Middleton, so the fact the purchase was made five days after he allegedly disposed of her was a moot issue.

The only evidence in their favor at this point was the time of death and the signs of sexual trauma found on Kathy Powell during the autopsy, but the D.A. would never prosecute based solely on those two facts. Time of death could be easily challenged, and Middleton left himself out for the rape allegations.

Middleton made a point of saying the front door was unlocked when he returned to Kathy Powell's apartment. That left open the allegation that an unknown person entered the apartment during his absence, and it was actually *that* person who tied up and raped Kathy Powell. As far-fetched as that seemed, the burden of *proof beyond a reasonable doubt* was often difficult to achieve in front of juries that were not always made up of reasonable persons.

The detectives needed more from Middleton, so they went back into the interview room after their dinner break to pick apart his lies. As hard as they tried to trip him up and get him to admit what actually happened to Kathy Powell, they could not get him to budge from his story. By midnight, the two exhausted detectives stood in the hallway, actually thinking it was possible Kathy Powell *hadn't* been murdered.

They'd been collectively dealing with hardcore criminals for almost forty years, but Middleton was unlike any other person they'd ever met. Were it not for Eddie Dixon pointing out that anyone short of a contortionist couldn't tie themselves up as Kathy Powell had been, they might have actually begun to believe Middleton. He was inside their heads, and he was good.

Jenkins and Douglas went back inside the interview room and tried to crack Middleton one more time. This is when he laid his trump card on them. The following excerpt is from the transcripts dealing with the final stages of this interview:

MIDDLETON: "I laid this all out for Specchio before I said I'd talk to you. I put it in a little more detail for you, but I laid it all out for him, too."

DOUGLAS: "I'll bet it was more detailed for us. Eight hours' worth."

MIDDLETON: "Anyway, Specchio says it ain't a murder, but you're gonna charge me with first-degree murder anyway and make me prove otherwise."

JENKINS: "Well, I hate to disappoint him, but from the story you've told us, I don't see a murder or sexual assault either."

MIDDLETON: "Then why would he say that?"

JENKINS: "Because he has to. He's covering himself to avoid a malpractice suit. If somewhere down the road you get three days or three hundred days and you think it's too much, you can't go back and say he didn't warn you."

MIDDLETON: "Why can't lawyers just do like other people?"

JENKINS: "Because they can't. It's the system we work in. I'd rather have my kid grow up to sell cocaine than be a lawyer. I say that in jest, of course."

MIDDLETON: "Well, it doesn't matter anyway cause I can't get a fair trial in this town. You might as well just book me for first-degree murder and get it over with."

JENKINS: "Why do you say that?"

MIDDLETON: "Because of the publicity! I mean, this has been told to me since I was arrested. I have no chance of winning because I'm black and because of the town I'm in. You said it yourself when you got when you arrested me. You said this is the Mississippi of the West!"

JENKINS: "No, that isn't what I said. I remember talking to you about racism and agreeing with you that racism is alive and well in some places today."

MIDDLETON: "No, you might have forgotten what you told me, but I didn't. When you jumped me and had me in the front of your car in front of my house, you said this is the Mississippi of the West, and that was a white school teacher. You don't stand a chance." (little laugh from Middleton)

JENKINS: "No, I never tied those two together."

MIDDLETON: "Whatever you say. I need some sleep."

DOUGLAS: "This is silly. This is ludicrous. I'm tired and cranky, and I don't want to be here anymore. I need out."

JENKINS: "Yes, we've gone too long. Transcriber, the time now is 1:10 A.M. on Friday, March 3, 1995. This interview is terminated."

They left Middleton inside the interview room while they waited for a uniformed officer to take him back up to jail. Douglas said, "Tell me you didn't really say that Mississippi of the west shit to him. He just played the race card, and now his whole defense is gonna head in that direction."

"Of course, I didn't say that," Jenkins said. "Didn't you hear that sick laugh after he made that accusation? He knows exactly what he's doing. He knew we were recording that interview and his statements are on record. Now, it doesn't matter whether I said those things or not. He's said I did, so that's going to go down as his mindset if we go in front of a jury."

Douglas exclaimed, "That's just perfect! We don't have shit on him as it is, and now it's gonna look like us rednecks are persecuting the poor innocent black dude because he screwed the white school marm."

Dixon had joined them and asked, "Do you want me to back up the tape a little bit?"

Jenkins smiled and replied, "Thanks, but no thanks, Eddie. Middleton's game is the act of a guilty man, but fortunately for us—my partner's neck is anything but red."

Chapter 24:
The End Of The Line

By 9:00 the next morning, the local news reporters were hovering around the station like vultures over carrion. They were already asking questions about the all-night interview of Middleton and if an arrest for the Kathy Powell case was on the horizon. One reporter even made mention of the racial undertones and the alleged "Mississippi of the West" statement made by a lead investigator in the case. This same reporter asked the department spokesperson if it was true a detective said he'd rather see his kids dealing crack than become an attorney.

Since the only law enforcement personnel who had witnessed the interview were people Jenkins trusted, he was reasonably certain the information had been leaked to the press by the Middleton defense camp. Fortunately, the higher-ups in the department trusted Jenkins' investigative and interview techniques enough to stand behind him. The department's official comment to the allegations was no comment at all. The P.I.O. told the morning gathering of reporters that Middleton had been questioned in the Kathy Powell case, and the investigation was continuing. This investigation—like *all* Reno Police investigations—would remain unbiased in regard to the race or ethnicity of all involved parties.

This boilerplate answer did little to appease the press buzzards. They left the station, but Jenkins had been around long enough to know they would now ad-lib with information from their sources since they smelled a story. He attended the morning administrative staff meeting and assured the department heads he would come up with something concrete on the case soon. How he was going to do that was the unanswered question of the day.

The Friday after payday Thursday is usually very quiet at a police station since civil servants often develop vision problems after cashing their checks – some of them just couldn't see coming into work when they had money in their pockets. This Friday was no different, and even Douglas called in to say he was taking the day off. It was his weekend to fulfill his monthly training obligation with the Air Guard, and the all-night interview had left him drained. He said he wanted to be well rested in case a foreign country decided to take over Arkansas while he was training there.

Jenkins had a task to create a suspect profile for David Middleton, so he used the quiet time in the office to accomplish it. He spent several hours on the phone with police departments in Boston, Montrose, and Miami.

David Middleton was born in Boston, Massachusetts on June 25, 1961. Coincidently, his father was a police officer at Tufts University in the suburban Boston area. Middleton's mother was a stay-at-home mom who raised him in their home in a town called Tucksbury, just outside of Boston.

His parents divorced when he was eleven years old, but his mother re-married two years later. He had a step-father, a step-brother, and a step-sister, but didn't associate with them after his mother's death from cancer in 1988.

Middleton attended Boston Tech High—a school for academically superior students. Upon graduation in 1979, he earned a full-ride scholarship for basketball and academics at Suffolk University. He attended Suffolk for one year and then transferred to the University of Massachusetts. He quit school in December of 1981 and never completed his degree.

When Middleton was eighteen years old, he attended the Boston Police Department's Police Cadet Academy. He served as a police cadet from 1979 through 1981 while attending college classes. Although this was a non-sworn position, it was considered a prerequisite for persons wishing to get hired by the Boston Police Department.

A Boston P.D. lieutenant named Frank Armstrong was still working at the department and remembered Middleton from his cadet years. Armstrong went through the Cadet Academy with Middleton, and the two became friends while serving as cadets together. The police cadets performed clerical desk duties and were often used to run errands for the brass. Times were tight in Boston in the early 80s, and the only way to get hired into the department was by performing well as a cadet.

Armstrong had vivid memories of Middleton. Since he grew up in a predominantly white Irish-Catholic Boston neighborhood, he said it was out of the ordinary to have a black person come to your house. Middleton had been to his home several times for dinner, but Armstrong said he had to do some fast talking to convince his old-school mother that he was OK.

He described Middleton as a well-liked and charismatic young man who quickly became earmarked as a future rising star in the department.

He said Middleton was very athletic, and at the time, minority hiring was being pushed in the department. It was said Middleton would be able to write his ticket in the Boston P.D., but then a chance happening changed all of that.

It seems Boston's mayor in the early 80's was a corrupt individual who was keeping two sets of books on the city's budget. In 1981, the Boston P.D. experienced its first and last layoffs in the history of the city. A hiring freeze was initiated, and no new police officers would be hired until all officers who had been laid off were re-hired. It was said that would take at least three years.

At the same time, the Miami Police Department sent fliers to Boston soliciting applicants from the officers who had been laid off. An estimated 125,000 Cuban refugees from the Mariel Boatlift had been dumped on the shores of South Florida within six months in 1980. A good deal of these refugees had been released from prison by Fidel Castro before making the journey to Florida, so Miami was experiencing an unprecedented surge in crime. They were begging for police officer candidates, and anyone with a police background stood an excellent chance of getting hired.

By then, both Middleton and Armstrong were strapping young twenty-one-year-old men with their sights set on careers in law enforcement. Since prospects looked bleak to fulfill that dream in Boston, they both headed to Florida and took the test for the Miami Police Department. They both passed, but before they were hired, the police union in Boston uncovered the second set of books the mayor had been keeping. The laid-off officers were put back on the payroll, and the police hiring freeze was lifted.

Armstrong had family roots in Boston, so he elected to stay there and eventually got hired by the police department. Middleton, on the other hand, found Miami to his liking. The warm weather was a definite plus after spending twenty-one long cold winters in Boston, but two other things attracted him. The girls on the beach and the Miami nightlife were unequaled anywhere else in the world. He packed his belongings and took the position with the Miami Police Department in January of 1982.

Armstrong hadn't heard from Middleton since then and was surprised to learn he'd been in trouble. Armstrong said he was the last person anyone would have expected to be suspected of rape and murder, although he did have an almost macabre fascination with the Boston Strangler case. He used his father's police connections to research the case in the Boston P.D.

records section for a college paper, and he spoke about the infamous murders often.

The information went a long way to explain how Middleton ended up in Florida, and the Boston Strangler story was also an interesting twist. Jenkins sat at his desk and wondered how many lives had been adversely affected by one corrupt Boston politician who set that chain of events in motion. At least three that he knew of—an eighteen-year-old girl in Montrose, a school teacher in Reno, and a sixteen-year-old girl in Miami. Had Middleton remained in Boston, chances are he never would have crossed paths with *any* of his victims.

In speaking with the Montrose P.D., Jenkins learned there was nothing new with the Buffy Rice Donohue investigation. Detectives from Montrose and Delta, Colorado, were interested in coming to Reno to question Middleton in the near future. In addition to the Buffy Rice case, there was the missing fourteen-year-old girl from Delta and the remains of an unidentified woman in her forties that were found in a shallow grave in the area. All of these crimes coincided with the time Middleton was in Colorado. It was agreed between the detectives that keeping the lines of communication open during the investigation was important.

Jenkins' phone call to the Miami P.D. was met with a bit more apprehension. He was told that several of Middleton's former coworkers were still with the department, but phone interviews with them would not be allowed. Also, any information included in Middleton's personnel file had already been sealed, so an administrative subpoena from the Dade County Court would be needed to access it. After completing the call, it appeared a road trip to Florida might be necessary before the investigation was over.

Jenkins was able to get through to the attorney who prosecuted Middleton in Florida, Kathleen Hoague. She was able to confirm most of the information the detectives had read in the Internet news articles but also gave her own opinion of Middleton.

She described him as a bad cop, twisted enough to use his badge and uniform to hunt down women and sexually abuse them. She used the words "smug" and "cocky" to describe Middleton, adding that he used his job as a warrant's detective to prey on the most defenseless women he could find. It was her opinion Middleton had problems that centered around the control and dominance of women. Although she doesn't think he killed anyone in Florida—he was definitely headed in that direction.

Ms. Hoague said when they arrested Middleton they confiscated two videotapes from his police locker. One tape was of him and a civilian Metro-Dade secretary having sex in an empty department D.U.I. room. Middleton told this lady he was a Santeria priest, and having sex with him would act as a natural anti-depressant for her. As if that wasn't bad enough, her husband was also a Metro-Dade cop.

The other tape was even more disturbing. It showed Middleton having sex with several women who were obviously prostitutes. Some of the women were in handcuffs, and at least one of them appeared to be in a great deal of pain. The tapes were shot in a room at Middleton's house and in some other unidentified locations—possibly a storage shed. In the tapes, Middleton didn't appear to be enjoying himself but looked more like he just wanted to tape himself doing sadomasochistic stuff. Since the tapes couldn't be introduced as evidence at his trial, the origin and filming locations were never explored. The Internal Affairs Division never investigated the civilian employee's claims against Middleton, so they never looked into the tapes either.

Ms. Hoague was also familiar with Evonne Haley and said she was working as a topless dancer in a club Middleton frequented when the couple first met. Middleton was married, but he started an affair with Haley long before his arrest in Miami. Ms. Hoague described Haley as being supportive of Middleton's unconventional passions and believes this is what helped them form a strong bond. Although she thinks Haley shot at least some of the video footage of Middleton, she was never able to prove it. It was her theory that Haley actually got women for Middleton, but she was never able to prove that either.

The last thing the prosecutor told Jenkins was that Middleton scared her to death, and she would have buried him under the courthouse if she could have. A bureaucratic snafu with a rape crisis center employee prevented evidence needed to convict Middleton from being introduced at his rape trial. She said the victim was credible, and there was no doubt in her mind Middleton was guilty. When she tried to press for additional federal charges against him, she was shut down by her boss, Janet Reno. She was forced to watch Middleton plead to the lesser charges and take his five-year sentence. Ms. Hoague seemed reluctant to get into more detail, and Jenkins didn't push. He thanked her for her help and said he would keep her updated on the Middleton case in Reno.

Jenkins now had a much better understanding of his adversary and was glad he'd taken the time to put together the profile. Before leaving for the weekend, he briefed Sergeant Burns on his progress and made copies of his notes to give to the other detectives at their Monday morning briefing.

Everything he'd heard throughout the day from people who knew or had dealings with David Middleton confirmed what Jenkins already knew: he was a sociopath career criminal who had spent his life slipping through the cracks. It was now time to make Reno the end of the line for him.

Chapter 25:
The Holy Grail

At 7:00 P.M. on Saturday, March 4, 1995, Dave Jenkins was standing at his kitchen sink helping his wife with the dinner dishes. When the phone rang, his wife gave him the sideways, squinty-eyed look that all married cops who are subject to callouts have grown to know and fear. Since he was not the on-call Major Crimes detective that weekend, he was not obligated to answer the call, but his theory was that when you took the job, you took the baggage that came along with it.

Dodging his wife's mad-dog stare, he stepped around her and picked up the phone. The call was from a police records clerk named Lynn Austin, who had just received a secret witness call regarding the Kathy Powell case she thought Jenkins would want to know about. Most secret witness reports coming in this long after a crime occurs are routinely filed away for the detectives to go through when time permits. But like the detectives handling the Powell case, Ms. Austin was also a veteran at her job, and her gut instincts told her this secret witness report was different.

A male caller had telephoned the secret witness line and said he had read about Powell's death in the local newspaper. In one of the press releases put out about the case, information was included about detectives looking for leads regarding Middleton possibly renting a storage shed. This caller said Middleton and Haley were associated with a company named Hal-Data, and the detectives should check local storage facilities under that name.

The caller was vague with his information, but Ms. Austin pressed him for the reason he knew this in order to establish his credibility. He finally told her he worked for the Post Office and delivered the mail to Middleton and Haley at their Carlin Street apartment. He said that in addition to mail addressed to them personally, he remembered the company name of Hal-Data Research with their address on some of the mail.

The caller gave his name so detectives could contact him if they had to, but said he could get in trouble at work if it was learned he released this type of information. He then told Ms. Austin he had delivered mail to Middleton's address the day before addressed to Hal-Data Research, and the return address was from a business called Sierra Royal Mini Storage in Sparks, Nevada.

After thanking Ms. Austin for the call, Jenkins hung up the phone and found the listing for Sierra Royal Mini Storage in the Yellow Pages. The address was 450 Howard Drive in Sparks, but when Jenkins called the number listed for the business, he got the after-hours recording. He decided to wait until the morning to check out the lead and called Sergeant Burns to fill him in. Since Douglas was still out of town, he called Eddie Dixon and made arrangements to meet at the station in the morning to assist him.

Before heading to the storage facility in the morning, Jenkins had an evidence custodian meet him at the station. He checked Middleton's keyring out of evidence and took it with him on the off chance he might locate a storage shed. At 11:00 A.M., Jenkins and Dixon met with the resident managers of the facility, Verrel and Freddie Tucker. The Tuckers had recently moved to the area and took over management of the facility sometime after the canvass of the local storage units had been done by Douglas and Jenkins. They were not familiar with the Kathy Powell case but said they would be more than happy to help the detectives.

Mrs. Tucker checked her computer for a storage shed registered to either David Middleton or Evonne Haley and came up with no results. Dixon gave her the name Hal-Data Research, and when she checked under that, she got a hit for unit #16-28. The actual name of the renter was not on the computer, and both detectives waited anxiously as Mrs. Tucker hand-searched the rental applications.

After a long two minutes, Mrs. Tucker walked back to the counter, looking pleased with herself, and handed the rental application to Jenkins. He and Dixon both experienced the kid on Christmas feeling when they read it. The owner of Hal-Data Research and the renter of the storage shed was David Stephen Middleton. He listed his social security number on the application and 1425 Carlin Street #3 in Reno, Nevada, as his business address. He even had his sister in Milton, Massachusetts, listed as the emergency contact.

Middleton had rented the ten-by-ten-foot storage unit on August 8, 1994. Prior to that, he had a smaller unit in the same facility, but he listed the reason for the move as a need for more storage space. Mrs. Tucker made a copy of the rental agreement, and Jenkins tried to hide his excitement as he folded it and placed it under the clip in his notebook. Mrs. Tucker then walked the detectives down to storage unit #16-28.

They stood outside the roll-up door to the unit for a moment before Jenkins removed Middleton's key ring from the pocket of his suit coat. He moved the keys around the ring until he came to the one that had attracted his attention during his first interview with David Middleton. Bending down, he inserted the key into the keyhole on the security lock and turned it to the right. When the lock opened with a metallic snap, Detective Dave Jenkins experienced the euphoric feeling King Arthur *never* got to experience in his lifetime quest to find the Holy Grail. It was now time to call a judge.

Chapter 26:
Chamber Of Horrors

At 2:45 in the afternoon on Sunday, March 5, 1995, Detective Jenkins returned to the Sierra Royal Mini Storage facility carrying a signed search warrant authorizing the search of unit #16-28. The warrant listed the scope of the search to include anything related to the murder of Kathy Powell as well as any evidence related to the Good Guys crime.

Eddie Dixon had remained behind to guard the storage shed and was waiting when Jenkins returned with the warrant. In addition to him, Sergeant Burns, Detective Hunt, and a detective from the Robbery Homicide Unit named Mike Cleveland were there to assist. Cleveland was there to take initial photographs. Sergeant Burns did not want to call out a C.S.I. team from the Sheriff's Office until he was sure there was something worthwhile in the shed.

After showing the search warrant to Mr. and Mrs. Tucker, Jenkins removed the security lock and pulled up the overhead door to the shed. The five detectives stood outside of the opened door and peered inside. At first glance, it appeared to be cluttered with nothing more than miscellaneous household junk, but then something in the right-hand corner caught Jenkins' eye.

A red hand truck was leaning against the wall of the shed, partially concealed behind some boxes. A yellow windbreaker with the words "Sunshine State Messenger Service" written on it in black lettering was draped across the handle of the hand truck. On top of a pile of boxes next to the hand truck was an unopened box with the words "Yamaha Model DSP-A2770 Stereo Amplifier" stenciled on it. Before Jenkins could celebrate the discovery of the evidence from the Good Guys crime, his attention was drawn to something else.

Lying on its back on the left side of the storage shed was a single-door upright refrigerator about five feet tall. A fifty-five-gallon cardboard drum and several boxes were stacked on top of the refrigerator's single door. Irreparable damage would be done to a refrigerator from storing it lying down like this one was, so there was a good chance it was not being stored for future use. Jenkins then saw a small hole drilled through the side of the refrigerator, and a horrific feeling came over him.

He shared his suspicions with the other detectives, and they carefully began removing the items stacked on top of the refrigerator door. Detective Cleveland videotaped the process, and when the door was cleared, Jenkins jerked it open. The five men stared into the filthy interior of the empty refrigerator, and it was Jenkins who first realized what they were looking at.

The inside of the refrigerator had been gutted of its food trays. All that remained was the freezer compartment covered by a blue plastic door, separated from the main part of the refrigerator by a metal shelf. It was the metal shelf of the freezer compartment that held Jenkins' attention and caused the hairs on the back of his neck to stand up.

The metal had been cut and peeled back in a semi-circular pattern to allow an opening between the freezer and the main refrigerator compartment. The opening was the right size for a human neck, and the blue cloth fibers covering the jagged metal around the opening were exactly the same as the ones Jenkins had seen around Kathy Powell's neck at her autopsy. He now knew where David Middleton had kept Kathy Powell during the last days of her life. Even more disturbing was he also now knew what caused the look of horror to be frozen on her face for eternity.

A large blue foam rubber ball with obvious teeth marks on it was lying on the floor next to the refrigerator. As Eddie Dixon so astutely put it, "That was used as a gag, and there ain't no reason to gag a dead lady. If she was here—she was alive for a while."

Sergeant Burns called for a C.S.I. team, and the detectives backed out of the shed while they waited for them. Thirty minutes later, Deputy Chuck Lowe and his boss, Lieutenant Don Means from the county forensics team, arrived, and the detectives went back inside the shed to continue their search.

The refrigerator was the initial focal point of the search. After first photographing it in place, the forensics investigators began to process the inside. Trace evidence of the blue fibers, as well as small particles of skin, were collected from the edges of the metal freezer tray cutout. There was not much visible to the naked eye, but the refrigerator was carefully loaded into the evidence truck so it could be moved to the crime lab and checked more thoroughly.

When the detectives stood the refrigerator upright, they saw that in addition to the small hole drilled on the right side, a cutout with another small hole had been drilled on the left side. They surmised these to be air holes, lending more credence to the theory Kathy Powell had been alive if she had, in fact, been held inside the refrigerator. Once the refrigerator was moved out of the shed, they began to make one morbid discovery after another.

Middleton had run a series of ropes and pulleys throughout the shed. The rope started at a hand winch mounted to a heavy wooden speaker box. The speaker box measured four feet by four feet and was the type that might be seen on the stage of a Broadway play. Although the interior of the speaker box was hollowed out, they estimated it still weighed about three hundred pounds. It was definitely heavy enough to anchor the winch that operated the pulley system in the shed.

From the winch, the rope ran through a series of industrial-strength pulleys mounted to the ceiling beam inside of the shed. There was a clasp hook attached to the free end of the rope, and human restraint devices were strewn around the floor near the hook. The forensic technicians found traces of hair and what appeared to be human skin on the restraint devices. With the way the restraint devices were rigged, it appeared the pulley system had been used to suspend a human body. As dark as cops' sense of humor can be, there was no joking as the detectives silently went about their search of the shed.

Underneath the blue plastic tarp, the detectives located an opened bag of Warp's Brothers Banana Bags with one bag missing. A bag of Ace Hardware brand black plastic bags matching the one that had been used to cover Kathy Powell's head was lying next to the banana bags. Receipts for the Commercial Hardware purchase of the bags and the original receipt for the Good Guys purchase were also located. White rope matching the one used to bind Kathy Powell, as well as a roll of duct tape were also found under the tarp.

Kathy Powell's answering machine, cordless phone, computer printer, and portable computer were found toward the front of the shed. There were some compact discs and cassette tapes that had obviously belonged to Kathy Powell in a box on top of her computer printer. Jenkins reached into the box with a gloved hand and removed the top compact disc. It was titled "Trust Theory, 1992." Middleton had stolen her trust—figuratively *and* literally.

The detectives then began discovering things they really didn't want to find. A crate filled with sadomasochistic and bondage-type pornography, a box filled with assorted and well-used dildos and sex toys, and a machete with an animal skull and horns for the handle. God only knew what *that* was used for.

The last discovery of the day was two handguns in a box. One was a Smith and Wesson Model 15 .38 caliber revolver, and the other was a Smith and Wesson Model 659 .9mm stainless steel pistol with a fifteen-round magazine. Also in the box was a rubber Halloween mask in the shape of the cartoon character Jughead's face. The cops called that a 2-11 kit after the California penal code for armed robbery.

They were now treading into a grey area as far as the search warrant was concerned. They were legally searching the storage shed but were coming up with evidence that had nothing to do with either crime they came to investigate. After a brief discussion, the detectives decided to seal the storage shed and go back in front of the judge in the morning in order to expand the scope of the search warrant. They bought a new lock from Mr. Tucker and locked the shed with the remainder of the contents still inside.

They were not yet a quarter of the way through their search of the shed, but they'd all seen enough for one day. Eddie Dixon summed it up the best when he said, "I sure picked a bad week to quit drinking."

Before leaving for his weekend training mission, Douglas told Jenkins he'd keep his cell phone with him in case anything happened on the case. He would be returning from his trip later that night, but Jenkins knew he'd want to be filled in about the storage shed as soon as possible. It was a bittersweet phone call because the discovery was far too gruesome to warrant a celebration.

The detectives who were on scene at the storage shed on that cold and cloudy Sunday afternoon were hardcore veterans who had faced more than their share of death. Some of them had even faced their mortality on more than one occasion, but none of them were prepared for the picture they now had of Kathy Powell's death. Bound with rope, gagged with a rubber ball, sealed inside an airtight makeshift coffin, gasping for her last breaths of fetid air filtering through two small holes in the refrigerator, alone and surely afraid. A death like that was worse than any of them could imagine.

When Dave Jenkins recounted the grizzly finding of David Middleton's storage shed to this author over a decade later, an eerie calm came over the veteran detective. He stared off into space and said, "My feelings were mixed. Part of me was elated because as soon as I saw what was in that shed, I knew we had him. Another part of me was horrified thinking about what had been done to the victim in there."

They say if a person looks into the eyes of evil for too long, some of the evil is bound to seep inside of him. And so it was with David Middleton's chamber of horrors. Each man who entered it took away a little bit of the horror from within, and they will carry it with them forever.

Chapter 27:
Twists

The detectives went back into the storage shed with their revised search warrant at 9:00 the next morning. The first thing they did was open the sealed fifty-five-gallon drum that had been sitting on top of the refrigerator door when they originally entered the shed. They were surprised to find the drum half-filled with a variety of women's panties and lingerie.

At first, they thought the clothing might belong to Evonne Haley, but as Douglas pointed out, most people don't keep their underwear in a storage shed. Then Eddie Dixon held up a pair of tiny red lace thong panties and made another one of his astute observations. He said the only way these belonged to Evonne Haley was if she was using them as a nose warmer because there was no way she was getting them over her butt.

The moment of humor ended when Douglas exclaimed, "Shit! He's taking souvenirs."

They all knew what that meant. Murderers were grouped into different categories based on traits they exhibited, and it was the serial killer who took souvenirs from his victims. By the time they got through searching the drum, they had collected thirty-seven pairs of panties, thirteen bras, and six negligees. The garments varied in style, but most of them were designed for smaller women. Some were clean, but others had obviously been placed into the drum without being laundered since their last use. Each garment was cataloged and placed in an individual plastic bag for DNA analysis. It would be a tedious procedure, but one that needed to be done.

The detectives theorized Middleton had been stealing women's underwear from their homes while he was working. When Middleton first moved to Reno, he took a job working for Stanley Steamer Carpet Cleaners prior to being hired at the cable company. Both of those jobs would allow him unsupervised access to his customer's bedrooms where he would have had the opportunity to steal the undergarments. Even though this was a disturbing scenario, at least it would mean the women were live victims of perverse thefts instead of dead victims of a serial killer. What was buried underneath the clothing led them to believe they were dealing with more than just a thief with an underwear fetish.

At the bottom of the barrel were strands of long black hair, and not just a few of them. The hair was human, and the strands were all at least twenty-four inches long. They pulled hair out of the barrel in clumps and laid it out on the folding table the forensics investigators were using to tag and bag the evidence. The split ends of the hair told them it obviously did not come from a wig, and since the roots were still attached, the hair had been pulled out of a person's head.

The hair was too long and too dark to belong to either Kathy Powell or Middleton. The only other female they'd dealt with in the case was Haley, and the hair definitely was not hers. The fact the hair was in the same drum as the women's underwear raised the possibility of another grim scenario for Middleton's souvenir collection. The detectives backed out of the storage shed and once again took the search warrant back to the judge for a revision. This time, the scope of the warrant would include "any evidence connected to murder victims presently referred to as Jane Does A through Z."

The search of the storage shed was completed on Tuesday, March 7, 1995, at 11:00 A.M. After everything had been removed from inside of the shed, the forensics team went over every inch of the interior with a black light, looking for traces of blood or fingerprints. The place was clean—too clean for the inside of a storage shed.

A nearly empty industrial size jug of Clorox bleach was found inside of the shed. The detectives surmised Middleton would know from his police experience that bleach would obliterate DNA trace evidence, so he had probably scrubbed the interior of the shed with it. This was another drawback of dealing with a suspect who was an ex-cop. They often knew how to get away with crime.

Kathy Powell's brother was allowed to view the property taken out of the shed to see if he recognized any of it. In addition to the items the detectives already knew of, he identified several distinctive pieces of jewelry, a camera, and a hunting rifle that he said belonged to his sister. He said he had never seen the two handguns found in the shed, but he was certain they did not belong to Powell.

Both the revolver and the semi-automatic pistol looked like the types of guns cops carried as duty weapons. A brown leather shoulder holster for the revolver was also found in the shed. In addition to these items, they found Middleton's Boston P.D. cadet badge and police I.D. card in an official-looking black leather badge wallet. The silver badge looked like a real police badge, and the word "Cadet" on the I.D. card was small enough to be easily overlooked if the credentials were flashed quickly. The photo on the I.D. card was of a much younger David Middleton, but it still looked like him.

There was a possibility Middleton either had in the past or was planning in the future to pose as a cop in order to commit crimes. They knew he'd used his badge to gain his victims' trust and lure them to him in Florida, so there was no reason he wouldn't try the ploy again. Someone who looked like a cop and flashed police credentials would certainly gain compliance if he approached the right person. They added sending a West Coast law enforcement teletype checking sex crimes and unsolved murders where the suspect posed as a cop to their to-do list.

The talk of Middleton's guns looking like cop guns gave Jenkins an idea. It was nearly 5:00 P.M. on the East Coast, but he took a chance and called the homicide division of the Miami Police Department. He was put in contact with a detective and, after explaining the case they were working on, asked if he would check the serial numbers on the guns found in Middleton's shed against their records. The detective said he would research the guns with the department range master and call back.

Fifteen minutes later, Jenkins got a call back from the slightly embarrassed Miami detective confirming that both of the handguns had been issued to Middleton while he was with their department. Both weapons were listed as the property of the Miami Police Department and still showed to be in service. The detective said their records also showed Middleton was issued a Remington Model 870 .12-gauge pump shotgun and asked if they had come across that weapon as well.

After flipping through his notes and comparing serial numbers, Jenkins confirmed the shotgun taken out of Middleton's apartment was the same one that the Miami Police Department had issued. The detective assured Jenkins he would look into how Middleton had been allowed to keep his guns and was relieved to hear they had not actually been involved in the crimes he was suspected of committing.

The phone call was followed by jokes about how great it must be to work for a department that let you keep your guns after going to prison so you could have something to fall back on when you got out and how they should list the Miami P.D. as an accomplice to the ex-felon in possession of a firearm case. The jokes stopped when the detectives realized they didn't know if Middleton really *had* used the guns in the commission of a crime. They had no idea what Middleton was involved in before they found him. And even though Kathy Powell hadn't been shot, the possibility existed that Middleton used one of the guns to coerce her into submission. As Douglas put it, the case was getting twisted faster than a rattlesnake on speed.

Chapter 28:
The Ace Of Spades

Even with the gruesome discoveries in the storage shed, there still wasn't enough information or evidence to charge Middleton with the murder of Kathy Powell. All the detectives had at this point were their own theories and conjecture about what had happened in the homemade torture chamber, and that wouldn't be enough to convince a judge to sign a warrant for a murder arrest. They needed more concrete evidence and made it their mission over the next weeks to get it.

On Wednesday, March 8, 1995, Jenkins and Douglas started the process of taking evidence from Middleton himself. Douglas obtained a seizure order to take blood and hair samples from Middleton for DNA analysis. The order also permitted them to take a dental impression from him for comparison to the bite mark on Kathy Powell's breast. The blood and hair samples were done at the County Jail, and they took Middleton to a local dentist to have the dental impression done.

Middleton had invoked his rights so they could not discuss the case with him without his lawyer being present. The discovery of the storage shed had been a leading story in the local news, so the detectives were certain Middleton knew about it. But since he did not bring the subject up there was no discussion about it. Middleton made mostly small talk with the detectives. On their return trip from the dentist, Middleton complained about the small portions of food at the jail, so Jenkins did a drive-through at a Burger King. Douglas told Middleton it was the least they could do since he used to be *one of them.*

The other detectives were also busy trying to tie up loose ends. Dixon was assigned to go to the storage facility and establish a timeline for Middleton's visits to his shed during the days Kathy Powell was missing. Each tenant had their own key code used to enter or exit the facility, so tracking him was just a matter of looking for his code and putting a time to his visits. There were also video surveillance cameras at the facility, but going through the tapes and matching them to the times would be time-consuming. The right man was on the job, though.

Hunt and Depsynski interviewed Evonne Haley about the storage shed. She denied any knowledge of it and said she had never heard of a company called Hal-Data. This was unfortunate since no identifiable fingerprints were found on the box of stereo equipment from Good Guys. They had nothing to charge her with unless she admitted knowledge of the crime.

The detectives also spoke to Haley's twelve-year-old daughter Natasha, who, like her mother, denied knowing about the storage shed. The young girl's hair did not match the hair found in the shed, but the possibility that the hair belonged to her or her mother would have to be eliminated since hair color and length can be changed. Without telling Haley the reason, Hunt told her they would eventually be getting a seizure order to take hair and DNA evidentiary samples from both her and Natasha.

Haley became upset and accused the detectives of ruining her life. She told them she'd already sent her ten-year-old son back to Colorado to stay with her parents, but her daughter wanted to stay in Reno with her. She told them due to the publicity the case was causing; she couldn't stand having the neighbors staring her and her daughter down, thinking they had been involved in murders, so now they were being forced to move. The detectives left without telling her most of the publicity was being caused by Middleton himself.

The local papers had once again hit the story with a feeding frenzy after the discovery of the storage shed was made public. Making the case even more of a media nightmare was the fact the Colorado newspapers had also picked up on Middleton's arrest and were running stories on his connection to the unsolved disappearance of Buffy Rice.

Walt and Bonnie Rice had been following the Reno case very closely and were fueling the media fire in Colorado. When the storage shed torture chamber was discovered in Reno, they were quite vocal with their opinion that if the Montrose Police Department had done its job with Buffy's case, these horrible things would never have happened in Reno. It had been sixteen months since Buffy disappeared, and she still hadn't been found.

The case was picking up enough press interest that articles began filtering out across the country through the Associated Press. Middleton was making noise about being framed because he was black, and it wasn't being confined inside the white brick walls of the Washoe County Jail. The nation was still reeling from the Rodney King incident, so police-related racial issues were big news. Since Middleton wasn't talking to the press, there was little doubt that his defense team was helping get the word of possible racial overtones of the case out to the media.

Even though Middleton had not yet been charged with killing Kathy Powell, it was plain to see that that was the direction the investigation was heading. So far, Middleton refused to do any jailhouse interviews with the local media, but he jumped at the chance to tell his story to television's *Inside Addition* reporter Tony Cox. The interview wouldn't actually air until September 29, 1995, but Middleton made it a point to throw in the "Mississippi of the West" comment. As an added bonus, he told the reporter the police said they were going to "hang his black ass for the murders." Even though the police categorically denied both statements, the public still got to hear them.

The detectives tried their best to continue their investigation and build a case against Middleton in spite of the negative publicity they were getting. It was statements made by Middleton's attorney Mike Specchio two weeks later that caused them to pull out what Douglas called their "Ace of Spades."

In an interview with *The Reno Gazette-Journal, Specchio was quoted as saying, "To me,* it stinks. They have nothing but circumstantial evidence on my guy. He admitted to dumping her body, and that was a terrible thing. If they want to charge him with that or with being in possession of some of her property, that's one thing, but they want to go farther than that. This guy didn't kill anybody, and he's not going to admit to killing anybody. We have to play by the rules, and the question is, do the rules apply equally to whites and blacks?"

He ended the interview by saying, "Just because he's a black guy and a convicted felon doesn't mean he killed anybody. If this guy was a white college professor the case would be thrown out before it ever got to court."

At 3:00 in the afternoon on Wednesday, March 23, 1995, Detectives Jenkins and Douglas leisurely strolled into the office of the Public Defender and asked to speak to Mike Specchio. After waiting about fifteen minutes outside of his office, his secretary told them he was available to see them. The attorney had never bothered to ask who the lead investigators were on the case, but he was about to find out.

Douglas walked into the office ahead of Jenkins and stopped in front of the desk Specchio was seated behind. With one of his best Eddie Murphy smiles, he said, "Let me introduce myself. I'm Detective John Douglas—the man who's gonna eventually be arresting your client, David Middleton, for the murder of Kathy Powell. Now, we both know this ain't about race, so let's stop the foolishness. It's just gonna be me and

Middleton in the newspaper photograph when we arrest him, and I'm even *blacker* than he is! Now how's that gonna look for you if you keep up this 'my client is a poor black man being framed' bullshit. We're doing our job clean, so how about you try that too?"

When telling this story later, Douglas said, "It was like the blood drained from the guy's face, and we just walked out and left him sitting there at his desk. It was the only time in my career I ever saw a lawyer speechless. Race was never an issue after that because he knew his smokescreen wasn't gonna work. I almost felt sorry for him. *Almost...*"

Chapter 29:
Lines In Time

On Friday, March 31, 1995, the detectives assigned to the case held their last briefing of the week at 2:00 P.M. in the Detective Division conference room. Sergeants Burns and Tolliver were seated at the front of the room, and four of the detectives were seated at the oval table looking over their notes. Eddie Dixon was standing at one of the white dry-erase boards mounted on the wall in front of the room, putting the finishing touches on the storage shed timeline he'd developed. When he finished writing, he began explaining what was known about Middleton's activities at the storage unit during the days Kathy Powell was missing.

According to the storage facility records, Middleton rented a five-foot by ten-foot storage unit under the name Hal-Data Research on June 30, 1994. On August 8, 1994, he requested a larger storage shed and moved into unit #16-28, which measured ten feet by ten feet. The entry records dating back to August were not available due to a change in security systems. Still, Dixon was able to accurately research back to February 3, 1995—the last day Powell was seen alive. The storage facility security system did not track exit times, but Middleton's entry times into the facility were outlined as follows:

- Friday, February 3, 1995: entered at 8:06 P.M.

- Saturday, February 4, 1995: entered at 12:37 A.M., 5:47 A.M., 6:49 A.M., 8:45 A.M., 11:53 A.M. and 5:38 P.M.

- Sunday, February 5, 1995: entered at 6:19 A.M., 11:09 A.M. and 3:30 P.M.

- Monday, February 6, 1995: entered at 9:26 A.M. and 3:15 P.M.

- Tuesday, February 7, 1995: NO ENTRIES

- Wednesday, February 8, 1995: entered at 6:49 P.M.

- Thursday, February 9, 1995: NO ENTRIES

- Friday, February 10, 1995: entered at 7:45 P.M.

- Saturday, February 11, 1995 (date Powell's body was discovered): entered at 7:26 P.M., VIDEO IS AVAILABLE OF THIS VISIT

- Sunday, February 12, 1995: entered at 12:53 A.M., VIDEO AVAILABLE OF THIS VISIT. THE SECOND PERSON IS WITH THE SUSPECT AT THIS TIME.

- NO FURTHER VISITS WERE MADE BY THE SUSPECT TO HIS STORAGE SHED BETWEEN 12 FEB 1995 AND THE DATE OF ARREST ON 23 FEB 1995.

Dixon went on to explain that the security system at the facility does not allow one car to follow another through the gate without entering a gate code. If a car tries to tailgate another one through the gate, an alarm sounds. That would mean only the times listed for Middleton's code number were the times he was actually at the storage facility.

Additionally, the video surveillance system is activated 24 hours a day, but it scans the entire facility and does not fix any one area. Middleton's truck was seen at the shed during most of the listed entries. During his visit to the shed on Monday, February 6th, at 9:26 A.M., he was seen driving his T.C.I. Cable Company truck. Mr. and Mrs. Tucker both remembered seeing the T.C.I. truck there on other occasions. Two other notable pieces of evidence were found on the videotapes.

During Middleton's visit to the shed on Saturday, February 11th, he can be seen loading a large, cumbersome package into the rear of his International Harvester pickup truck. The quality of the tape and the lighting conditions were poor, but the package is clearly identifiable as the sleeping bag containing Kathy Powell's body. Middleton uses the ropes tied around the outside of the sleeping bag for handles as he carries the bundled body out of the storage shed and loads it into the back of his pickup truck. The time on the tape when he is seen loading the body is 7:40 P.M.—approximately two hours before it was discovered inside the dumpster.

The video also captured Middleton when he made his next trip to the shed five hours later on Sunday, February 12, 1995. His truck can be seen pulling through the front gate at 12:53 A.M. He is then seen walking out of his storage shed and getting into his truck to leave at 2:05 A.M. The interesting thing about that video clip was that Middleton was not alone during this visit.

A female was seen leaving the shed with him and getting into the passenger seat of his truck. Once again, the lighting and quality of the video were too poor to make out who the female was. It would never hold up in court, but judging from the height and weight, Dixon was reasonably certain the female was Evonne Haley. The tape had been sent to the F.B.I. for assistance with enhancement, but since the camera angle was bad, they weren't hopeful that they could help.

After some discussion, the timeline was updated with the other information they had. Since Kathy Powell had made phone calls to her fiancé in Philadelphia at 7:38 P.M. and to another friend at 8:00 P.M. the night she was last seen, they were certain she was still alive when Middleton stopped at his storage unit at 8:06 P.M. that night.

During the marathon interview, Middleton told Jenkins he had arrived at Kathy Powell's house for his date with her at 9:00 P.M. on Friday, February 3, 1995. Since Powell was never heard from after her 8:00 P.M. phone call that estimate was probably accurate. That meant Middleton stopped at his storage unit on his way to Kathy Powell's house, which is something a man doesn't normally do when he is on his way out for a date.

The probable reason for that stop was to retrieve the rope Middleton used to bind Powell and some type of weapon used to coerce her into submission. In addition to the other weapons discovered in the shed, they'd also located an electric stun gun. No marks from the prongs on the stun gun had been found on Kathy Powell's body, but the weapon was fully charged when it was recovered from the shed. The intimidation factor alone from a weapon such as that could cause a person to acquiesce to unreasonable demands, so not finding marks didn't rule out the possibility the stun gun had been used in the crime. The reason for Middleton's stop at the shed might never be known, but their logical conclusions were good enough for now.

Based on what they knew so far, the detectives pieced together what they thought was a reasonable scenario for Kathy Powell's abduction and murder. Middleton had Powell with him when he returned to the shed at 12:37 A.M. on Saturday, February 4, 1995. Whether she had accompanied him there willingly or not will never be known because the video camera at the storage facility did not capture his arrival. What was known for certain was that Kathy Powell never left that storage shed alive again.

Middleton bound and restrained Kathy Powell during this initial visit to his storage shed and then left her there while he returned to her apartment to steal her belongings. With Powell out of the way, Middleton would be able to take his time going through her apartment without fear of interruption. This would account for Powell's missing garage door opener, as he would have taken that with him in order to enter the condo surreptitiously through the garage. It would also explain why Powell's neighbors returning from their late night out at 4:00 A.M. saw Middleton's truck parked in front of her condo and loaded with what they described as household goods.

Since there were nine entries into the storage unit over the next two days, Kathy Powell was most likely alive and held captive during that timeframe. Middleton would have used his frequent visits to perform whatever depravities the poor woman had been subjected to before her death. Exactly what he'd done might never be known. Still, the image of the homemade pulley system, human restraints, and the rubber ball gag gave them a good enough idea to paint a morbid mental picture of the probabilities.

And then there was that horrendous refrigerator. Their original theory that Middleton bound Kathy Powell and kept her naked and gagged inside of the refrigerator when he was not at the storage unit was confirmed by the forensics evidence report. The blue fibers found on Kathy Powell's neck matched the fibers around the cutout in the freezer tray inside the refrigerator. The origin of these fibers was a shredded blue towel found on the floor next to the refrigerator.

It appeared Middleton had placed the towel around the cutout so Kathy Powell would not cut her neck on the jagged aluminum. It was an insanely humane gesture for a madman who was torturing his victim, and it apparently did not work. The skin fragments found on the cutout belonged to Kathy Powell, too, so sometime during her struggle for freedom, the towel placed there for her comfort became dislodged.

The forensics investigators also identified traces of skin and blood belonging to Kathy Powell on the interior of the refrigerator door. After taking measurements, they found these skin and blood traces matched the ante-mortem bruising discovered on Kathy Powell's body during the autopsy. DNA evidence and teeth marks taken from the blue ball gag also matched Kathy Powell. All of this meant she had been alive and struggling to get out of the refrigerator while held captive—a thought more horrific to the detectives than any other aspect of the case thus far.

Moving back to the timeline they saw there was a noticeable decrease in activity starting Monday, February 6, 1995. Their assumption was that Kathy Powell had died sometime between Middleton's last visit at 3:30 P.M. Sunday and his next visit at 3:15 P.M. on Monday. This timeframe would also coincide with the time of death placed by the coroner. Even though Powell had been murdered, a strange sense of relief came over the detectives when they realized her suffering would have ended by that time.

Middleton's next visit to the storage unit was the same day he purchased the plastic bags from Commercial Hardware—Wednesday, February 8th. It would have taken him a good deal of time to wrap Kathy Powell's body up in the manner it was found, so the detectives theorized he used his visits on February 8th and February 10th to do this. His visit to the shed when he removed the body on February 11th only lasted twelve minutes, so he must have had the package ready for travel before he got there.

Dixon had driven the most direct route he could think of from the storage facility to the location where Kathy Powell's body was found, making sure to take the drive at 7:40 P.M. on a Saturday so traffic would be comparable to what Middleton faced. It was 14.3 miles, and doing the speed limit, the drive took him twenty-one minutes. That meant Middleton dumped the body at roughly 8:00 P.M., so he had plenty of time to formulate his plan before going back to the storage facility.

Middleton's last visit to the shed at 12:53 A.M. Sunday, February 12[th,] could have only been for one purpose—evidence eradication. Somewhere along the way, he picked up the female who was seen leaving the shed with him. Dixon passed around some grainy black and white photos he made from the videotape of the woman seen leaving the storage unit with Middleton. The detectives were all convinced it was Evonne Haley, but they knew a jury might see it differently since the person in the photo was almost unrecognizable.

The one nagging question was why Middleton did such a good job cleaning up his shed but left things like the blue ball gag, the restraints, and trace evidence inside the refrigerator. After much discussion, they came up with the only answer that made sense. If it *was* Evonne Haley who came back to the shed with Middleton, then maybe he just told her part of what happened. Admitting to having sex with Kathy Powell and her subsequent death inside of the shed might have been easy for him to explain away as an accident—just like he explained it to the police. But if he told Haley of the sadistic torture Kathy Powell endured before her death, he might have risked shocking her into going to the police herself.

The detectives thought they had more than enough circumstantial evidence to justify charging Middleton with Kathy Powell's murder—even without a cause of death determination. All they needed to do was show criminal agency had been involved in her death to prove murder in the first degree. The fact they could show she had been kept alive inside of that horrid refrigerator for a period of days and then died while she was being held captive seemed more than enough to prove her death resulted from a criminal act.

Unfortunately, District Attorney Gammick disagreed. There were too many loopholes in the law when it came to prosecuting a murder case with an undetermined cause of death, and he didn't want to lose this case through one of them. Middleton had already admitted to having sex with Kathy Powell, finding her dead, and dumping her body. A good attorney could make it look like that was exactly what happened, and Middleton's attorney was good.

Gammick wanted more evidence before he approved charging Middleton with murder. If their case wasn't strong enough, there was a chance they would lose it and let Middleton go free to kill again. Double jeopardy was a concern, so if they lost him once, they'd lose him forever.

The same went for charging either Middleton or Haley with the crimes related to the Good Guys incident. There was enough evidence now to arrest them on that, but it was much smarter to wait until the murder charge was brought against Middleton so everything could be joined together in one all-encompassing case. The use of the credit card was just one step in the progression of criminal elements involved in the case. If they charged him with that crime prematurely, the case would have to be tried separately, and they might not be able to use evidence from it at Middleton's subsequent murder trial. Waiting was the right thing to do, but it wasn't easy.

Middleton was a captive audience, so the detectives weren't overly concerned with the District Attorney's decision. He was scheduled to go to court on his ex-felon in possession of firearms case on May 17th, and it looked like he would be pleading guilty in exchange for a one-year sentence. The detectives still had time to come up with more evidence to support the murder charge, but they needed another lucky break. As they left for the weekend, they had no idea that break would come from a Golden Retriever named Nugget.

Chapter 30:
Sticks And Bones

Verdi, Nevada, is a quaint little town nestled in the foothills of the Sierra Nevada Mountains twenty miles west of Reno on the California-Nevada border. The icy waters of the Truckee River, fed by the mountain snowmelt, flow swiftly through the Verdi Valley, making it lush with green vegetation. The hills are covered with Pinion Pine trees and Bitterbrush sage bushes, so the air always has a clean, crisp smell to it.

Bridge Street is the main thoroughfare running through Verdi. The two-lane road was aptly named for the wooden bridge spanning the Truckee River that connects Verdi to the main part of the valley. From Bridge Street, a dirt road runs north into Dog Valley—a fifty-square-mile recreation area that is home to hikers, campers, horseback riders, and off-road enthusiasts. On April 9, 1995, at 10:00 A.M., seventy-two-year-old Verdi resident James Warner* was walking his dog on the dirt road leading into Dog Valley. Unbeknownst to both man and dog, they were about to help turn the tide of the David Middleton investigation.

Warner was a retired cardiologist, so he knew the value of daily exercise. His routine was to take his eight-year-old Golden Retriever, Nugget, for a three-mile walk every morning at 9:00 sharp. During the winter, they kept to the lower-lying trails along the river, but on this sunny Saturday morning, he decided to hike into Dog Valley. Spring was in the air, the wildflowers were beginning to bloom on the hillsides and the snow had already melted off of the ground at the lower elevations in the valley.

Warner and his dog were on their return trip about a mile from town, playing a game they both enjoyed immensely. Warner would throw a stick as far as he could into the sagebrush, and Nugget would rummage around until he found it. The dog would faithfully return the stick to his master, who would then throw it again to start another round of fetch. The wind was with Warner when he threw the stick for the last time, and it landed in a grouping of Pinion Pines about thirty yards off the trail. He watched Nugget bound through the sagebrush toward where the stick landed, only this time the dog didn't return right away.

After foraging around in the high sagebrush for a full minute, Nugget returned to his master, holding his prize in his mouth—only it wasn't the stick he had originally gone after. Instead, clamped in the dog's teeth was what Warner instantly recognized as a human femur bone. Warner gently removed the bone from the dog's mouth and placed it on the ground beside the trail. He stuck a large stick into the semi-frozen ground as a marker and then snapped a leash onto his dog's collar before following him to where he had found the bone.

When Warner was thirty feet from the copse of trees where he had thrown the stick, he began to smell the distinctive odor of decay associated with death. The odor grew stronger as he got closer to the trees and was almost unbearable by the time he got to them. As Warner stepped into the clearing in the sagebrush directly underneath the pine trees, he saw where Nugget had found the femur bone and where the stench of death was emanating from.

Human skeletal remains had been partially unearthed from a shallow grave. Bones and bits of material were scattered around the site, which had apparently been dug up by scavenging coyotes. The skin that had once covered the bones had long since decomposed, but the clumps of long black hair still attached to the skull made the skeleton appear to have been from a female. Warner remembered from medical school that skin and organ tissue decomposed rather quickly, but hair sometimes remained for years after death.

The part of the skeleton still covered with dirt appeared to be enclosed in what looked like a sleeping bag. At first, Warner thought this might have been a transient who had died while sleeping in a makeshift encampment and was then covered in dirt by a windstorm. But before backing out of the burial site to call the authorities Warner noticed something to change his mind. The white rope was looped around the hands and neck of the skeleton, and Warner's morning walk turned into a jog as he rushed to call the police.

The site where the skeletal remains were discovered was in the jurisdiction of the Washoe County Sheriff's Office, so they responded when the jogger Warner flagged down for help called them. Warner remained on scene and led the first responding deputies to the site, then left after vowing to himself to keep to the river trails for his morning walks from now on.

By the time Lieutenant Don Means from the Forensic Investigation Unit arrived, a good-sized portion of Dog Valley Road had been cordoned off with yellow crime scene tape. Bodies dumped in the desert are not that strange of an occurrence—especially near gambling towns. But as soon as

Lieutenant Means looked down at the partially exposed skeleton, he knew this one was different.

Means noted a lot of animal activity at the site. In addition to the part of the skeleton still remaining in the shallow grave, there were bones and bone fragments scattered for several hundred yards. Intermingled with the bones were pieces of black plastic and shreds of fabric that appeared to have come from a sleeping bag.

Means helped investigate the discovery of Kathy Powell's body, so he was familiar with that case. He immediately saw the white nylon rope running through the matted hairpiece and around the hands of the skeleton was the same diameter and texture as the rope used to bind Kathy Powell. The knots in the rope were also strikingly similar in both cases.

As Means later put it, "Body dumps aren't that uncommon. But finding two of them where rope, trash bags, and sleeping bags were used in this short of a period *is* uncommon—even in Reno."

Detective Larry Canfield was the lead investigator on the scene for the Sheriff's Office. After conferring with Means, they agreed there were many similarities between the two cases, so they notified Reno P.D. and asked for the detectives working on the Kathy Powell investigation to respond.

Jenkins and Douglas were called in from home and met at the police station so they could drive out to Verdi together. They brought along a binder containing every report of a missing female that had been filed with local police agencies since Middleton moved to Reno. Of the nineteen total reports, six were teenage runaways who had already returned home, three were elderly Alzheimer patients, and two were disgruntled housewives who had fled their husbands and were now accounted for. After eliminating these, they were left with eight missing females, but only four of them fit into the category of Middleton's past victims. These were the four cases they were in the process of following up on when they broke for the weekend.

The skeleton had not yet been exhumed from its shallow, earthen grave when Jenkins and Douglas arrived. They stood in the interior of the crime scene with Detective Canfield and Lieutenant Means, oblivious to the smell of death around them. After they were briefed, they were allowed to take a closer look at the skeletal remains. It was then that they saw the long black hairs attached to the skeleton's skull cap, and they both instantly knew they'd seen that hair before.

The coroner was on the scene and said the body would have had to have been buried there before the onset of the cold winter weather in order for that degree of decomposition to occur. The grave was only about six inches deep, so decomposition would have occurred quickly in the hot summer months. His best guess was the body had been buried for at least seven months, but it could have been longer. Using that timeframe, Jenkins eliminated all but one of the missing person's reports in the binder.

They studied the Sparks Police Department missing person report of forty-two-year-old Thelma Davilla. An officer named Rocky Triplett took the initial report, and was experienced enough to have collected hair from Ms. Davilla's hairbrush to be used for later comparison. The case had then been assigned to Sparks Detective Dave Adams, who, according to the report, had dental records for Ms. Davilla on file. In addition to the hair still remaining on the skeleton, the jawbone and teeth were still intact. Because of the excellent preliminary investigation done in the missing person case, it would be easy to confirm whether the remains actually were Ms. Davilla quickly.

The date Ms. Davilla was last seen was August 8, 1994. Douglas looked up from the report and asked, "Why does that date sound so familiar?"

"Because we've seen it before," replied Jenkins. "Eddie Dixon had August 8, 1994, listed on his timeline as the day Middleton moved into his new and larger storage unit. Now we know the reason he needed more room."

"Shit! We should have seen that earlier."

"Well, we didn't," replied Jenkins. "But we see it now, and that's what matters. From the looks of our decedent, it wouldn't have mattered if we had noticed it when we got this report last week anyway."

Canfield said, "Well, it's gonna save us a lot of leg work if you've got both the victim *and* the suspect identified in this case."

"I believe we do," said Jenkins. "But we need to be sure before you focus entirely on Middleton. If you will be so kind as to call Detective Adams from Sparks and have him bring the hair samples and dental records from his case, John and I will go to our department and retrieve the hair samples we took from Middleton's storage shed. We'll meet you at the crime lab in about an hour and see if things match up the way I think they will."

As the two Reno detectives were heading back to their car, Canfield called to them. "Hey, D.J., how many more do you think there are?"

Jenkins looked at the binder in his hand and answered, "Only God and the devil can answer that question."

Douglas added, "And the devil ain't talkin' without his lawyer."

Chapter 31:
Thelma

The search of the Verdi gravesite and recovery of the skeletal remains were halted at 4:30 P.M. due to darkness. Forensic investigators spent the entire next day performing a painstakingly thorough grid search of the entire area where the remains had been located. By Monday morning, April 11, 1995, the exhumed skeleton and all of the scattered bones collected at the site were in the custody of the Washoe County Coroner's Office. All of the forensic evidence was taken to the Sheriff's Crime Lab.

Washoe County Coroner Vernon McCarty positively identified the skeletal remains as Thelma Davilla through a comparison of dental records. Additional identification came from Dr. Berch Henry, a criminalist for the Washoe County Sheriff's Crime Lab. Dr. Henry compared DNA taken from the skull cap of the skeleton to the hairs taken from Thelma Davilla's hairbrush and got a positive match. The hairs found at the bottom of the drum in Middleton's shed also matched Ms. Davilla's DNA. The detectives had anticipated this, but the DNA comparison yielded one surprising discovery.

Hair and small amounts of blood and skin had been located inside the hollowed-out portion of the large speaker box inside Middleton's storage shed. This trace evidence also matched Davilla's DNA. The only logical explanation for this was that Thelma Davilla had, at some point, been placed inside the speaker box. The space was easily large enough to hold her small-framed body, and since she had been bound, she more than likely was alive when placed inside the box. The detectives envisioned Middleton using the speaker box to hold Davilla captive the same way he used the refrigerator to hold Powell.

Investigator Richard Berger from the Sheriff's Forensic Science Division examined the rope found on and near Davilla's remains. Mr. Berger had also done the evidentiary analysis in Kathy Powell's case and said the rope used on both victims was consistent and similar in all manners. The rope was also consistent with the rope recovered from Middleton's storage shed.

An autopsy on Davilla's remains was not possible due to a lack of tissue, but Dr. Frederick Laubscher performed a medical examination from the Coroner's Office. Since the skull and other bones were intact, Dr.

Laubscher ruled out gunshot, knife wound, crushing injury, or any type of trauma as the cause of death. However, he could not rule out suffocation or most other possible causes of death. After thorough examination, his summation of cause and manner of death consisted of one word—*undetermined.*

The Davilla case now involved all three of Northern Nevada's biggest law enforcement agencies. She had been reported missing to the Sparks Police Department, her remains had been found in an unincorporated area under the jurisdiction of the Washoe County Sheriff's Office, and her death was directly related to a Reno P.D. case. Since they were once again dealing with an undetermined cause of death, the detectives would have to prove criminal agency was involved. They had their work cut out for them and decided it would be beneficial to both investigations to pool their resources.

A multi-jurisdictional task force would require the approval of the heads of all three agencies, and that would take time. As Douglas put it, if you put three police chiefs in the same room together, they're not even going to agree about the time of day, never mind who's going to be lead agency on a task force. But nothing was preventing the detectives from holding an impromptu meeting to discuss the cases between themselves, so that is what they did at 9:00 A.M. on Tuesday, April 12, 1995.

They met at the Sparks Police Department since Detective Adams was the lead investigator on the Davilla case. Jenkins and Douglas had a vested interest in helping tie Middleton to the death of Thelma Davilla. If they could show Middleton had a predisposition for kidnap, torture, and murder six months before he ever met Kathy Powell, it would make proving criminal agency in their case much easier.

In addition to Jenkins and Douglas, Sheriff's Detective Larry Canfield also attended the meeting. The three detectives listened intently as Detective Adams briefed them, each wanting to learn as much about the victim as they could.

Thelma Davilla was a Guatemalan immigrant who shared a one-bedroom apartment at 2244 Greenbrae Dr. in Sparks with her older sister, Dora Valverde. At the time of her disappearance, she was forty-two years old and unmarried. She had a sixth-grade education, spoke very little English, and worked bussing tables at the Hickory Pit Restaurant inside of the Circus-Circus Casino in downtown Reno.

She occupied the living room of her sister's apartment and slept on the couch. She enjoyed simple pleasures, like going to the mall or watching T.V. Since Davilla grew up in poverty in Guatemala, she was never able to indulge in those types of activities. According to her sister one of the first things Davilla did after getting a job was buy a television and get cable installed in the apartment. Her cable T.V. provider was listed as T.C.I. Cable Company.

Davilla worked the 4:00 P.M. to midnight shift at the Hickory Pit Restaurant on Sunday, August 7, 1994, and was scheduled to be back at work at 4:00 P.M. the next day. When Ms. Valverde left for work at 8:00 A.M. on Monday, August 8, 1994, Davilla was asleep on the couch. The television was on, and a multi-colored Mexican-style blanket covered her.

When Valverde returned home after work at 5:30 P.M. that same day, she found the front door unlocked, which she said was unusual. The T.V. was still on, but Davilla and the blanket she had been using were gone. A plant near the couch had been knocked over, but that was the only thing appearing out of place. Davilla kept several hundred dollars in cash from tips in a coffee can near the couch, and the money was still there.

Valverde was not overly concerned until she checked her telephone messages. There was a message from Davilla's dentist saying she had missed a morning appointment and another from the Hickory Pit Restaurant asking why she wasn't at work. Valverde knew her sister would not have willingly missed the dental appointment since she had been complaining of a toothache. She also knew Davilla had not missed a day of work during the six years she had been employed at the restaurant—a fact she was extremely proud of. Davilla was in good health and would not have missed work without calling.

When Valverde still hadn't heard from Davilla by the next morning, she notified the Sparks Police Department. Due to the uncharacteristic behavior of Davilla, the responding officers believed foul play might be involved. Detectives were called to the apartment and began their missing person investigation.

Davilla's checkbook was on the living room table, and the last check she wrote was dated August 8, 1994. The check was for seven dollars, and it was written to the T.C.I. Cable Company. The detectives checked with T.C.I. and found Davilla had not been billed for a seven-dollar charge. They also had no record of anyone from T.C.I. going to her apartment to collect any type of payment. Additionally, there was no specific service they provided where a seven-dollar charge would have been billed. The information did not seem important at the time, so it was logged into the report with no further follow-up.

Davilla had only three close friends she socialized with and did not have a steady boyfriend. One of her female friends said they often frequented a Latin nightclub called Cheers on West 4th Street in downtown Reno. She said Davilla liked to dance and occasionally dated men she met at the club. She added that Davilla had a preference for black men. Davilla and the friend had gone to Cheers on Saturday night, August 6, 1994. The friend could not remember who Davilla had danced with, but they did leave the club together.

All three friends said Davilla never opened the door to her apartment without looking through the peephole to see who was there, even when she was expecting someone. They said it was unlikely she would open the door for a stranger while she was home alone. The detectives noted in their report there was no sign of forced entry into the apartment.

Davilla did not own a car and used Citifare busses to commute. After canvassing the bus drivers, the detectives found one driver who knew Davilla because she was a regular passenger on one of his routes. The driver remembered seeing Davilla at the Sparks bus station in the early evening on Friday, August 5, 1994. She was quite dressed up and told the driver she had plans to go out to dinner with friends. The driver recalled seeing a light-colored pickup truck pull up to where Davilla was waiting. A black male was driving, and a white female with curly reddish-blonde hair was in the passenger seat. The male got out, and Davilla jumped in and slid into the middle of the front seat. The male then got back into the truck and drove off.

All investigative leads in Davilla's disappearance eventually turned into dead ends, and the case was subsequently listed as open and inactive. Detective Adams said until Davilla's remains were discovered, it was like she just vanished without a trace.

The words *vanished without a trace* echoed inside of Jenkins's head because he'd heard them before. News reporters in Colorado used those same words when telling the story of the disappearance of Buffy Rice-Donohue in Montrose, Colorado, nine months before Thelma Davilla disappeared. But before he could dwell on that thought the phrase was chased from his brain by two words even more horrific. *Serial Killer!*

138

Chapter 32:
Body Count

Sergeant Burns called Jenkins as he and Douglas were leaving the Sparks Police Department to tell him that Lieutenant Tom Chinn of the Montrose Police Department and two other Colorado detectives were flying into Reno that afternoon. They hoped to look over the evidence taken from Middleton's storage shed and discuss similarities in the cases they were working on.

The Colorado detectives arrived at the Reno Police Station at three in the afternoon, and a meeting was set up in the Detective Division conference room to discuss their respective cases. Detectives Canfield and Adams, representing the Sheriff's Office and the Sparks Police Department, joined Jenkins, Douglas, and Sergeant Burns for the meeting.

After being filled in on the Middleton investigation in Reno, Lieutenant Chinn brought the detectives up to date on the Buffy Rice-Donohue investigation. There was still no trace of Buffy and no new leads on the case. Chinn hoped something in Middleton's storage unit might link him to Buffy's disappearance and shed new light on his investigation. Their case was still listed as open and active, but they held little hope of finding Buffy alive after seventeen months.

Lieutenant Chinn alluded to the fact that Walt and Bonnie Rice had provided them with bad information that delayed their initial investigation in an attempt to steer the police away from any possible drug connection to Buffy's disappearance. Middleton and Haley had been questioned during the investigation, and they both took polygraph tests prior to leaving Colorado. The results for both of the polygraph tests were inconclusive. Since that time, additional witness interviews had been done, and Middleton and Haley were now considered the only viable suspects in the case.

The two questions the Nevada detectives had on their minds sat heavily in the room like invisible elephants. Why had Middleton been allowed to leave Colorado when he was the main suspect in Buffy's disappearance, and why hadn't he been arrested on the weapons charge when they had their chance to hold him? Those questions would remain unasked because it just didn't matter now.

Detective Sergeant John Musick from Delta, Colorado, next discussed the disappearance of fourteen-year-old Cindy Booth from his city. The teenager had last been seen riding her bicycle to the home of a family friend after school on the afternoon of August 4, 1993. Neither the girl nor her bicycle was ever seen again.

The family friend whose house Booth went to was forty-year-old Eugene Marvin Smith. The man was questioned after Booth's disappearance and was still the primary suspect in the case. Since a body had never been discovered and there was no physical evidence linking Smith to Booth's disappearance, he had not yet been charged with any crime related to the case.

Delta is twenty miles west of Montrose, and the police department was interested in Middleton because Booth's disappearance occurred during the time he lived there. Eugene Smith and Middleton knew each other through construction work, so they wanted to explore the possibility that Middleton might have been involved in the disappearance. Smith refused to talk to the police and had since been convicted on unrelated charges of molesting his three-year-old niece in 1992. He was due to be sentenced to fifteen years in prison, so, like Middleton, he was off the street while they investigated the disappearance of Cindy Booth.

Montrose P.D. Detective Kevin Walters then discussed a case he was working on in conjunction with the San Miguel County, Colorado Sheriff's Office. On November 13, 1994, the skeletal remains of a female in her early forties were found buried in a shallow grave in a rural area of Colorado about fifty miles east of Montrose. Her estimated time of death was in the early fall of 1993. This would have been just after the disappearance of Cindy Booth, and during the time Middleton and Haley were living in Montrose. The woman still remained unidentified, but it was believed she may have been a transient prostitute who was never reported missing. Detective Walters was working the case with the Sheriff's Department since the crime may have originated in Montrose.

The San Miguel County Coroner was able to establish blunt force trauma as the cause of death for the unknown female, so the case was classified as a homicide. The fact that Middleton preyed on street prostitutes in Miami had not gone unnoticed by the investigators, but it was the discovery of Kathy Powell and Thelma Davilla that really got them interested in him. Much like the Reno victims, the Jane Doe victim in the

San Miguel County case had been bound with rope and placed inside a sleeping bag before being disposed of.

The Colorado detectives brought DNA and hair samples from all three victims with them. Thus far, two hair samples and DNA evidence from five pairs of women's panties found in Middleton's shed were not matched with their owners, so arrangements were made for comparisons of all samples to be done at the Washoe County Crime Lab the next morning. There were no plans to charge Middleton with any of the Colorado crimes yet since he was already in custody in Nevada, but that could change if additional evidence was discovered. The Colorado detectives were also interested in interviewing Haley and Middleton while they were in town.

During the ensuing discussion, Jenkins asked about the polygraph tests Middleton and Haley took. He had never before heard of a case where the polygraph results from two suspects involved in the same crime showed inconclusive, and he asked Chinn if he had a theory for the anomaly.

Chinn let out a sigh and said that question had come up before, but he didn't have an answer for it. He did say a lot of people were conned by Middleton, and most people in Montrose thought he was an honest ex-cop who had to get out of Miami after going undercover in prison. Jenkins had spent enough time talking to Middleton to be reasonably certain the Colorado lieutenant was probably a member of the group he had conned.

Several things were discussed by the Nevada detectives after their counterparts from Colorado left for their hotel. First and foremost, they all agreed a task force needed to be formed to investigate Middleton's crimes in Nevada. Part of the responsibilities would be to do an independent inquiry into Middleton's criminal activity in Colorado and Florida. They were not out to burn anyone—they just had to establish a pattern of criminal activity to support their case.

They needed to do this without stepping on the toes of the Colorado cops. None of them thought the Montrose Police Department had intentionally bungled their case against Middleton. Mistakes are sometimes made when small-town cops get involved in big-time investigations, but the mistakes have to be rectified.

The follow-up in Florida was another matter, but it was just as essential. Somewhere along the line, Middleton went from respected cop to serial killer, and they all believed Florida was where they would find the answers. A road trip to Florida would definitely need to be made, and the detectives would carry more clout if they represented a multi-jurisdictional task force. Sergeant Burns agreed and said he would start the procedure first thing in the morning.

The conversation then turned to Evonne Haley. They all agreed she was currently more valuable to them as a free person than she would be if they arrested her on the theft charges from the Good Guys case. They had enough to proceed with the charges now, but her rights to an attorney would kick in if they questioned her about any of the murders while she was in custody. They decided to let her enjoy her freedom for now, but they all knew her days were numbered.

As they broke for the evening, Douglas joked that if Middleton's body count got much higher, he was going to make Norman Bates look like a boy scout. The detectives laughed, but inside, they knew Middleton had already passed the magic number to be considered a serial killer. None of the men in the room had ever worked with a confirmed serial killer before, but it was every homicide detective's dream to go up against one. Middleton was good, but now it was time to prove they were better.

Chapter 33:
Heads Or Tails

The Colorado detectives flew home on Thursday, April 14, 1995. They had located nothing of evidentiary value to their cases during the search through the contents of Middleton's storage unit, and no DNA matches were found.

Speaking through his attorney, Middleton refused to talk to the detectives. When they called Haley for an interview, her message to them was also quite clear. She told them to either arrest her or leave her the hell alone. The only things the detectives took with them were hair and DNA samples from Middleton. These might be useful for evidence comparison if the bodies of the two missing women should be discovered.

On Friday, April 15, 1995, Jenkins was flipping through the investigative report on the Buffy Rice case Lieutenant Chinn had left him. His instincts told him something was missing, so he got the phone number for the Rice family from the report and decided to call to see if they could shed some light on the case. He didn't know it at the time, but it would be the first of many conversations he'd have with the family throughout the course of the investigation.

Bonnie Rice was home when Jenkins called and was more than happy to talk to him about the case of her missing daughter. For the next hour, Jenkins listened to the story of Buffy Rice-Donohue's disappearance while taking notes on a yellow legal pad. Some of what Bonnie Rice told him he'd already read in the papers, but most of it was new and useful information.

The first bit of interesting information Jenkins learned was that Haley's father was an ex-cop with the Mesa County Sheriff's Office in Grand Junction, Colorado. According to Mrs. Rice, Haley's father had been fired for his involvement in some type of cover-up during a murder investigation of a wealthy businessman in Telluride, Colorado. The adage about women being attracted to men like their fathers popped into Jenkins's mind when he listened to the story.

Buffy knew that Haley's father was involved in law enforcement in Colorado and that Middleton had been a cop in Miami. She didn't know at the time Haley's father had been fired, and she believed Middleton had been an undercover operative while in prison in Miami. Buffy told her parents she trusted Middleton and Haley due to their involvement with law enforcement. Once again, the word *trust* was used by one of Middleton's victims.

Bonnie Rice described Buffy as a good student and an all-around good kid through her high school years. Buffy got engaged to her boyfriend, Mason Donohue, shortly after she graduated from high school. Bonnie said she and her husband would have rather seen her wait until she was older, but they liked Mason and were supportive of their daughter's decision. Buffy planned to become an X-ray technician, so she took the job at the Sizzler to raise money for school. Mason worked construction, and the young couple moved into a rented mobile home in Montrose after they were married.

Buffy became involved with drugs three months before her disappearance. Mrs. Rice blames Middleton and Haley for this, as it became well-known that the two of them were involved in selling methamphetamine. Two weeks before Buffy disappeared, she told her parents she had found out Middleton had raped a girl in Florida. She said she was terrified of Middleton and asked if she and Mason could move in with her parents. The young couple abandoned their mobile home and moved in with Bonnie and Walt Rice.

Bonnie had her own theory about Buffy's disappearance on the afternoon of Sunday, November 21, 1993. Evonne Haley had come to the Rice residence earlier that day to talk to Buffy, possibly about money Buffy owed her. Haley was parked in front of the Rice house talking to Buffy when Walt Rice yelled to Buffy that he wanted her to get the family car washed later that afternoon. Bonnie Rice felt Haley heard that exchange.

The apartment Haley and Middleton shared overlooked the parking lot of the car wash, which was located in the same shopping complex as the Wal-Mart Buffy's car was later found parked in front of. Bonnie believed Haley waited for Buffy to pull into the car wash and then confronted her there. Witnesses saw Haley drive into the car wash parking lot in her red RX-7 and then follow Buffy to the Wal-Mart. The same witnesses saw Buffy get into the passenger seat of Haley's car but said it looked as though she was at first trying to walk away from Haley.

When Buffy did not return home by 4:00 that afternoon, her parents knew something was wrong and suspected Middleton and Haley were involved. They called the Montrose Police Department, and an officer responded to their house. Although the officer did not take an official report at that time, he did write down the address Mrs. Rice gave them for Middleton and Haley as a place they thought Buffy might be.

Mrs. Rice said she went to Middleton's apartment three times that night looking for Buffy, but no one answered the door. She went on to say that several of Buffy's friends gave statements to the police, including the store clerk Jenkins had read about who saw Middleton carrying bags out of the apartment that night. Not only did the police fail to follow up with some of these witnesses, a year later they contacted one of them and asked her to fill out another statement because they lost her original one.

On one of the visits Mrs. Rice made to Middleton's apartment that first night, she noticed a window screen had been partially pushed out, and she saw what looked like a bloodstain on the inside of the windowsill. She reported this to the police, but they did not go to the apartment until two days later. According to Bonnie, Lieutenant Chinn and two officers went to Middleton's apartment on Tuesday, November 23, 1993, to check her report. Lieutenant Chinn said the alleged bloodstain looked like paint, so no photos were taken, and no evidentiary sample was collected.

Lieutenant Chinn told Mrs. Rice it was during this visit to the apartment that he asked Middleton about the report of him loading bags into his car the night Buffy disappeared. Middleton said the bags contained laundry and showed Lieutenant Chinn several empty laundry bags inside the apartment. Lieutenant Chinn believed this story, even though Middleton offered no explanation for why he was loading heavy bags of laundry into Haley's car at midnight in a town that didn't have a twenty-four-hour laundromat.

Jenkins asked Bonnie Rice about the article concerning the nude photos of Buffy. She confirmed the story to be true and went on to explain how the police came into possession of the photos. Due to Rice's frustration with the way the police were handling the case, they hired a private investigator named Nelson Jennett on December 1, 1993, to help find Buffy. Unbeknownst to them, Jennett had close ties to the Montrose Police Department and was reporting back to them without the Rice's consent. The Rice's got word of this and fired Jennett on December 20, 1995.

Bonnie said Jennett notified Lieutenant Chinn that he was no longer working for Rice, but he asked if he could continue working with the police to assist on the case. Jennett received a phone call from a man named Ken

Newman on January 2, 1994. Newman was the manager of the mobile home park where Buffy and Mason Donohue had been living prior to moving in with the Rice's. He told Jennett he had found an undeveloped roll of film while cleaning out Buffy and Mason's trailer and wanted to know what to do with it.

Jennett went to the mobile home park and picked up the roll of film. While he was there, Newman told him there was a second roll of film still inside the trailer. Newman let Jennett into the trailer, and he retrieved the second roll of film. He then got the film developed and turned the photos over to Lieutenant Chinn. The photos were from Buffy and Mason's honeymoon and did, in fact, contain nude photos of Buffy. Not only did the photos have no possible evidentiary value to the missing person case, but the family actually did confirm the police had shown them around in public on more than one occasion.

The film was the property of Mason Donohue, and it was taken out of a trailer. The rent was paid. Mason made repeated requests for the police to give the photos to him, but thus far, they had refused. Bonnie said the situation was particularly frustrating because even if the photos did have some evidentiary value, it was her understanding that they could not be used in a court of law. The private investigator was acting as an agent of the police, so a search warrant should have been obtained before the film was taken out of the trailer. This last statement led Jenkins to believe perhaps Bonnie Rice had a better understanding of the law than did the people investigating her daughter's disappearance.

Bonnie went on to say it was shortly after the first confrontation they had with the police over their display of the photos that charges were filed against her husband for the Waterdog Mountain incident and against her for trespassing at Middleton's apartment. She said Haley admitted in a recorded phone conversation with her that the police who responded to the apartment the night Middleton pulled the shotgun on her told Haley to press charges against her. Bonnie was told by her attorney this tape was inadmissible in any court proceedings because it was recorded without Haley's knowledge. It was still enough to convince the Rice's that the police were siding with Middleton and Haley.

Jenkins then asked Bonnie to tell him more about the shotgun incident. She described the shotgun in great detail, and her description exactly matched the weapon taken out of Middleton's apartment. She said when Middleton pointed the shotgun at her, it was so close to her face that she could see clearly all the way down the barrel. She said she honestly believed Middleton was going to kill her, but at that point and time, she didn't care. Deep inside, she knew her daughter had been killed, so a part of her was already dead.

As an afterthought, Jenkins asked Mrs. Rice what her opinion was regarding Middleton and Haley both passing their polygraph tests. She surprised him when she immediately answered they hadn't passed the tests. The results were inconclusive, which was a big difference. She had obviously done her homework because she knew polygraph test results depended largely on how the operator posed the questions.

In the case of Middleton and Haley, the polygraph operator was the father of the owner of the construction company Middleton worked at. Both men were friends and members of the group of people Middleton had conned into believing he was an undercover cop when he was in prison. Bonnie had no doubts the polygraph test results were inconclusive because the operator *wanted* them to be so.

Bonnie then gave Jenkins one more piece of surprise information. She had been in Reno following Middleton and Haley the week Kathy Powell's body was discovered. Bonnie Rice, her mother-in-law and a family friend drove to Reno for the purpose of following Middleton and Haley in hopes they would do something to lead to the discovery of Buffy.

The three women sat in their car at the end of Middleton's Street and followed either him or Haley until they would lose them. They arrived in Reno two days after Kathy Powell was abducted, but they never saw Middleton go to his storage shed, and they were not following him when he dumped the body in the dumpster. They actually spent more time following Haley because they were convinced, she was dealing drugs out of a downtown Reno car repair shop.

Before hanging up, Bonnie said she wished Jenkins luck in bringing Middleton to justice for the murders he committed in Reno. She said not knowing who was responsible for her daughter's disappearance was a living hell, but seeing Middleton go to prison would make it a little easier. She said she would pray for the detectives, and Jenkins believed her.

By the time Jenkins hung up the phone, he'd accumulated more information than the entire case file Lieutenant Chinn left for him contained. It was not uncommon for animosity to develop between a victim's family and the police when a case went unsolved for an extended period of time. But in this case the story told by the police was completely different than the one told to him by Bonnie Rice. A story was much like a coin—each having two sides that sometimes bore no resemblance to each other. Now that he'd heard both sides of this story it was time to figure out which one was heads and which one was tails.

Chapter 34:
Task Force

It is a proven fact in law enforcement that the best way to screw up an investigation is to keep getting more police agencies involved in it. The old adage of "too many chiefs and not enough Indians" comes into play every time. By the end of April, this is exactly what happened with the Middleton investigation. Every police administrator wanted their department to be the one that broke the case, and they *all* were putting pressure on the District Attorney's Office to file murder charges against Middleton.

On Friday, April 21, 1995, at 8:00 A.M., a meeting was held at the Washoe County Sheriff's Office. In attendance were representatives from the Reno and Sparks Police Departments, the Washoe County Sheriff's Office, The Washoe County District Attorney's Office, and the State of Nevada Division of Investigation. The cops who were actually working on the case were finally going to get what they had asked for. A task force was being formed to investigate the murders of Kathy Powell and Thelma Davilla more efficiently.

Members of the task force would be Detective Dave Adams from the Sparks Police Department, Detective Larry Canfield from the Sheriff's Office, Investigator Mary Haugen from the Nevada Division of Investigation, and Detective Dave Jenkins from the Reno Police Department. Other detectives from those agencies would be utilized as needed, but they would take their assignments from these lead investigators.

District Attorney Dick Gammick and his assistant Dave Stanton would be following the case closely, but Deputy District Attorney Tom Viloria was assigned exclusively to the Middleton case. Even though Viloria was handling the case, Gammick made it perfectly clear that any decision to file murder charges against Middleton would need *his* personal approval. This would take some of the heat off Viloria, but it would also ensure the case was prepared the way Gammick wanted it before his office prosecuted it.

From the onset, it was decided the job of the task force would be to investigate *only* the Powell and Davilla murders. Their investigative efforts in Colorado, Florida, or anywhere else in the case led them would be confined to fact-finding inquiries to establish information that would aid them in the prosecution of Middleton for these two murders.

Any crimes Middleton committed in other jurisdictions either had been or were in the process of being investigated by the proper agencies. The task force would liaise with these agencies and render any assistance they were asked for, but that was it. The fear was that if the detectives uncovered possible malfeasance that allowed Middleton to remain a free man, his defense attorney would use that at trial. It was a very realistic possibility that a good attorney could turn everything around and point the blame at the police for not doing their jobs and allowing Middleton to continue killing people. It only took one juror with a grudge against the police to believe that type of ploy and poison the entire jury.

The task force was given one week to gather all the information known about Middleton, Haley, and both murder cases. Another meeting would then be held the following Friday to discuss the status of the investigation. The District Attorney would review the case at that time and make a determination about what else was needed to support murder charges against Middleton.

The next task force meeting was held at the Washoe County Sheriff's Office crime lab on Friday, April 28, 1995, at 10:00 A.M. The detectives had worked hard at putting their cases together during the week and felt they were close to having enough on Middleton to file murder charges against him. The refrigerator and several other items of evidence taken from Middleton's shed were displayed at the meeting. In addition to the task force detectives, representatives from the administrations of each agency and the District Attorney's office were in attendance.

Jenkins started the discussion by giving background information on what was known about Middleton's past criminal history in Florida and Colorado. He included Haley's involvement with Middleton and what they had learned from the Colorado detectives about the three open murders in the Montrose area while the couple was living there. He also told the group what he had learned during his conversation with Bonnie Rice.

Everyone at the meeting was familiar with the evidence gathered thus far linking Middleton to the two Nevada murders, but some important evidentiary findings had come in since the last meeting. Middleton's dental impression and the bite mark on Kathy Powell's left breast were examined by Dr. Raymond Rawson, a professor of dentistry. This comparison was important because no saliva had been found on the bite mark, possibly because Middleton had cleaned it with bleach. Dr. Rawson confirmed the bite mark had been inflicted by Middleton. He further concluded that this was a very hard and painful bite since it caused bleeding below the skin. Because of this bleeding, he determined the bite was inflicted while Powell was still alive.

Dr. Rawson also compared the teeth marks in the foam ball to Kathy Powell's dental impression. He confirmed the teeth marks in the ball were Powell's and that she had bitten into it extremely hard to cause those marks. From the positioning of the teeth marks, he concluded the ball had been shoved into Powell's mouth in its entirety. Since the saliva on the ball also matched Powell's, the ball would have been placed into her mouth while she was still alive. The body does not produce saliva post-mortem, and additionally, there would be no reason to gag a dead person.

The forensic report on the rope used on Powell and Davilla had also returned. White nylon twelve-strand rope with a one-quarter-inch diameter was used to bind both victims. This was the same type as the rope found in Middleton's storage shed, but the rope was a common type sold commercially. The knots in the rope were listed as "SS granny knots," which are very common knots.

Further analysis had also been done on the hairs found in Middleton's shed. In addition to the hair discovered in the barrel, hairs found on a blanket, in a rolled-up ball of duct tape, and on one of the human bondage restraints had also been identified as coming from Davilla. This was positive proof that Davilla had been held inside of the storage shed at some time prior to her death.

Detective Adams went on to further discuss the Davilla investigation. Davilla and her sister had T.C.I. Cable service installed in their apartment in June of 1993. Middleton was not the installer listed in the company records. The cable service at their apartment was serviced on July 23, 1994, approximately two weeks before Davilla disappeared. Middleton was not the listed technician on this service either. The technician who did the service recalls Middleton helping him on several occasions but could not accurately recall if the July service call was one of them. It was possible that Middleton was on this service call and met Davilla at that time.

Another possibility was that Middleton met Davilla at the Cheers nightclub in Reno. The manager of Cheers picked Middleton out of a photo lineup and recalled him being in the club on more than one occasion. He also recognized the photo of Davilla but could not recall if he ever saw the two of them together.

A third possibility was the Sierra Stix bar in Sparks. This was directly across the street from Davilla's apartment, and she sometimes went there with friends. Jenkins recalled from his interview with the bartender Suzanne Atkinson that she first met Middleton at the Sierra Stix Bar in the summer of 1994. When they re-contacted her, she said she believed this was either in late July or early August of 1994.

Where Middleton met Davilla was irrelevant because they could now show that he *had* known her on August 8, 1994. During a canvass of Davilla's apartment complex the week prior, one of her neighbors identified Middleton from another photo lineup. The neighbor said he recalled seeing Middleton at 6:45 A.M. the morning of August 8, 1994 at Davilla's apartment. He said he watched Middleton walk partway up the stairs leading to the apartment. He then saw Middleton stop and stand on the stairs as if he was listening to something, then turn and walk back down the stairs and away from the apartment.

In a follow-up interview with Ms. Valverde, she told detectives that 6:45 is the time she normally eats breakfast before going to work, and the kitchen is just inside the front door of the apartment. Detectives theorized that Middleton planned to make contact with Davilla during the 6:45 A.M. visit but left the apartment when he heard Valverde making noise in the kitchen. It was possible that he remained in the area and returned to the apartment when he saw Valverde leave for work. Records at T.C.I. showed Middleton was scheduled to work at 8:00 A.M. on Monday, August 8, 1994, but he called in sick.

The detectives also had a theory about how Middleton had taken Davilla from the apartment. Since the plant was knocked over near the couch where Davilla was sleeping, there was probably some type of struggle. Middleton could have used his stun gun on her, or he could have simply overpowered her. They were reasonably certain Middleton had carried Davilla out of her apartment wrapped inside a blanket. Ms. Valverde identified a large hand-woven Mexican blanket found inside Middleton's storage shed as the one her sister was covered with when she last saw her sleeping on the couch on August 8, 1994. In addition to the blanket, Ms. Valverde also identified a black lacy top and a red hair scrunchy found inside the shed as belonging to Davilla.

Since hair and DNA evidence from Davilla was found inside the large speaker box in Middleton's shed, that is where he most likely held her captive when he first took her to his old storage unit. Once there, Middleton must have realized his storage shed was too small for whatever he had planned for Davilla, so he rented the larger one. Since Davilla's hair was found in the balled-up duct tape, it was probably used as a gag. That meant she was kept alive in the storage shed for at least some period of time and was more than likely bound and gagged inside the speaker box while Middleton moved his belongings into his new storage unit.

What was done to Davilla and how long she was held captive inside Middleton's chamber of horrors might never be known. One thing that was certain is she never left that storage shed alive.

The discussion then moved to when murder charges would be filed against Middleton. A rather heated debate began between Sergeant Tolliver and District Attorney Gammick. Tolliver thought there was enough to move ahead with the murder charges and accused the D.A. of wanting the entire case gift-wrapped for him. The undetermined cause of death ruling was still a stumbling block, and Gammick would not budge on the issue.

Sergeant Burns intervened and suggested they meet again after Middleton's May 17th sentencing on the weapons charge. Middleton might slip up and give them something they could use against him during the court proceedings. The frustrated task force detectives agreed, but each of them felt there was a far better chance of Middleton slipping *away* than slipping *up*.

Chapter 35:
Death Of A Cheerleader

David Middleton pled guilty to one count of conspiracy to being an ex-felon in possession of a firearm on May 17, 1995. In exchange for his guilty plea, he was sentenced to one year in jail. He would be given credit for time already in custody and would be allowed to serve the rest of his term in the Washoe County Jail instead of the Nevada State Prison. The sentence was light, but prosecutor Tom Viloria knew other charges would be brought against him before he was ever freed from jail.

If Middleton behaved while incarcerated, he would be given credit for "good time" and be out in six months. The detectives could always charge him with the Good Guys crime to keep him in jail longer, but they wanted more. They knew Middleton had tortured and killed Kathy Powell and Thelma Davilla, and they wouldn't rest until he was made to answer for the unspeakable crimes he'd committed against them.

The next notable event in the Middleton investigation was as much of a fluke as Nugget's discovery of Thelma Davilla in Verdi. On May 24, 1995, a woman and her boyfriend were hiking in the rugged hills near Norwood, Colorado. Norwood is a small town about forty miles west of Montrose, and the outlying areas are a good place to find Indian artifacts and animal bones. The woman was looking for deer antlers and stopped underneath a tree where the brush had been disturbed. She used a small shovel to dig through six inches of loose dirt, but instead of finding antlers, she unearthed the remains of Buffy Rice-Donohue.

Jenkins first learned of the chance discovery that same day through a phone call from Bonnie Rice. The coroner had not made an official identification of the body yet, but investigators were certain it was Buffy. The living hell of the unknown was over for the grieving mother, but the investigation into Buffy's death would prove to be a different kind of nightmare.

Buffy's body was discovered in the jurisdiction of the San Miguel County Sheriff's Office, but the Reno detectives assumed the Montrose Police Department would retain the lead in the investigation since she was last seen in their city. The task force detectives in Reno followed the Colorado investigation closely because they were certain Buffy's killer was already in their custody. Any evidence the Colorado detectives could come up with linking Middleton to Buffy's murder would strengthen the Reno cases. The day after the remains were found, the medical examiner's office determined through a match with dental records that they were, in fact, the remains of Buffy-Rice Donohue.

The cold Colorado temperatures and the fact Buffy's body had remained buried slowed the decomposition process considerably. Unlike the Thelma Davilla case, the San Miguel County Medical Examiner was able to perform an autopsy on the remains of Buffy Rice-Donohue. By Friday, May 26, 1995, the preliminary report from that autopsy had been completed, and a copy was faxed to Dave Jenkins.

The task force detectives sat in the Detective Division conference room at the Reno Police Department, reading copies of the autopsy report with great interest. The coroner was able to determine a cause of death after examining Buffy. The death was caused by blunt force trauma and was officially listed as a homicide. That ruling alone would make the case much easier for the Colorado detectives to work.

Buffy had been bound with white nylon rope, and her body was covered with black plastic garbage bags. Duct tape had been wrapped around her head and mouth to gag her. Several deep teeth marks and tearing found on the gag showed that Buffy was alive for quite some time after being bound. Keeping his victim bound and gagged while engaging in sexual torture was another similarity between this and the Kathy Powell murder case.

Some hairs and carpet fibers were found inside of the plastic bags covering Buffy's body. The preliminary report showed the hair matched the samples from David Middleton and the carpet fibers were the same color as the interior carpet in Evonne Haley's RX-7. Since the hair samples used for comparison were given to the Colorado detectives by the Reno detectives, there was some question about their admissibility as evidence. To alleviate this problem the Colorado detectives would be returning to Reno in the near future to take hair and carpet samples under a court order. Until such time they could not officially say the hairs found on the body belonged to Middleton.

The murder of Buffy Rice-Donohue was a tragedy, but the task force detectives believed her death would not be in vain. Unlike the Reno murder cases, the Colorado case was strong. They had a confirmed cause of death, a coroner's ruling of homicide, a motive of sex and money for the murder, and forensic evidence on the victim's body. Added to this were the facts the victim was last seen with Haley, and a witness had seen Middleton loading a large bag similar to the one Buffy was buried in into the back of Haley's RX-7 the night of her disappearance. The detectives knew there was no such thing as a slam dunk case, but this was about as close to one as they could get.

The proper way to proceed with the investigation was obvious. Once the Colorado detectives officially matched Middleton's hair and the carpet samples from Haley's car to the evidence they found on Buffy's body, they would have enough to charge one or both of them with her murder. Middleton was still in custody for his firearms charge, but no other charges had yet been filed against him. The process of extraditing him to Colorado and trying him for Buffy's murder would be fairly easy since there were no pending court actions in Nevada.

The best-case scenario would be that Middleton would be found guilty in Colorado. The detectives could then file murder charges on him resulting from the Powell and Davilla cases and extradite him back to Nevada for trial. Since he would have already been found guilty of a murder that bore so many similarities to the Nevada cases, they would be able to use the Colorado case during Middleton's trial. Even if they were precluded from using it during their case in chief, they would surely be able to bring his conviction in during the penalty phase to show prior criminal acts.

The worst-case scenario was that Middleton would be found innocent in Colorado. That seemed unlikely, but stranger things than that had happened. The murder trial of O.J. Simpson was beginning its fifth month and adding a new twist to the adage of "anything can happen in a jury trial." The prosecutor in the Simpson case had called it a slam dunk, but she was losing ground on a daily basis.

Even if Middleton *did* beat the Colorado charges it would still help the Reno cases. There is no statute of limitations for murder, and the more time they had to gather evidence, the better. They could defer charging him until after the Colorado case was adjudicated so they would not have to worry about violating the time element dealing with Middleton's Sixth Amendment right to a speedy trial. The clock started ticking when they officially charged him, so time was on their side.

It was a win-win situation for the Nevada detectives, and they left for their weekend feeling good about the latest developments in Colorado. Their revelry was short-lived when they received updated information from Colorado on Monday, May 29, 1995. Montrose District Attorney Wyatt Angelo ruled that regardless of what evidence was gathered connecting Middleton to the murder of Buffy Rice-Donohue, no charges would be filed against him at this time.

Angelo's decision was based on the cost of extraditing and trying Middleton when he would surely be charged with the Reno murders soon. He estimated the cost of a murder trial to be $100,000 and said there was no reason for the taxpayers of Montrose to bear that type of expense if there was a chance Middleton would be found guilty of two murders in Nevada.

The detectives investigating the Powell and Davilla cases were amazed by the Colorado prosecutor's decision. Publicly, they had to be very careful not to express their opinions, so all press inquiries were directed to the Montrose Police Department for comment. Their private opinions were another matter. One of the detectives couldn't come close to mustering his Eddie Murphy smile when he called the prosecutor's decision *bullshit!*

Jenkins had been out of the room taking a call from Bonnie Rice, and after returning, he told the other detectives about his phone conversation. Bonnie had just finished an interview with the *Rocky Mountain News* about the district Attorney's decision, and after hearing it, the detectives all wished murders were prosecuted by mothers instead of lawyers. Her quote was, "This should never be a money matter at all. A murder took place in our county, and the murderer should be prosecuted."

Buffy Rice-Donohue's life was taken away from her at the age of eighteen. The perky former cheerleader for the Montrose High School Indians had aspirations of someday being a marine biologist. Those who knew her had no doubt she would someday achieve her goal. At her wedding, five months to the day before Buffy disappeared, she told guests her one wish was for happiness and a long life. Every cop sitting in the conference room knew who had taken that wish away.

Other detectives had crowded into the conference room to hear what was going on. Jenkins told them the Rice's were in the process of having a tombstone made for Buffy's grave. The inscription on the back of the heart-shaped stone read, "We promise you, Buffy, Mom and Dad will never stop fighting for you."

There was one detective in the group who was harder than the slab of marble that parental promise was chiseled into, but even the former Army Ranger had trouble keeping his emotions in check when he heard that. He said, "Nobody's gonna put this fuckin clam Middleton away for us, so let's get to work."

Chapter 36:
Girlfriend-En-Stein

The detectives were still unable to talk to Middleton without him first contacting them, so they decided to work the case from a different angle. At 9:00 A.M. on Tuesday, May 30, 1995, Jenkins called Evonne Haley and asked if she would agree to a follow-up interview. Haley said she would talk to him, but she did not want the police to come to her apartment. Jenkins made arrangements with Haley for him and Depsynski to meet her at a coffee shop two blocks from her Carlin Street apartment in forty minutes.

The detectives worked out their interview strategy on the way. They would mention nothing to Haley about the discovery of Buffy Rice-Donohue's body, but if she brought the subject up, they would listen and play dumb. They didn't want to tip Haley off to the fact the Colorado detectives would be in Reno the following week to take their evidentiary samples from her car and from Middleton.

The main reason for the meeting with Haley was to discuss the storage shed, her involvement in the Good Guys case and to ask her if she knew Thelma Davilla. In addition to the bus driver originally interviewed in the Davilla case, some of her coworkers also gave a description matching Haley as a person Davilla had been seen with just prior to her disappearance. Haley and Davilla worked in downtown Reno casinos that were only two blocks apart. Additionally, Haley's place of employment was only a block from the nightclub Davilla frequented. Bonnie Rice was convinced that Haley singled out female victims and brought them to Middleton, so this possible connection needed to be explored.

Another possible theory on how Middleton met Davilla recently surfaced, and the detectives wanted to ask Haley about it. The Cheers Nightclub on West 4th Street in Reno was in the middle of an area known for prostitution activity. The parking lot of the food and liquor store right next to Cheers was a popular congregating place for prostitutes. Since Middleton had been known to troll for streetwalkers in Florida, the detectives thought there might be a connection there.

When Detective Adams took a photo lineup to the store, one of the clerks recognized Middleton's photo as a man he knew as "Big Dave." He said Middleton often bought burritos at the store in the afternoon and parked his T.C.I. Cable Company truck in the parking lot while he ate his lunch. He also remembered Middleton coming into the store on occasion during the night to buy liquor. The store had a large plate glass window in the front, so the clerk had a good view of the parking lot. He said he had seen women he knew were prostitutes leave the lot with Middleton on more than one occasion in both his T.C.I. Cable Company truck and his International Harvester pickup.

There was no indication that Davilla had ever been involved in prostitution activity, but this was definitely a place where Middleton might have first seen her. The route from the closest bus stop to Cheers crossed directly in front of the convenience store parking lot. Davilla was known to dress nicely when she went out dancing and often wore short skirts that accentuated her legs. The possibility that she attracted Middleton's attention and he followed her inside the nightclub was worth exploring.

During the interview, Haley denied knowing Thelma Davilla. She said she read about the case in the newspaper and did not recognize Davilla from the news photo. She also read the news stories saying the police were looking into Middleton's involvement in the Davilla case and accused them of trying to frame him for the Davilla murder in order to make it look like he killed Kathy Powell. She was convinced Middleton never met Davilla and had nothing to do with her death.

Haley told the detectives she had no knowledge of the Good Guys' thefts and denied knowing anything about the existence of Middleton's storage unit. The conversation then moved to Haley's sexual relationship with Middleton. She said they had never practiced or discussed any type of bondage, sadomasochism, or any other type of unusual sexual activities.

Jenkins told Haley that information had been uncovered during the investigation that conflicted with her claims of ignorance regarding some of the issues they were discussing. Haley suggested that she might be better off if she took a polygraph test to resolve those conflicts. Jenkins hid his excitement about Haley making the offer and excused himself from the table so he could call the station to set a time for the test.

The polygraph test was set for the following Thursday morning at 9:00 A.M. Since the police still had Haley's car in custody at the evidence yard, Jenkins said he would pick her up and drive her to the station for the exam. She agreed but said she would be living at her new trailer in Sun Valley by then since she had to be out of her Carlin Street apartment by

160

the first of the month. Haley gave Jenkins her new address of 5722 Flynn Drive in Sun Valley and left the coffee shop.

The detectives knew through a jailhouse informant that Middleton made nightly phone calls to Haley from jail. They were hopeful she would tell Middleton about her interview and that he might make contact with them to see what was going on. They were also reasonably certain Middleton would tell Haley not to submit to the polygraph test. With an unbiased polygraph operator and Middleton not there to offer Haley guidance, they were certain she would not be able to defeat the test.

Their suspicions about the polygraph test were confirmed when Jenkins went to pick up Haley at her Sun Valley residence at 8:30 A.M. on Thursday, June 1, 1995. Haley was not home, and the trailer was locked. Sun Valley is only fifteen miles north of Reno, but it is sometimes referred to as the biggest trailer park in the world. Haley's trailer was located in the type of neighborhood where people get selective memories when dealing with the police. None of her neighbors admitted seeing Haley or anyone else around the trailer that morning, so Jenkins drove to Haley's Carlin Street apartment to look for her. She was not there, but he found her daughter Natasha sitting on the front steps of the apartment.

Jenkins asked the girl why she was not in school, or at least inside the apartment. She told him she had spent the night at a friend's house, and when she returned to the apartment, she found she was locked out. Natasha told him she had not eaten since the day before and she was very hungry. Jenkins agreed to take her to a local fast-food restaurant to get something to eat before driving her to school and notifying Child Protective Services of the situation.

During the drive, Jenkins asked Natasha if she had ever been to Middleton's storage unit in Sparks. She said she had not and wasn't even aware Middleton had a storage unit. She then asked him why the police thought Middleton had killed women. She said she was ready to hear about the investigation, so Jenkins gave her an abbreviated version of what the police knew so far. He then dropped her off with the principal of her school and made another unsuccessful attempt to contact Haley.

On Tuesday, June 6, 1995, the detectives decided to make another attempt at getting Haley to take a polygraph test. They did not have a new phone number for her, so Jenkins, Canfield, and Adams drove to her Sun Valley trailer. She was home when they got there and told them she would reschedule the polygraph test. When asked if she would take it that afternoon, she said she couldn't because she was trying to find a ride to take her to pick up her daughter from school.

Adams suggested they schedule the test at the Sparks Police Department, and they could pick up Haley's daughter along the way. Haley consented to this, but once at the Sparks Police Department, she said she had changed her mind. She said she was not mentally prepared to take a polygraph test and could not understand why the detectives could not take her at her word regarding the storage shed, the Good Guys case, and her not knowing Davilla.

Since the detectives' last meeting with Haley, two of Davilla's coworkers had picked her out of a photo lineup, saying they had seen her with Davilla on two separate occasions shortly before she disappeared. One other coworker said he saw Haley with Davilla at a doctor's office in Sparks in early August of 1994. Haley said they must have her confused with someone else and again denied ever meeting Thelma Davilla. She then started making a scene in the lobby of the police station and asked for her and her daughter to be driven home.

All three detectives got the same vibes from Haley. If the theory was true about sociopaths attracting other sociopaths, she and Middleton were a match made in hell. Except if Haley actually *was* bringing Middleton his victims, then who was the bigger monster? It went back to the Frankenstein theory. Was the *real* monster the creator or the created?

Even though the detectives knew Haley was lying, they could not force her to take the polygraph test. During the drive back to Sun Valley, Haley asked Jenkins why he hadn't spoken to Middleton recently. She said she talked to Middleton on the phone the previous night, and he told her he wanted to talk to Jenkins again but felt the detective didn't want to talk to him.

Jenkins smiled and was grateful Canfield was in the car with him to hear the exchange. He told Haley that if Middleton wanted to talk, he would be more than happy to oblige his request for contact. His plan to have Haley feed Middleton information was working, and he was about to get another crack at the devil.

Chapter 37:
True Lies

On Wednesday, June 7, 1995, Detectives Jenkins, Douglas, Canfield, and Adams drove to the Washoe County Jail to attempt an interview with Middleton. The secondhand request through Haley for Jenkins to talk to Middleton was questionable, but they decided to make contact with him and see how it went.

Middleton agreed to an interview but said he would only talk to Jenkins. The detectives knew Middleton was trying to play them, so they decided to use this to their advantage. Jenkins would take the lead on the interview and let Middleton believe there was some type of cop-like bond between the two of them. The other three detectives would video-record the interview from an adjacent room and act as a safety net for Jenkins. If they saw Middleton starting to get the upper hand in the interview, they could call Jenkins out and re-direct their strategy.

The detectives left Middleton alone in the interview room while they formulated their strategy. His hands were cuffed to a belly chain and his right leg to a steel eye bolt mounted in the floor. The idea was to make him as uncomfortable as possible while he was alone and then improve his level of comfort when Jenkins came into the room. Having him associate comfort with talking to the detectives might give them a psychological edge.

The interview room was devoid of furnishings with the exception of a square metal table and three chairs in the center of the room. The hard metal chair for the interviewee was slightly lower and smaller than the two padded chairs on the opposite side of the table designed for the interviewers to sit in. Taking the high ground was another mental game used to put the prisoner at a disadvantage during the interview.

Jenkins walked into the interview room and set two Styrofoam cups of steaming black coffee on the table. After removing the restraints from Middleton's hands and ankles he suggested the prisoner stand and stretch before starting. Middleton went to sit back down on the prisoner chair, but Jenkins pushed one of the more comfortable interviewer chairs around to the other side of the table for him to use. He told Middleton he wasn't going to insult his intelligence by playing cop games with him. While this small gesture put Middleton at ease, it also showed him Jenkins was in control of even the simplest things in his life right now.

Unlike the interview rooms seen on T.V. cop shows, there was no one-way glass built into the walls or video camera hanging from the ceiling in this one. The camera and microphone for the state-of-the-art video and audio equipment being monitored by the detectives in the next room were concealed in the smoke detector hanging from the ceiling. Even though the interviewees had to be advised they were being recorded, people sometimes talked more freely when the camera wasn't staring directly at them.

They sat sipping their coffee and making idle conversation for a few minutes, more about the NBA playoff games than about Middleton's time in jail. When the light on the smoke detector went from flashing red to solid green, Jenkins knew the recording equipment was on, and it was time for him to start talking about the real reason he was sitting in the room with a murderer.

Jenkins began the interview by asking, "So what's going on here, David?"

Middleton shrugged his shoulders and, in a soft voice, said, "I guess Evonne told you I wanted you to come up here and talk to me. I'm glad you did because I'm going crazy in here."

"I'm flattered," Jenkins said. "But that's not what I was asking about. I want to ask you some questions, and they're not related to Kathy Powell. Have you been reading the newspapers lately?"

Middleton replied, "I haven't read the papers or watched the news in the last three weeks. I plead guilty to the gun thing, so I'm gonna be in here for a while. If I read about things going on out there while I'm stuck in here, I just get more depressed."

Most people's eyes look up and to the left when they lie, but Middleton wasn't most people. He stared right into Jenkins' eyes when he gave his answer. Jenkins knew from the jailhouse informant that Middleton had watched the T.V. news story about his link to the deaths of Kathy Powell and Thelma Davilla. The informant described Middleton as becoming catatonic after seeing the news show. Jenkins didn't put much faith in informants, but the deputy assigned to Middleton's cell block had confirmed the story.

"Does the name Thelma Davilla mean anything to you?" Jenkins asked.

Middleton again stared Jenkins straight in the eyes. He said, "I never met the lady. Her name was in some of my plea agreement paperwork and my lawyers said you might be asking me about her. My lawyers also told me you make your living lying to people and that you were gonna lie to me. They told me not to talk to you."

Middleton was deflecting his guilt back to Jenkins, but the detective wasn't falling for the trick. He said, "If your lawyers say not to talk to me, then don't talk to me. I'll get us another cup of coffee, and we can bullshit about basketball some more before they take you back to your cell. If that's what you want, then it's fine with me."

Middleton smiled and said, "You're good, Jenkins. I'll talk to you, but I wouldn't mind another cup of coffee, too."

Douglas was waiting in the hallway when Jenkins stepped out of the room to get the coffee. The other detectives were satisfied the Miranda requirements had been met after Middleton's last statement agreeing to talk to Jenkins, so they decided it was time to push him. They also agreed that the way Middleton could look him in the eye and lie was nothing short of eerie.

Jenkins returned to the room with the coffee and got right back into the questioning. He asked, "Have you ever been to the Cheers nightclub, David?"

Middleton sipped his coffee while staring across the table at Jenkins. He answered, "I know where it is, but I've never been inside the place. I used to get my lunch at the store right next to the club sometimes while I was working. I'm not much of a bar person, though, so I never got the urge to go in the club."

"Would you be referring to the Al Collins Food and Liquor Store when you say you got your lunch near Cheers?"

"That's the one," Middleton replied. "They make a mean burrito there, and the price is right. When I was working in that area of town, I liked to sit outside the store in my truck and people-watch while I ate my lunch. There're a lot of interesting characters hanging on 4th Street."

Jenkins took a sip of his coffee and then asked, "What if I told you the manager from Cheers picked your photo out of a lineup and said he remembers you being inside the club?"

Without hesitation, Middleton replied, "I'd say all of us brothers look alike to you white people, so the manager's statement wouldn't hold up in court."

Jenkins smiled and said, "I never mentioned that the manager was white. You're slipping, David."

For a fleeting second, Jenkins saw a panicked look on Middleton's face, but it was gone as quickly as it had appeared. Middleton stared at Jenkins with his cold, dark eyes and said, "Like I said before, Jenkins, you're good. That's why I like you. But for the record, I was just guessing the bar manager was white because most of them are. I've never been inside of Cheers, so I have no idea what the manager looks like."

"Fair enough," Jenkins said. "Let's move on. Have you ever been inside of the Sierra Stix Bar in Sparks?"

Middleton's gaze didn't move when he said, "Nope. I've never been inside of that one either."

It then became crystal clear to Jenkins how Middleton could lie so convincingly. He was a true pathological liar, and in his demented brain, he wasn't lying at all because he'd convinced himself he was telling the truth. Jenkins had studied this phenomenon and had even crossed paths with pathological liars on occasion, but none as deviant as this one.

Middleton had the ability to move the real truth across a bridge inside of his brain and store it in a place where there was no return route in the informational journey. He was well aware of his evil deeds, but his lies seemed truthful because he was able to answer questions with the part of his brain that was guilt-free. This is why he was such a good con man and why he was able to defeat the polygraph test. It was also why Jenkins now knew he could beat the devil.

Jenkins decided to try an experiment. He made a face like he just smelled something sour and asked, "Did you brush your teeth today, David?"

Middleton looked confused and replied, "Of course I did. I brush my teeth every day. Why?"

Jenkins shrugged and said, "No reason, really. It's just that your breath is so rotten I can smell it clear over here. I think you're lying about brushing your teeth, but that's your prerogative."

Middleton jumped up and yelled, "What the hell are you talking about? Why would I lie about brushing my teeth?"

Jenkins remained seated. He knew the line of questioning would confuse the other detectives who were watching him, but they wouldn't intervene unless they thought he needed help. He calmly said, "Sit down, David. Perhaps I'm mistaken."

Middleton's anger calmed as he sat back in his chair. He said, "Damned right, you're mistaken. It's probably just this rank cop-shop coffee that's making my breath bad. Now I've got a question for you. Did you tell Evonne I was having a homosexual relationship in jail?"

Jenkins had made mention of this to Haley the day before, mainly to see is she would leak it back to Middleton during her nightly conversation with him. He answered, "I received information from a jailhouse informant that you were having a homosexual relationship with someone in jail. I don't normally believe much of what I hear from informants, so I asked Evonne if you may have had any proclivity to homosexual involvement in the past. Not that it matters to me—I just wanted to confirm the credibility of the informant."

"Well, I ain't no punk," Middleton said. "You can tell your informant to go fuck himself and tell Evonne that whole thing is bullshit."

Jenkins said, "I'll do that. Have you spoken to Evonne lately?"

"Not in a few days. Sometimes, the lines are long at the jail phones."

Jenkins knew this was also a lie since Middleton must have spoken to Haley sometime since he leaked the information to her. There was no reason for him to lie about this, but another trait of a pathological liar was they lied even when they didn't have to. Middleton was passing every test Jenkins threw his way.

Changing the subject, Jenkins said, "Tell me about your storage shed, David."

Middleton looked straight at him and said, "I store shit in there. Sometimes, I do a little work in there, too."

"Were you working on that old Tappan refrigerator you had in the shed?"

A smile slowly spread across Middleton's face, and he responded, "I got a good deal on that thing. I thought I could fix it up, but now I think it's beyond repair. You can throw it out if you get back over there. I can always get another one when I get out."

Jenkins nodded his head slowly and said, "Let me think about that. How about all the clothes in the shed? Where did they come from?"

"That stuff all belongs to Evonne and Natasha," Middleton replied.

This was another lie. Hair and DNA samples had already been taken from Haley and her daughter. Nothing from the shed matched either of them, and they both denied having anything stored anywhere other than their apartment. Jenkins let the lie go and continued, "What if I told you Thelma Davilla's sister identified a blanket and some clothing found in your shed as belonging to her sister?"

Middleton said, "I'd tell you that I got that blanket in Nogales, Mexico when me and my old Metro partner Harvey Honig were down there for an extradition about seven years ago. Anybody who says differently must be mistaken. A lot of those Mexican blankets look alike."

Jenkins continued smiling but said nothing. There were several different kinds of blankets inside the storage shed, and he'd never mentioned the one he was talking about was a Mexican blanket. Moving along, he asked, "Did you ever bring Evonne, Natasha, or any other woman to your storage shed?"

Middleton held the detective's gaze, "No."

Jenkins looked at his notes and said, "I have a statement from the storage facility manager that says he saw you bring a woman to your shed."

"What did he say she looked like?"

Jenkins leaned back in his chair. "Why would that matter? If you said you never took a female to your storage shed, then the manager must be mistaken, right? Just like the informant was wrong about your homosexual relationship in jail, Ms. Davilla's sister was erroneous about the blanket, and I was incorrect about your forgetting to brush your teeth. Everybody makes mistakes in your life except you, right, David?"

Middleton looked away from Jenkins and once again became visibly upset. He exclaimed, "Hey! All this stress I've been under has been giving me terrible headaches! I forget shit sometimes. I did take a girl to the storage shed, but only one time and one girl. She was a black girl I met when I was eating lunch outside of that store one day."

Jenkins raised his eyebrows and asked, "The store next to cheers?"

"That's right. I was in my company truck eating lunch, and the girl came up to the window and started talking to me. All I remember is her name was Jennifer or something like that. I gave her a ride to Sparks, but we stopped off at my storage shed first."

"And why would you take a girl you just met to your storage shed, David? I've been there, and I can honestly say there is not much to do that would appeal to a girl you just met."

Middleton calmed down again and slipped back into his macho role. He said, "That depends on what you're planning on doing. Sometimes, when girls get around me, they can't control themselves. This girl said she wanted to have sex with me. I couldn't take her to my place because Evonne was home, and the girl said she lived with her parents or something. The storage shed was close to where she was going, so I figured it was as good a place as any."

Jenkins hid his excitement at the fact Middleton had just admitted to taking a girl to his shed for sex. Now was the time to play up to his ego to keep him talking. He continued, "There are a lot of prostitutes that hang out around that store, David. The romantic tryst you've just described to me sounds surprisingly similar to a prostitution deal. Was this girl Jennifer a 4th Street prostitute?"

Middleton gave Jenkins a smile evil enough to make the real Satan take a step backward. "I didn't ask, but do I look like a man who needs to pay for it? I never paid for pussy in my life."

Jenkins smiled back and said, "That may be true, but when you get things on credit, the payment comes due sooner or later. I think your bill has just been sent to a collection agency."

"We'll see," Middleton said. "I'm getting another headache, so I want to go back to my cell now."

Once the prisoner requests to end a voluntary interview, anything else said cannot be used as evidence. Jenkins stood up to get the jail deputy, but before he got to the door, Middleton said, "Hey, Jenkins. I heard they found Buffy. Is that right?"

"That's right," Jenkins answered. "A couple of your old friends from Montrose are coming to visit you on Friday, so I'll let them tell you about it. And speaking of old friends, it seems I'll be in Miami on Monday. Is there anyone you'd like me to say hello to for you while I'm there? Maybe an old partner, ex-wife, former female co-worker, or girl you met when she was sixteen? I'll be glad to give them your regards. Call me when you'd like to talk again, David."

Jenkins walked out of the interview room, leaving his statement about going to Florida hanging in the air for Middleton to think about. Jenkins himself had plenty of new information to think about before his pending trip to Miami.

They now had to research any missing person cases or unidentified dead bodies that could possibly be the girl Middleton admitted to taking to the shed. They would also have to show Middleton's photograph to *every* street prostitute they could find to see which of them had contact with him. If he admitted to taking a black girl to his shed, that meant she was probably a white or Hispanic girl. The legal prostitution ranches east of town would also need to be checked since some of those girls moonlighted as streetwalkers on their days off.

All this was running through his head when Douglas stepped out into the hallway and said, "I've got twenty bucks bet with these clowns that Middleton's bad breath has something to do with the murders. You better not let me down."

Jenkins looked at him and said, "Have I ever?"

"Not today," Douglas replied. "Let's talk."

Chapter 38:
Your Own Worst Enemy

The four detectives went to the first-floor cafeteria to discuss the interview. After ordering coffee and sandwiches, they sat at a table in a far corner of the room, away from the other patrons. The cafeteria was for employees only, but people talked about things they overheard, and privacy was important.

When they were seated, Canfield asked, "So what was that all about in there?"

"I was giving our boy a series of tests," Jenkins replied. "I now know we are dealing with a true pathological liar, and that fact will shape the way we handle him from now on."

Douglas swallowed a mouthful of turkey and cheese and then said, "I could have told you Middleton was a liar, even *without* asking him about his teeth."

Jenkins said, "Not just a liar, John—a *pathological* liar. There's a big difference between pathological liars and your run-of-the-mill *slimeball* liar. I'll show you."

Looking at Adams, Jenkins said, "I'm going to ask you a very simple question, Dave. I want you to take your time answering it, but I want the answer you give me to be something you know to be an obvious lie."

"OK," Adams said. "Just don't ask me if I ever thought about screwing a chicken. That's the one question they always ask you on those police psych tests that there's really no way to answer without making it look like you thought about screwing a chicken sometime."

"You're reading too much into this little test," Jenkins said. "The question I'm going to ask you is much simpler than your thoughts on animal husbandry. What is your name?"

Adams paused in thought while he stared at an imaginary spot on the ceiling to his left. He then looked at Jenkins and answered, "John Douglas."

"That's original," Douglas said.

"It may not be original," Jenkins said, "but it proves my point. Did you see the way he looked up and to his left before he answered with a lie? That is because a *normal* person needs to go into the prefrontal cortex of their brain to retrieve information they know isn't true. In Dave's case this action was overt—probably because lying doesn't come easy to him."

"You wouldn't say that if you ever played golf with him," Canfield interjected.

"Well, now you know what to look for the next time he tells you his score," Jenkins said. "The looking to the left action is sometimes much more subtle than we just witnessed. It's often nothing more than the eyeballs looking up and left for a fraction of a second, but it's always there in a normal person. Pathological liar have increased amounts of white matter and decreased amounts of gray matter in the prefrontal lobe of their brains. The study I read said this is the reason they can look you straight in the eye and lie like it was second nature."

Douglas said, "You know entirely too much shit that a cop just ain't supposed to know about."

Jenkins smiled and said, "I find if I learn a little about a lot of things and not too much about any one thing in particular, then I can at least *sound* fairly intelligent in most settings. At any rate, the way Middleton handled the question about brushing his teeth was a typical behavior for pathological liars. They can't always tell the truth from a lie, so when you call them on something small that they haven't had a chance to process yet, they will go into a rage. It didn't matter whether Middleton brushed his teeth or not. What mattered was that I called him on it, and his brain wasn't prepared for a response to the unexpected question."

Canfield said, "So why can he lie so easily about murder and torture but then can't deal with something as insignificant as brushing his teeth?"

"Because the pathological liar re-writes history in their brain, so to them, it never really happened. Some normal people do this, too, but pathological liars take it to the extreme. Lies are normally unplanned and impulsive. But pathological lying is a behavior, and a behavior needs to be repeated over a long period of time."

"Are you sure we should even be talking about shit like this?" Douglas asked. "We might be opening the door for an insanity defense if his lawyers get wind of this psychobabble."

"Middleton is just as sane as any of us sitting at this table," Jenkins assured. "Well, that might not be the best comparison to use, but he *is* sane. Just because someone fits this definition doesn't mean they are necessarily evil, either. Some very famous and charismatic people throughout history were pathological liars—including a couple of our most popular presidents."

Douglas said, "You're not referring to our current president, are you? Who in the hell doesn't inhale when they smoke pot?"

"I'm not referring to anyone in particular. I'm just saying a pathological liar may not readily recognize truth from lies, but he certainly knows right from wrong. The McNaughton rule says the prosecution only needs to prove the defendant knew his criminal acts were wrong in order to meet the burden of proof. If Middleton didn't think what he did was wrong, he wouldn't have lied in the first place, so that just strengthens our case."

"So now that we know Middleton is a pathological liar, how do we use it against him?" Adams asked.

"Several ways," Jenkins responded. "I am by no means an expert on this, but there *are* some out there who would be willing to testify to this phenomenon. The class I took was put on by a professor from USC and I'm sure he would offer expert testimony if needed. After that, the defense would never be able to bring up the fact Middleton passed a polygraph test, and they *certainly* would never risk putting him on the witness stand.

"In addition to that, there are traits exhibited by pathological liars we can use to our advantage. They need a crowd to perform in front of and to always be the center of attention. The more times they tell their story—the more improved their lies get. They are manipulative, egotistical, and legends in their own minds. Where is Middleton currently housed in the jail?"

"He's in G.P.," replied Canfield. This was the jail terminology for the general population housing units.

"Can that be changed?"

Canfield thought for a moment and then answered, "I could get him moved to the SHU," again using a jail acronym to refer to the Special Housing Unit. "He'd be in a solitary cell there and would only be let out one hour a day for exercise. He wouldn't be allowed to go to the recreation yard, either. I'll need a reason to keep him there, though. If I just get him moved without cause, his lawyer will file a writ for cruel and unusual punishment."

Jenkins said, "How about threats of suicide and the potential for violence as the reason for the move? You heard him talking about depression, and we all know he's going to snap when we finally charge him with the murders."

"I'll give it a try. The worst the jail commander can do is say no, but I think I can call in some favors and make it happen. Why do you want him out of G.P.?"

"We need to take away his audience," Jenkins answered. "Middleton will go crazy if he can't be on stage. Did you see the look on his face when I told him we were heading to Miami? He has no idea what we've dug up on him, and that is going to eat away at him twenty-four hours a day if he doesn't have a diversion. If I remember right, he won't be able to make nightly phone calls to Haley while he's locked up in the S.H.U., so his information pipeline will be cut off, too. I want David Middleton alone and worried for the rest of this investigation. He can share a cell with his own worst enemy from now on, and that enemy is the devil's incarnate himself."

Chapter 39:
Welcome To Miami

When Jenkins, Canfield, and Adams stepped outside through the front doors of the Miami International Airport at 5:15 P.M. on Monday, June 12, 1995, they instantly learned the meaning behind the phrase, "It's not the heat, it's the humidity." The ninety-three-degree air temperature was only slightly warmer than what they left behind at home, but Reno's humidity level normally hovered in the area of five percent. The informational T.V. monitor in the baggage area said Miami's current humidity was ninety-eight percent—a mere two percent from the air turning into water.

By the time they found a taxi and made it to the Miami Airport Holiday Inn, they were hot and clammy, and their clothes were sticking to their skin. They decided to stop at the lobby bar and enjoy some cool, conditioned air and even cooler beers before checking in. Since it is impossible to stop for *a* beer when two or more cops get together, they were still in the bar enjoying steak dinners and libations at eight o'clock that night.

Their investigative plans for Miami were based on information obtained during a series of phone calls made the prior week. Middleton had been well-liked for the most part during his police career, and they wanted to keep their interviews as neutral as possible. On the list of officers they would talk to were five of Middleton's former partners, his supervisor at the time of arrest, and the detective who investigated his rape case.

There were also three civilians they would interview who might be able to shed light on Middleton's past. This list included the civilian records clerk who he videotaped himself having sex with, his ex-wife, and the victim of the rape that brought Middleton's criminal activities to light.

Jenkins also made phone contact with Metro-Dade County District Attorney Kathleen Hoague prior to leaving Reno. There were no plans to interview her while they were in Miami, but she would be providing them with some valuable assistance. They would need to review the case files for Middleton's rape arrest, his personnel file, and his Internal Affairs file. They would need an administrative search warrant to get some of this information, and the D.A.'s office would help with that.

The combination of their late-night planning session, jetlag, and the intense morning humidity made the detectives feel like they were moving in slow motion when they met in the hotel restaurant at 7:00 the next morning. Nevertheless, by 8:30 they were pulling out of the Airport Hertz lot in their rented white Crown Victoria headed for Downtown Miami.

None of them had ever been to Miami before, and they took in the sights as they drove along Highway 836, better known as the Dolphin Expressway. The morning commuter traffic was heavy even though it was the off-season, but the cold air blasting out of the dashboard vents felt good while they crept along the highway at a steady twenty-five miles per hour. When they neared the end of their nine-mile drive to the courthouse, the ocean came into view on the other side of the Miami skyline.

The sun was shining through the hazy morning sky over the ocean, which seemed out of place to the three west coasters. The detectives were used to the Pacific Coast, where the sun was over the ocean in the afternoon. They felt sorry for the people living near the East Coast beaches since they didn't get to see the spectacular sight of a bright orange sun setting into the ocean. It was almost a ritual in coastal areas on the Pacific to toast the ocean sunsets with some type of adult libation. Tossing back a couple of cold ones while watching the early morning sun pop up over the Atlantic Ocean could also be considered a ritual of sorts—albeit one that might require substance abuse therapy.

The twenty-eight-story Dade County Courthouse was built in 1928, making it the oldest building in downtown Miami. For many years it was the tallest building south of Baltimore, but those times were long gone. The early twentieth-century architecture of the beautifully constructed white building made it stand out like an ancient stalagmite in the midst of the modern glass-walled skyscrapers. Since it was the only building of its kind in the city, it was easy for the three tourist detectives to locate. They parked in a downtown parking structure and endured the heat and humidity one more time during their half-block walk to the courthouse.

Jenkins met with the assistant district attorney who was assigned to help with the required paperwork while the other two detectives researched Middleton's court case in the first-floor records section. The attorney's office was on the twenty-sixth floor and had a view of downtown Miami. The six-lane MacArthur Causeway with Miami Beach and the Atlantic Ocean beyond it could be seen in the distance. Jenkins considered checking out the famous Miami Beach nightlife while they were in town

176

but then thought better of it. The Holiday Inn bar was better suited to their tastes than a nightclub would be. He'd heard the South Beach nightlife didn't start until midnight, and unless he was being called out for murder, he was normally asleep long before then.

With signed warrants in hand, Jenkins met the other two detectives in the courthouse lobby at 11:30. They decided to have lunch at a restaurant next door and discuss what they learned before heading to the police station. The restaurant had a sidewalk dining area where patrons sat underneath misters to stay cool, but the three desert-dwelling detectives opted to sit inside and take advantage of the air conditioning.

Adams and Canfield had copied several of the reports in Middleton's court files, but they didn't learn anything new. They'd already obtained most of the information through news articles and phone conversations with the prosecutor.

Judging from the court transcripts, it looked like the jury did their best with what they had to work with when reaching the verdict in Middleton's trial. Pre-trial defense motions kept some of the most damaging evidence from ever making it to the jury. It appeared the jury had come to the only verdict they could because they were never allowed to hear about the evidence of the rape. There were some questions about the judge's decisions and jury instruction, but since he had been removed and prosecuted himself, those questions would never be answered.

The next step for the detectives was to get into Middleton's personnel and I.A. files, which were kept in the main police station located twelve miles inland in the city of Doral. Afternoon traffic was light, so they made the drive in fifteen minutes. The four-story glass and marble building was easy to find, and they parked in the visitor's lot adjacent to the building. The Metro-Dade Sheriff's Department had changed its name to the Miami-Dade Police Department in early 1994, but shading from the old lettering could still be seen over the door as they walked through the main entrance.

They were escorted to the Investigative Services Division, and the first thing they noticed was they were highly overdressed. All the Miami detectives wore summer-weight short-sleeved shirts and slacks. None of them bothered wearing suit coats to cover their guns and badges as the Reno detectives did, and they decided an evening clothes shopping trip might be in order.

The Reno detectives sat shooting the breeze with some Miami detectives while they waited for their warrant to be reviewed by the dayshift lieutenant. They were treated cordially, and the Miami cops were very curious about the case since none of them actually knew Middleton. After twenty minutes the detectives were led to a conference room where they were allowed to review Middleton's personnel and I.A. files in private.

According to the documents in Middleton's personnel file, he had been an outstanding police officer during his early years with the Miami Police Department. During his first year, he earned a series of commendations and above-average performance evaluations, which resulted in a promotion to detective in the Warrants Bureau. After that it looked like he was on the fast track for upward movement in the department.

The records showed he continued to excel in his career during the next six years, but in early 1988, he began having trouble with tardiness and unexplained absences from work. The first major incident they found was documented in March of 1988. Middleton was removed from his detective job and assigned to station duty while being investigated by Internal Affairs. This stirred their interest, so they switched over to Middleton's I.A. file to learn more.

The I.A. investigation began when a detective from the County Prosecutor's Office in Somerset, New Jersey, contacted the Warrants division at the Miami Police Department on February 17, 1988. The detective had received a letter from the Miami-Dade Warrants section in support of a suspect named Jaabir Muhammad, who was incarcerated in New Jersey on narcotics trafficking charges. Muhammand was being held without bail due to the serious nature of his crimes. The letter in question was a request to have Muhammad granted a low bail amount since he had proven to be an asset to the Miami Police Department in the past.

The New Jersey detective found the request strange and called to verify the authenticity of the letter. It was written on official letterhead from the Metro-Dade Warrants division and signed by Detective David Millington, badge number 3261. The Metro-Dade Warrants division sergeant who had taken the call told the New Jersey detective they didn't have anyone named Millington working there, but they did have a David *Middleton,* and, coincidently enough, his badge number was *3361.* He also said any request for bail assistance from within the department would be highly unusual and would, at the very least, have to be approved by the division commander.

The New Jersey detective then asked if the sergeant had ever heard of Ms. G.A. Thomas or a company named Total Concept Cleaning Inc. The detective also received a letter in support of Jaabir Muhammand from Ms. Thomas the same day he received the letter from Detective Millington. Ms. Thomas said in her letter that Muhammand was a business associate of hers and that she would vouch for his credibility should he be granted bail. Although she listed her address as a post office box in Delaware, the letter was postmarked in Miami. The detective said Muhammand was a hardcore criminal, and it was odd to get even *one* letter in support of him, never mind two on the same day bearing the same postmark.

Neither G.A. Thomas nor the company name sounded familiar to the Metro-Dade sergeant. He also didn't think Detective Middleton would write a letter such as the one described, but he told the New Jersey detective he would ask a few questions and get back to him.

Those few questions turned into a full-blown one-year Internal Affairs investigation. The investigative report read like a dime-store crime novel, and if the three detectives didn't know what they did about Middleton, they would have thought they actually were reading a work of fiction instead of a police document.

It turned out that Ms. G.A. Thomas was actually an alias for Gerrilyn Smith, an ex-felon for fraud and narcotics-related offenses. Smith had served a year in the Tennessee State Prison after being picked up on felony warrants in Miami in early 1984. The arresting officer when she was picked up in Miami was Detective David Middleton from the Miami Police Department Warrants Division.

When the I.A. investigators checked with the prison officials in Tennessee, they discovered Middleton had later written a letter in support of Smith, vouching for her and guaranteeing her employment if she should be released on early parole. The letter was written on Miami Police Department letterhead, and the employment Middleton guaranteed was at a company he owned called Total Concepts Cleaning Inc. in Miami. As a result of this letter, Ms. Smith was paroled and allowed to move back to Miami.

The investigators then researched Total Concepts Cleaning Inc. and found it was a Delaware-based company with an office address in Miami.

Since Delaware has the most liberal state tax laws in the country, it is not uncommon for companies to register there and then base offices in different states. What *was* uncommon was Total Concepts Cleaning Inc. listed David Middleton as the president and his brother-in-law Albert Heredia as vice president. Gerrilyn Smith and New Jersey prisoner Jaabir Muhammand were listed as board members. It was later determined Smith and Muhammand were sister and brother.

The I.A. file contained transcripts from several interviews with Middleton where he denied writing the support letters for Smith and Muhammand, knowing either one of them, and involvement in Total Concepts Cleaning Inc. He said the company was formed by his brother-in-law as a tax shelter, and he had no idea his name was on the corporate paperwork. A polygraph test given to him during the investigation, surprisingly enough, proved inconclusive.

At the end of the investigation it was determined that Middleton did write both of the support letters and had been lying about them from the start. He changed his name to Millington on the New Jersey letter to avoid getting caught. It was also determined that Middleton had been having a long-term affair with Smith that began when he arrested her in 1984.

Research was done on Total Concepts Cleaning Inc. and it showed to be an active company—at least on the surface. Money was moving through the company, but they did not actually have any customers. There were allegations that profits from Muhammand's drug trade might have been laundered through the company, but the detectives could not find any supporting documentation in the files showing a follow-up investigation was done in this area.

The Internal Affairs investigation determined Middleton was guilty of associating with known criminals, assisting known criminals, misrepresentation and falsification of police documents, lying during a police investigation, and not reporting outside employment. He was given a suspension of ten days without pay but was allowed to give up vacation days in lieu of some of them. Middleton had been assigned to desk duty throughout the investigation, but he was returned to his position in the Warrants section on February 15, 1989. This was nineteen months *before* he kidnapped and raped the sixteen-year-old girl in Miami.

A criminal investigation was not initiated on Middleton even though several crimes almost jumped off the pages of the report at the detectives. Even if the only crimes investigated were tax evasion and money laundering, Middleton still would have been at least fired, if not put in prison. In most departments just a sustained allegation of lying during an investigation warrants termination because the officer's credibility during court testimony is diminished.

The Reno detectives knew if this original investigation had been handled differently, they would not be sitting in Miami right now, and several women might still be alive. Before leaving the room they gathered up their notes and reminded each other they were here to investigate their own case, not critique the handling of the Miami case seven years earlier. They would keep their opinions to themselves, but they also decided to cancel their shopping trip to buy clothes better suited for the Miami weather. Not fitting in with the Miami cops didn't sound like a bad idea at the moment.

Chapter 40:
Seven-And-O

The detectives were given use of the conference room in the Robbery-Homicide division at the main station in Doral for their interviews. Their plan was to interview all seven Miami cops that day, and the first one met them at 9:00 A.M. on Wednesday, June 14, 1995.

Sergeant Harvey Honig was currently working in the Auto Theft Bureau, but he had been Middleton's partner in the Warrants division from 1983 to 1987. The first thing he told the detectives was that he was shocked by the possibility Middleton was involved in a serious crime. But he then added he was equally shocked when Middleton had been arrested in Miami for rape.

Sergeant Honig described Middleton as being very personable, intelligent, and a hard-working police officer. He said he had not worked or socialized with Middleton for over a year before his Miami arrest and realized that people do change. He said he'd never known Middleton to do anything that would be considered illegal, although he did have some questionable ethics when it came to his sexual behavior.

Jenkins asked Sergeant Honig if he recalled the extradition trip to Mexico where Middleton said he bought the Mexican blanket found in his shed. Sergeant Honig said he distinctly remembered the trip because out-of-country extraditions were unusual. He and Middleton had flown to Nogales, Mexico, to pick up a wanted drug trafficker who had turned himself in at the U.S. Consulate there. While in Mexico, Sergeant Honig said he bought several Mexican-style blankets but was reasonably certain that Middleton did not buy any or any other souvenirs. Middleton's transference of the blanket purchase from his partner to himself also fits the profile of a pathological liar.

The next scheduled interview was with Middleton's former supervisor in the Warrants division. Sergeant Wesley Dallas currently worked in the Miami-Dade Narcotics Bureau. Due to the nature of his assignment, the task force detectives drove to his Miami office instead of asking him to come to the main police station.

Sergeant Dallas also used the words intelligent and personable to describe Middleton but added he wasn't an easy employee to supervise. He said Middleton was constantly late or absent from work, and he had to discipline him twice for this. Aside from these problems, he said Middleton was a good cop, and he never suspected any drug, alcohol, or ethical problems.

When Middleton was identified as a suspect in the Miami rape case, Sergeant Dallas was assigned to bring him in for questioning. It was Sergeant Dallas who tracked Middleton down and located him in Mississippi after he'd skipped town. He was also one of the two Miami cops who flew to Mississippi after Middleton was arrested to extradite him back to Florida.

While in Mississippi, the local police detectives gave Sergeant Dallas two videotapes that had been in Middleton's possession when they arrested him. The sergeant said he was by no means a prude, but these tapes could only be described as sexually deviant in nature. One tape showed Middleton having sex with several women who appeared to be prostitutes. The tape was obviously recorded in Miami, and most of the sex was rough bondage type.

The other tape showed Middleton having sex with a civilian Miami Police records clerk inside the department's main station. Sergeant Dallas recognized the woman and said in addition to her being an employee, she was also married to a Miami Police officer. The tapes were not pertinent to Middleton's rape case, so they were returned to him. These were the same tapes found in his storage unit during the Reno investigation.

At the end of the interview, Sergeant Dallas added one more interesting piece of information. Middleton's brother-in-law and corporate vice president, Albert Heredia, was currently in prison for drug trafficking charges. The charges stemmed from money laundering allegations associated with Total Concepts Cleaning Inc. Middleton was out of state by the time Heredia was arrested, but it still raised questions about his involvement in the drug trade while he was in Miami.

Officer Art Wellons was waiting for the detectives when they returned to the conference room at the Doral station. Officer Wellons was currently assigned to an elementary school as a school resource officer, but he had worked in the Warrants division with Middleton shortly before his arrest on the Miami rape charges.

When asked to describe Middleton, Officer Wellons replied, "He's weird." He then went on to say Middleton seemed obsessed with sex and often bragged about video tapes depicting him having sex with various women. Officer Wellons said he never personally saw any of these tapes, but other detectives in the unit told him they had seen them. Aside from his sexual peculiarities, Officer Wellons described Middleton as a personable and likable officer.

Detective Greg Benjamin was waiting outside the conference room for his interview when Officer Wellons left. Detective Benjamin was currently working in an auto theft task force, but he had been Middleton's partner in the Warrants division at the time of his arrest on the rape charges.

Detective Benjamin said he had limited contact with Middleton away from the job, but he was familiar with his relationship with Evonne Haley. Detective Benjamin coached the junior league football team Haley's son was on, so he knew Middleton was having an affair with her. He knew Middleton was married but also was aware he was involved in several extra-marital affairs. He said Middleton had a post office box where he used to keep things from his wife but never knew him to have any type of storage unit while they were working together. Without putting it into words, the detectives could tell Detective Benjamin did not think too highly of his former partner.

Detective Paul Kuiper still worked in the Warrants division and had been partnered with Middleton at times during 1985 and 1986. He said he became fairly close to Middleton at work but did not socialize with him away from the job. He said Middleton was married at the time but was very sexually active and always hitting on someone. At one time, Middleton confided in him that he was having an affair with his wife's sister and often had sexual trysts with her and other women in his house when his wife was not home.

Detective Kuiper described Middleton as a schemer and as always talking about ways he could make a lot of money. He also said he knew Middleton drank heavily and had become very sloppy in his appearance during the months just prior to his arrest. Detective Kuiper described a pattern of worsening behavior in Middleton, which eventually caused him to ask his supervisor to break up the partnership. He said he no longer wanted to travel or work with Middleton. He didn't expand on this and the detectives didn't push him on it. They'd already heard enough Middleton stories to form an opinion about his police days, and this detective did not sound like a big fan of Middleton's.[6]

The next interviewee was *definitely* not a member of the David Middleton fan club. Detective Ellen Christopher was the lead investigator in Middleton's rape case. She had nothing good to say about Middleton, or the way his investigation was handled at the levels above her. She said the victim in that case was credible, and she had no doubt Middleton was guilty of the rape.

Detective Christopher seemed agitated and said she could not go into the details of the case or the subsequent prosecution. The task force detectives didn't push her on this because they got the impression she wanted to talk to them but had possibly been told not to. Before leaving the brief interview she did tell them she was certain Middleton had been involved in previous cases similar to the one that resulted in his arrest. She said it was her opinion these cases either went unreported—or uninvestigated.

Their last interview of the day proved to be the most informative. Detective Linnard Broom was also still assigned to the Warrants division and had known Middleton from his first day in the division until the day he was arrested. He had never been permanent partners with Middleton, but they had been friends and went on several extradition trips together. Detective Broom described Middleton as personable and likable but wasn't surprised at all that he was in trouble with the law.

Detective Broom said it was his opinion that Middleton had no morality when it came to his sexual activities and described him as having a very large sexual appetite. Middleton often bragged about his extra-marital sexual encounters to Detective Broom and showed him several videos he'd taped of himself having sex with other women. One of these was the tape of him having sex with the civilian police employee, and Middleton joked about her husband being a Miami police officer. Detective Broom was also aware of Middleton's affair with his wife's sister.

---

[6] Detective Kuiper was interviewed for the updated edition of this book. He confirmed the information contained in the section, and contributed to other sections of this book with additional information.

According to Detective Broom, Middleton was well-liked and highly respected in the division prior to his arrest. But he added, "I always knew his joint would end up getting him in trouble."

The rape allegations shocked Detective Broom, so he asked Middleton about them while visiting him shortly after his arrest. Middleton admitted having sex with the juvenile but denied raping her. He said the girl willingly had sex with him and then made up the rape allegations later. Middleton was so convincing when telling the story that Detective Broom went back to the station and told his coworkers the whole thing was no big deal and Middleton would probably be back to work soon. It was after that he learned Middleton had been wearing his uniform at the time of the alleged rape incident.

He told the task force, detectives, "That was the one thing above everything else that made me doubtful of Mr. Middleton's innocence. Officers in the Warrants division wear plain clothes, so there was no reason he should have been on the street in uniform. I went back and asked him about it, but he had no explanation. He actually went into a rage, so I just wished him the best and never saw him again."

The three tired detectives sat in the Airport Holiday Inn restaurant that evening, discussing the day's interviews over dinner and drinks. Although some opinions varied about Middleton's personality, one thing was certain. All seven cops said Middleton had sexually deviant tendencies long before he ever reached Reno. They were 7 and 0, establishing the groundwork for Middleton's premeditated behavior, and any team would be proud of a win-loss ratio like that.

Chapter 41:
Oedipus

Thursday, June 15, 1995, would be the detective's last full day in Florida. They had three more interviews to conduct and were looking forward to escaping the Florida weather. Their first interview of the day was with Middleton's ex-wife Julia "Tina" Heridia.

Ms. Heridia agreed to talk to the detectives at her home located twenty miles south of Miami in an area called Cutler Ridge. The detectives arrived at the modest two-story home Ms. Heridia had once shared with Middleton at 10:30 in the morning. Ms. Heridia answered the door wearing a white cotton sundress and white sandals. The thirty-five-year-old single mother of two was pretty in a wholesome sort of way. Her long dark hair, dark complexion, and slight stature matched the characteristics of all the victims attributed to Middleton thus far.

A pitcher of iced tea with lemons floating in it was in the middle of the kitchen table Ms. Heridia led the detectives to. Once they were seated she poured them each a glass before sitting down herself. Her demeanor was quite cordial, and her conversation was candid. She told the detectives she and Middleton had been high school sweethearts while growing up in Boston and had gotten married right after graduation. They moved from Boston to Miami after Middleton took the job with the Miami Police Department.

Shortly after they moved to Miami, Ms. Heridia said she became aware Middleton had been involved in several extra-marital affairs. She described Middleton as a chronic liar and said he would often tell her unbelievable stories to cover his relationships with other women. She also said he would lie about everything.

She then told the detectives she believed her ex-husband's life began to change for the worse after his mother's death in 1987. She noticed he began drinking excessively, and his affairs became more blatant. When asked to describe Middleton's mother, the detectives noted Ms. Heredia could very well have been describing an older version of herself—or any of Middleton's other victims.

It was also around this time that Middleton's sexual appetite and aggressiveness began to gradually increase. Ms. Heridia said on several occasions, Middleton requested that she hurt him, scratch him, or bite him.

He also wanted to handcuff her and even bit her on a couple of occasions. She said she had been unwilling to participate in these types of activities and refused to have sex with him when he became insistent that she try these things. She also said Middleton told her that her unwillingness to participate in unusual sex practices resulted in him leaving home to find more willing partners.

When Middleton was arrested in Miami, Ms. Heridia said she questioned him about the allegations made by the police. Even though Middleton steadfastly denied the charges and said the young female victim was lying, she always knew in her heart her husband was guilty. The couple had a son and a daughter, but both were very young when their marriage began to fail.

Ms. Heridia filed for divorce while Middleton was in prison. Her uncontested request was granted in January of 1999 and she legally changed back to her maiden name. Middleton stayed at her house for two weeks when he got out of prison but then left to join Evonne Haley in Colorado.

Since that time, he had not been in contact with either her or their children. There were no child support payments, and Middleton did not request visitation with his children. Since he gave up his parental rights, the children's last names were also legally changed to Heridia. When asked if she would be willing to testify in court about the things she had just told them, Ms. Heridia answered yes without hesitation.

Their next interview was forty miles north in the city of North Miami with Alyssa Cervantes*, the sixteen-year-old runaway Middleton had raped in 1990. She was now twenty-one years old and lived with her husband and two-year-old daughter in a small house in North Miami.

The detectives made the drive up the Florida Turnpike in a little under an hour and were pleasantly surprised when they got out of the car in front of Ms. Cervantes's house. A cool breeze blowing in from Biscayne Bay had caused the air temperature to drop to eighty-eight degrees and the humidity to plunge to eighty-five percent. This was considered a cooling phase for the Miami area, but the Renoites still felt like they were walking through a steam room as they made their way to the front door.

Ms. Cervantes was visibly nervous when she opened the door for the detectives and asked that her older sister be allowed to remain with her during the interview. They sat at a table in a small but very neat dining room, and Jenkins began the interview by asking generic background questions to put Ms. Cervantes at ease. She said she was employed as a full-time customer service representative at a local firm and was also attending night school for physical therapy. On the outside, it looked like Ms. Cervantes had moved on with her life, but something in her eyes told the detectives this was just a façade.

As Ms. Cervantes began telling the story of what happened to her when Middleton picked her up on September 29, 1990, there was no doubt she was still haunted by the nightmare. She did her best to maintain her composure as she recounted the events, but as she described being brutally raped by Middleton while she was handcuffed and helpless in the back seat of his police car, she lost control and began sobbing heavily.

The detectives offered to cease the interview, but Ms. Cervantes said she wanted to continue. After calming herself she went on to say the only reason she was out that night in the first place was that she had had a fight with her boyfriend and decided to walk home from a party they were attending. She had always been taught to respect the police, so when Middleton pulled up and told her to get into his police car, she did as she was told.

She said, "I wasn't aware that I had to be cautious with this man. He had a uniform on. I was supposed to respect him, so that's what I did."

The young girl had the same long dark hair, the same dark Latina skin, and the same small build shared by Middleton's mother, his ex-wife, and all of his other victims. She said when Middleton climbed into the back seat of his police car and started undressing her, she resisted, but he easily overpowered her. She said she pleaded with him, but he just kept telling her to shut up.

After Middleton raped her, he opened the car door and told her she could run if she wanted. He made no offer to take off the handcuffs or let her get dressed, and she had no idea where they were. She asked him if he could drop her off closer to her home and remained in the back seat while they drove to the area where he picked her up. Ms. Cervantes said Middleton was like a different person during the drive. He made no mention of the attack and talked about his daughter and family. She said it was like he was two different people.

Ms. Cervantes did not initially report the rape out of fear no one would believe her. Two days later, she broke down and confided in her sister, who was a corrections officer at a nearby state prison. Her sister persuaded her to go to the police and took her to the Miami-Dade Police Department to make the report.

After Middleton's conviction, Ms. Cervantes' sister found out he was being allowed to serve his time in a county facility as part of a protective custody program for former law enforcement officers convicted of non-violent crimes. Her sister was outraged and went to the administration of the prison where she worked to complain. Middleton was soon transferred to the very same prison where Ms. Cervantes' sister worked to serve the remainder of his time. Judging from the smile on the correctional officer's face as she told the story, the detectives were reasonably certain his time spent in her prison was not easy.

As the detectives were leaving the house, Ms. Cervantes told them she had pangs of guilt about testifying against Middleton now that she knew he had killed some of his victims. She said, "Because I came forward, he lost his job and went to jail. He learned from that, so he wasn't about to take the chance of letting his victims go again. The only difference between what he did to them and what he did to me is he made sure they couldn't testify against him."

They assured Ms. Cervantes she had done what was right by coming forward and testifying against Middleton, but each of them knew she was right about one thing. Middleton was a man who learned from his mistakes, and in his mind, letting his victim live was the only error he ever made.

When they were back in the car, Adams said, "Freud would have a field day with Middleton's mommy issues. First, he married a girl who looked like his mother, and then after she died, he started raping and killing girls who looked like her. What do they call that?"

"A friggin psycho," Canfield replied.

Jenkins said, "Actually, Dave, it's funny you should mention what Freud would think. He called what Middleton has the Oedipus Complex. He named it after the Shakespearian character Oedipus Rex, who allowed his sexual feelings for his mother to control everything else in his life."

"Douglas is right," Canfield said, "you do know too much shit a cop ain't supposed to know about."

Adams asked, "So, do you think all that Freudian crap will help Middleton's defense out?"

"Nope," Jenkins answered. "People lose their loved ones every day, but they don't go out killing people who look like them. From here on out, we will never mention Freud again. We're cops, not shrinks. We'll be much better off going with the Larry Canfield theory that Middleton is just a friggin psycho. Is anyone besides me hungry?"

Chapter 42:
Father Dave

After a seafood lunch at a bayside restaurant, the detectives called the work phone number for their last interviewee. Ms. Barbara Fortunato* was the former civilian employee for the Miami-Dade Police Department who had had sex with Middleton in the station's D.U.I. room. She did not want the detectives coming to her place of employment, but she agreed to meet them at a North Miami McDonald's a block from her office.

The three detectives were sitting inside the McDonald's sipping Mc-milkshakes when Ms. Fortunato walked into the restaurant. They knew it was her because her looks were interchangeable with the other two women they had talked to that day. She was very pretty and had long dark hair, dark skin, and a petite build. She also recognized the detectives upon sight because they were probably the only three people in Miami wearing suit coats and ties during the current heat wave. Ms. Fortunato sat down at the table and introductions were made all around. She began telling the detectives the strangest story they had yet heard during the weirdest investigation any of them had ever been involved in.

Ms. Fortunato was a thirty-one-year-old Cuban immigrant when she met Middleton while working at the main Miami-Dade Police station in 1989. Ms. Fortunato was a practicing member of a local Santerían religious sect—a fact she often discussed with Middleton. Santeria is a West African-based religion imported to South Florida by Cubans who were used as sugar plantation slaves in the early 1800s. Some of their voodoo-type rituals include animal sacrifices, putting people into trances, and worship of gods.

One day, Ms. Fortunato confided to Middleton that she was having marital problems with her husband, who worked in the Patrol division in one of the Miami-Dade substations. It was then that Middleton informed Ms. Fortunato that he was a practicing Santerían priest and could help her solve her problems. Ms. Fortunato told the detectives a Santerían priest is called an Ifa, pronounced *ee-fah*. She said an Ifa is the most powerful person in the religion and receives knowledge and wisdom directly from the gods. She said she was honored to be in the presence of an Ifa and told Middleton she would do whatever he told her.

The detectives let Ms. Fortunato continue without interruption. They knew Middleton was conning her but did not want to make her feel foolish. Middleton was no closer to being a priest than Satan himself, but there was no sense pointing out what was surely obvious to her by now.

Ms. Fortunato said one afternoon, shortly after Middleton revealed his religious secrets to her, he phoned her in the Records section and told her to meet him in the department D.U.I. room. Middleton was alone when she got there. He locked the door and handed her a chicken egg. He then told her to insert the egg into her vagina as the first part of the ritual. He said that if the egg remained inside her for ten minutes without breaking, it would show she was pure enough to continue with the remainder of the cleansing rituals. Ms. Fortunato explained that chickens and chicken blood are common in Santerían rituals, so the request did not seem odd to her.

Ms. Fortunato did as she was instructed. After ten minutes, she removed the unbroken egg from inside of her and gave it back to Middleton. The detectives didn't have the heart to tell the woman she had most likely not been handed a raw chicken egg. Father Middleton, or whatever his official title was at the time, had probably bought a hardboiled egg at a local deli while preparing for the ritual and then ate it for lunch after he was finished cleansing her.

The next thing Middleton told the woman was that his semen contained wisdom and power bestowed upon him by the Santerían gods. He said she needed to accept his semen into her body in order to be helped with her marital problems. Once again, she did as instructed and accepted his magical bodily fluids both orally and vaginally. What she didn't know was the religious acts were being captured on video courtesy of Father Dave.

The following week, Ms. Fortunato told Middleton her marital problems were continuing, so he suggested she come to his house where he could perform a more detailed cleansing ritual. Ms. Fortunato was reluctant to go to his house until Middleton assured her his wife and children would be there. He said his entire family practiced Santeria, so she would be among friends.

Ms. Fortunato went to Middleton's house the following Sunday and was surprised to see he was the only one at home. He assured her his wife would be home shortly but suggested they begin the Santerían cleansing rituals without her. Middleton excused himself from the room, and when he returned, he was wearing a black hooded priest's robe and some type of white rubber mask and had a machete with an animal head for a handle attached to his belt. Ms. Fortunato said the skull handle had a sharp horn about eight inches long attached to it. Based on the description, the detectives knew this was the same machete they had found in Middleton's shed.

The room they were in had animal heads mounted on the walls and large plants in each corner. The tile floor had been covered with a large plastic tarp, and Middleton told Ms. Fortunato it was for the ritual. She became nervous and asked him about the priest's robe, the mask, and the large machete. He told her it was all part of the ritual and would need to draw blood from her before they continued.

Middleton had Ms. Fortunato strip naked and stand in the middle of the plastic tarp. He then took out the animal skull machete and cut her finger to draw blood. She was telling the story as calmly as if she were describing a day at the beach, and the detectives were on the edge of their cheap plastic seats waiting to hear what happened next. As she continued they certainly were not disappointed.

After a small puddle of blood had dripped out of the cut on Ms. Fortunato's finger, Middleton retrieved a burlap bag from the backyard and brought it into the house. He pulled a live chicken out of the bag and handed it to the naked, bleeding woman. He then instructed her to hold the chicken by the neck and swing it around until the neck broke. Ms. Fortunato did as she was told and then handed the deceased chicken back to Middleton. The masked priest then took out his machete, decapitated the dead chicken, and covered Ms. Fortunato with chicken blood.

Ms. Fortunato said things began getting a little strange after that. Middleton made her put on a pink dress and told her he was going to handcuff her while he introduced more magical semen into her body. Since Ms. Fortunato was familiar with the use of animal slaughter and chicken blood as normal parts of Santerían religious rituals, she didn't give them much thought. But she had *never* heard of handcuffs being used in *any* religion, so she decided to make a hasty retreat out the front door.

Unfortunately for Ms. Fortunato, Middleton was much quicker than her. He caught her before she was able to get out of the house and struck her across the back of the head with the animal skull handle of his machete. She was knocked unconscious but said she remembered Middleton sexually assaulting her vaginally and anally. He used the horn on his animal head machete handle for the anal penetration.

When Ms. Fortunato went to Internal Affairs to complain about the incident, they did not believe her story. They told her it was their opinion she made up the bizarre tale to cover up the fact she had sex with Middleton in the D.U.I. room. Ms. Fortunato volunteered to take a polygraph test, but the department elected instead to fire her for having sex in the workplace. Perhaps if they had looked a little harder and found the animal skull machete and Jughead Halloween mask currently sitting in the R.P.D. evidence room, they might have put more credence in the story.

The detectives were eerily silent in the car as they drove back to their hotel after bidding farewell to Ms. Fortunato. Each one of them believed her story, but they'd had the advantage of meeting the David Middleton no one knew existed when she reported it to the Miami cops. They could all picture Middleton running around his house with his black hood partially covering his Jughead mask, swinging a machete in one hand and a headless chicken in the other. It was a sight they'd all rather forget.

Canfield said, "Middleton's one hell of a marriage counselor. I wonder if she ever straightened out her problems."

"I don't know," said Jenkins. "But I've gotta call Douglas as soon as we get back to the hotel."

"To tell him about that weird shit?" asked Adams.

"No, to say I told you so," replied Jenkins. "He was swinging that machete around the evidence room like he was some kind of Samurai warrior, and I told him he should have been wearing gloves. Maybe he'll listen next time."

Chapter 43:
The Arrest

The investigation in Reno progressed nicely while the three detectives were on their Florida fact-finding trip. The lab reports from Thelma Davilla's remains were now officially completed, and several DNA matches had been located on items found in Middleton's storage shed. The most damning of these evidentiary matches was hair and blood from Davilla found on the Mexican blanket her sister had identified as coming from their apartment. The rope used to bind Davilla was also now positively matched to the type of rope found in Middleton's shed.

During a task force meeting on Monday, June 19, 1995, District Attorney Dick Gammick said he was finally convinced there was enough evidence to file murder charges against Middleton. He wasn't certain how much of what the detectives learned in Florida could be introduced at trial, but the story of the Santeria ritualistic rape was something he would like to get in front of a jury.

A meeting was set with Deputy District Attorney Tom Viloria for Thursday, June 22, 1995. The arrest warrants would be written on that day and presented to the judge for his signature. The decision was made to file all charges against Middleton in one single indictment instead of charging each murder separately. This way, only one jury would hear everything connected to both cases. That would eliminate taking the chance of two juries considering the evidence differently and arriving at conflicting verdicts. Since juries were unpredictable, it was better to keep exposure to them as limited as possible.

The legal term for bringing separate cases together was called a *joinder,* and there were pros and cons involved in using the process in this case. On the one hand, the prosecution would not have to worry about evidence from one of the murders being excluded from the other case if it was ruled prejudicial to the jury. On the other hand, they stood a chance of losing their strong case in the Powell murder due to the weaker case in the Davilla one. They still hadn't proven a solid link between Middleton and Davilla, and the only man who knew what that link was wasn't giving it up.

The final decision on the joinder of the cases was left up to Tom Viloria since he would be prosecuting them. To him, this decision was another no-brainer. If there was ever a case worthy of the death penalty, this was it. In Nevada, the same jury that hears the case-in-chief also sits for the penalty phase, so he would prosecute one case in front of one jury. The joinder wouldn't be easy, but he welcomed the challenge.

The law said two or more offenses could be charged in the same indictment with a separate count for each if the prosecution could prove certain things about the crimes. In this case, Viloria would have to prove the criminal acts were either connected together or were parts of a common scheme or plan. Since there was no obvious connection between the two murders, the latter would have to be proven in order for the cases to be joindered.

The common scheme or plan displayed by Middleton in the two murders was to meet women, abduct and hold them captive, abuse and kill them, and then dispose of their bodies. The similarities between Powell and Davilla were that both were unmarried women of about the same age and physical stature, alone at home when they disappeared, and their homes had been serviced by T.C.I. Cable Company. Middleton had also met both of the victims before they disappeared. Even though Middleton hadn't admitted knowing Davilla, Viloria would be able to introduce witness testimony that would suggest he had met her at least once.

The storage shed was the key piece of evidence to prove a common scheme in the murders. He visited that shed on the day each victim disappeared; DNA evidence and property from both women were found inside the shed, and a rope similar to the one used to bind both victims was also stored there. Viloria was confident he could successfully joinder all of the charges together into one indictment, and Judge Fidel Salcedo agreed with him when he signed the arrest warrants at 11:30 A.M. on Thursday, June 22, 1995.

Detective Canfield met Jenkins and Douglas in an interview room at the Washoe County Jail. After Middleton was brought into the room, they sat him down at a table and let him read through the arrest warrant and the affidavit in support of it. The detectives did their best to hide their jubilance while they watched Middleton deflate like a used Mylar balloon as he read through the papers detailing his crimes.

After Middleton was through reading the documents, he was officially placed under arrest for two counts of murder in the first degree, two counts of kidnap, and charges of credit card fraud related to the telephonic purchase at Good Guys. The arresting officer listed on the paperwork was Detective John Douglas, and it would be his face smiling his best Eddie Murphy grin that would appear on the front page of the local paper the next morning when the story of the murderous cable guy ran. Any racial overtones left lingering around the case would then be gone forever.

Middleton asked no questions until the jail deputies were leading him out of the room. His cockiness returned when he stopped at the door, looked over his shoulder at Jenkins, and said, "This ain't over. Not by a long shot."

Jenkins and everyone else involved in the case knew that was an understatement. A major part of the investigation had just come to a close, but they were far from finished. A preliminary hearing was set for July 15, 1995, to determine if there was enough evidence to bind Middleton over to the District Court for trial on the charges against him. This would be their first hurdle in what would surely be a long and complicated legal battle, and they still had work to do if they were going to make it over the top.

The task force detectives planned to meet for a victory dinner at the Harrah's Casino Steak House at 6:00 P.M. None of them would rest until Middleton was convicted in court, but arresting him for his criminal acts was the first reason the detectives had to celebrate since Kathy Powell's body was discovered nearly five months earlier. Before Jenkins and Douglas could join the others for the impromptu victory party, they had one more job to do.

The decision had been made earlier in the day not to charge Evonne Haley with any crimes related to the Good Guys case, even though they would have no problem proving her involvement in them. Tom Viloria wanted her to testify against Middleton, but if they arrested her before the preliminary hearing, they would run into trouble with co-conspirator testimony. For the time being, she would remain free, but they would subpoena her as a witness for the State. There was no doubt she would perjure herself on the stand in order to save Middleton, but exposing her lies would be more damning to the defense than if she actually told the truth.

It was 4:00 in the afternoon when Jenkins and Douglas pulled their unmarked detective car into the rundown Sun Valley trailer park where Evonne Haley shared a rusted forty-foot single-wide trailer with her daughter. Jenkins instinctively parked two spaces down from Haley's trailer so they would not be seen as they walked up to serve the witness subpoena on her.

When Haley opened the door, she was once again highly agitated. The living room floor of the small trailer was covered with broken glass, and a table in the center of the room was overturned. Haley said she had flown into a fit of rage when one of Middleton's attorneys called to tell her of the murder arrest. She accused the detectives of framing the man she loved and ruining her life. As an almost insignificant afterthought, she then told Jenkins it was *his* fault her daughter had just threatened to commit suicide.

Jenkins asked Haley what she meant by that statement, but she dismissed the question without answering and asked why the detectives were at her home. Douglas explained the witness subpoena to Haley while Jenkins wandered around the trailer looking for her daughter. He found the girl crouched in a corner of the small, cluttered bathroom. She was crying and using a large pair of scissors to slice through the veins in her right wrist.

Blood was already dripping from a wound on her left wrist, and Jenkins knew better than to rush in and try to grab the scissors from the girl. He kept his voice as calm as he could as he talked the young girl into putting down the scissors and stepping away from them. The wounds were deep enough to need stitches, but fortunately, she had not yet cut all the way through her veins. Jenkins wrapped towels around the girl's wrists and then called out to Douglas, asking him to radio for backup and an ambulance. It looked like their victory dinner would have to wait for another day.

Chapter 44:
People vs. Middleton

David Stephen Middleton was formally arraigned in Judge Fidel Salcido's courtroom on Thursday, June 22, 1995. He was dressed in an orange jail-issued jumpsuit and stood stoically next to his attorney behind the defense table as the judge read the charges against him. When Judge Salcido asked if Middleton understood the charges, he nodded his head and quietly answered, "Yes, sir."

When the judge asked Middleton if he wished to enter a plea, the question was answered by his attorney. Mike Speccio's booming voice echoed off the wooden walls in the courtroom when he said, "My client pleads not guilty to *all* of the State's charges."

Judge Salcido looked down at Middleton from his perch behind the ornate judge's dais. He said, "Mr. Middleton, I hereby order you to remain held in custody without bail at the Washoe County Jail. You will return to this courtroom at 9:00 A.M. on July 14, 1995, for a preliminary hearing. At the conclusion of that hearing I will make a determination on whether you should be bound over to the District Court of Washoe County for trial. Do you have any questions?"

Middleton answered no and was led out of the courtroom by two jail deputies. A photo of Middleton with his head hanging low, shoulders slumped, and wrists shackled to a belly chain as he shuffled out of the courtroom was on the front page of the local newspaper the next day. Even though Middleton had held several different jobs in the six years since he ceased being a police officer, the headline in bold print above his photo read, "EX-COP CHARGED IN DOUBLE MURDER!" The task force detectives figured there just wasn't enough sensationalism in reporting the arrest of a cable guy, so an ex-cop was better for sales.

Pre-trial publicity was heavy during the three weeks prior to the preliminary hearing. In a last-ditch effort, Middleton's attorneys filed a motion to get Judge Salcido removed from the case. They cited that the judge's involvement from the onset of the investigation would prejudice him, but their appeal was overruled. Salcido remained the presiding judge, and the hallway outside of his courtroom was crowded with spectators and reporters on the morning of Friday, July 14, 1995.

The preliminary hearing was expected to last at least three days. Dave Jenkins was scheduled to be the first witness for the prosecution, and his testimony was expected to take up most of the first day. Jenkins had been meeting with Tom Viloria on a daily basis preparing for the hearing, and when he arrived at the courthouse at 8:30 in the morning he wasn't surprised to see the crowd waiting to get inside the courtroom.

Evonne Haley had contacted Tom Viloria and said she would refuse to testify in the hearing. She cited her Fifth Amendment right against self-incrimination as the reason since she would be asked to testify in a case she might later be charged in. Jenkins spotted Haley and her daughter seated on a wooden bench in the hallway outside of the courtroom, and he knew they were there as spectators—not witnesses. Viloria had initially wanted to subpoena Haley's daughter but thought better of it after Jenkins explained the girl was currently in therapy after her botched suicide attempt. She'd already been through enough, so they would spare her the added trauma of testifying against a man she once trusted.

Jenkins recognized several family members and friends of both Kathy Powell and Thelma Davilla in the crowded hallway. He'd met most of them during the investigation and exchanged somber greetings with them as he worked his way toward the courtroom. A man and woman standing quietly in the corner attracted his attention. He didn't recognize them, but the large buttons bearing the smiling face of a once-popular cheerleader they wore pinned to their shirts immediately told him why they were interested in the case.

Jenkins walked over and shook hands with Bonnie and Walt Rice. They had driven fourteen and a half hours through three states in order to hear testimony against a former Miami cop who they knew in their hearts had taken their daughter from them. Underneath the beaming photo of Buffy on the pin they wore over their hearts were written the words, "WE WON'T FORGET YOU BUFFY."

Bonnie Rice told Jenkins they would be staying in Reno for the duration of the court proceedings. She said, "I want to see Middleton, and I want him to see me. I want him to know that we know what happened to our daughter. He took the most precious thing in our lives away from us—our only daughter."

Walt Rice added, "It's going to hurt to see him knowing what he did to our daughter, but knowing that he's locked up and can't hurt anyone else will give us some satisfaction."

After hearing that, the hardened homicide detective who was about to testify about dumpster diving and death whispers was so overcome with emotion he could barely talk. Jenkins fought to regain his calm veneer and assured Bonnie and Walt Rice he would do his best to make sure David Middleton never walked the earth as a free man again. He then introduced them to the Powell and Davilla families and left them alone to bond in a way that only survivors of common tragedies can understand.

The deputy guarding the courtroom door recognized Jenkins when he approached and stepped aside so he could enter before the doors were opened for the public. The room was designed to hold about a hundred people, but there were more than that waiting outside the doors. Jenkins found the court bailiff and arranged to have a row of seats close to the front of the courtroom reserved for the victim's family members through the proceedings. Since he was a witness, he knew he would be unable to stay inside the room and listen to the testimony of other witnesses, but he wanted to make sure the family members heard what they had come for.

Judge Salcido had denied the defense motion to bar the press from the proceeding, and at 8:45 A.M., members of the media were allowed to take their places in the section of the courtroom reserved for them. After that, the general public was allowed to enter, and by 9:00, the room was filled to capacity. Tom Viloria walked in and placed his briefcase on the prosecution table located to the right of the defense table in the front of the courtroom.

Jenkins walked through the swinging gate of the wood rail separating the attorney tables from the rows of wooden spectator benches and approached Viloria. After a hushed conversation, Viloria followed Jenkins to where the victims' family members were seated. He introduced himself to Bonnie and Walt Rice, Kathy Powell's mother and brother, and Thelma Davilla's sister and uncle. The emotional moment ended abruptly when the side door opened, and David Middleton was escorted into the courtroom.

Middleton walked into the room with the confident stride of a man on a mission. During the trial phase of the court proceedings he would be allowed to dress in street clothes so the jury would not be predisposed to thinking he was a criminal due to his mode of dress. But since the judge presides over a preliminary hearing without a jury being present, Middleton was still dressed in his jail overalls. His curly black hair was pulled back into a short ponytail, and the sleeves of his jumpsuit were rolled up tight over his muscular arms. Even though his hands were still cuffed to the belly chain around his waist, he presented an intimidating figure as he stared around the packed courtroom.

Mike Speccio was already seated at the defense table with the two attorneys from his office who would be assisting him. Before Middleton got to his designated seat next to his attorney, he spotted Bonnie and Walt Rice sitting in the second row on the prosecution's side of the room. He locked eyes with Walt Rice and then leaned down to whisper something to his defense team. The three attorneys representing Middleton turned and looked at the Rices and then engaged in a hushed conversation between themselves.

Jenkins and Viloria witnessed the exchange, but before they could discuss it, the bailiff exclaimed, "All rise! The preliminary hearing related to the matter of the People of the State of Nevada versus David Stephen Middleton will now begin."

Chapter 45:
The Black Cloud

Judge Salcido walked into the courtroom through the rear door leading to the judge's chamber and took his seat behind the ornate oak dais. He told the crowd to be seated and asked the defense and prosecution attorneys if they were ready to begin. Attorney Mike Speccio stood and asked to approach the bench for a sidebar conversation before the proceeding started. His request was granted, and he and Viloria walked to the front of the room to speak to the judge out of earshot of the spectators.

Jenkins was seated in the first row of spectator benches and watched nervously as the two attorneys stood to the left side of the judge's dais, speaking in hushed tones. Criminal cases were more often won or lost by legal maneuvering than by testimony and evidence. Jenkins knew Speccio was good at what he did, and didn't like the fact he was raising legal questions before the proceedings even started.

The topic of the sidebar conversation was the buttons being worn by Bonnie and Walt Rice. Speccio argued this would be prejudicial to Middleton since it implied, he was already guilty of murdering their daughter in Colorado. Since Middleton had never been charged in that case, Speccio claimed it was unfair to bring anything related to it into this proceeding. His first request to have the Rices removed from the courtroom was denied by Judge Salcido since this was an open proceeding. His second request to order them to remove the buttons bearing the photo of their murdered daughter was also denied due to the possibility of First Amendment rights violations.

The judge's ruling was binding, and Speccio was clearly frustrated. Before leaving the bench, he was overheard telling the judge, "This will gain media attention that is going to prejudice Mr. Middleton in both Nevada and Colorado. Maybe that's what we should do: have Mr. Middleton tried in the public opinion polls instead of court!"

The attorneys returned to their respective seats, and Judge Salcido told Viloria to call the prosecution's first witness. When Viloria called Detective Dave Jenkins to the stand, he walked purposefully to the witness chair attached to the right side of the judge's dais and stood erect as the bailiff swore him in. The courtroom spectators and media representatives watched intently as Jenkins took his seat in the witness chair, but it was

Middleton who the detective locked eyes with as he adjusted the microphone in front of him.

Speccio stood and asked Judge Salcido to invoke the exclusionary rule before Viloria began questioning his witness. This rule was commonly used to keep witnesses from hearing each other's testimony, so all persons testifying in the case would have to leave the room unless they were currently on the stand.

Since Viloria knew Jenkins would be testifying throughout most of the day, he did not have any of his other witnesses scheduled to come in until the afternoon. The only other prosecution witness in the room was Thelma Davilla's sister, Dora Valverde. It had to be explained to Ms. Valverde several times why she would not be able to remain in the room, and she was visibly upset by the fact she would not be able to hear testimony in the case. Viloria waited until she was escorted out of the courtroom and then began his questioning.

The prosecution's job in a preliminary hearing is to prove a crime has been committed and that there is enough probable cause of the defendant's guilt in that crime to bind him or her over for trial in District Court. Once the defendant is bound over, the burden of proof beyond a reasonable doubt kicks in before a jury can find him guilty of committing the crime. This is the reason the prosecution introduces as little testimony and evidence as possible during the preliminary hearing. If they show the defense too much too early, it can hurt their case in chief when it gets in front of a jury.

Viloria skipped having Jenkins introduce his resume into the record since he was already well known to the judge and defense attorneys. He would save that impressive show of credentials for the jury in order to lend credence to the detective's testimony. He asked only if Jenkins was employed as a homicide detective with the Reno Police Department on the night of Saturday, February 11, 1995. When Jenkins answered yes to the question, Viloria began leading him through the initial steps of the investigation.

During the next three hours, Jenkins took the judge and courtroom spectators on a journey that began with the discovery of Kathy Powell's body and ended with the subsequent arrest of David Middleton. Viloria acted as the tour guide for the audience, using a series of questions and answers designed to extract the information that led Jenkins and the other detectives down the winding path the investigation followed. Most questions were designed to be answered with a simple yes or no reply to avoid giving the defense too much information. Viloria had prepared his questioning well, but his timing was the most important aspect of his presentation.

The noon lunch break actually starts at 11:30 in most court proceedings, and it was precisely 11:00 when Viloria's questioning led Jenkins to the discovery of Middleton's storage shed. It was at this point in the detective's testimony that Viloria stopped leading him and let him describe in narrative what was found inside the shed. This style of testimony would give the horrific torture shed the most descriptive value, and Viloria wanted the impact to settle in on all who heard it during the ensuing lunch break.

Middleton's attorneys had sat quietly through Jenkins' testimony thus far, but they raised their first objection when Viloria asked him about the discovery of the storage shed. Court documents showed the detectives used Middleton's keys to determine this shed actually belonged to him. Since Middleton specifically told Jenkins he did not want the police to have his key ring, the defense argued they were illegally in possession of his keys. Therefore, any evidence discovered by using the keys should be dismissed.

This was a reasonable objection, and Jenkins tried not to appear nervous as the attorneys for the defense and prosecution argued the point of law. He knew their case would be severely damaged if they were not able to introduce the contents of the storage shed into evidence, but Viloria handled the objection perfectly. Since Middleton had relinquished custody of the keys to Evonne Haley and she subsequently gave them to Jenkins, Judge Salcido ruled the police legally possessed the keys. Jenkins spotted Evonne Haley seated in the audience and noticed her face had turned a bright shade of red after realizing the error she had made in turning over the keys to him.

Jenkins was allowed to continue his testimony. He told of discovering the storage shed and outlined for the judge some of the items located inside. He described finding the Warps Brother's Banana Bags, bondage devices, gags, a stun gun, and sexual paraphernalia. The last thing Jenkins described was the refrigerator they theorized Kathy Powell had been held captive inside of. This drew the second defense objection because they said it was only speculation on the part of the investigators that Powell had been alive when she was placed into the refrigerator.

This was another area of testimony carefully planned out by Viloria, as he had anticipated the defense objection. The judge granted Viloria's request to clarify the statement, so he asked Jenkins what led him to believe Kathy Powell had been placed inside of the refrigerator while still alive. Jenkins went on to describe the air holes drilled into the refrigerator, how the blue fibers found around the freezer cutout matched the fibers found around Powell's neck, and how the blood and skin fragments found inside of the refrigerator were linked to her by DNA comparison.

He finished by saying, "That transfer of fiber, blood, and skin could only have been caused by the decedent thrashing about inside of that refrigerator. It has been my experience through many years of homicide investigation that when a person stops living—they also stop moving. Therefore, the only logical conclusion to be reached is that at some point prior to Ms. Powell's death, she was held in a horrible captive state inside of that refrigerator."

The statement exploded in the room like a bomb, and loud sobs could be heard coming from the audience. Jenkins looked over and saw Kathy Powell's brother putting his arm around his mother to comfort her. This was the first official mention of how the refrigerator had been used, and Jenkins knew the grizzly picture of Kathy Powell being held inside of it would be forever ingrained in the minds of her family members.

What the prosecution planned to introduce into evidence next was even more horrific than Jenkins' description of the refrigerator. Before Viloria brought out blowup photos of the crime scene and the refrigerator itself, he told the court the photos would be highly disturbing in nature. He asked the judge to ban the press from photographing the evidentiary photos and gave anyone who might be bothered by them a moment to leave the courtroom if they so desired. The judge granted the request, but everyone in attendance remained in their seats.

Several eight-by-ten photos mounted on heavy white poster boards were placed on easels in the front of the courtroom. Judge Salcido swiveled his chair to better view them, and Viloria asked Jenkins to describe what was depicted in the photos.

The first set of photos was of Kathy Powell as she was found inside the dumpster. In the second set she had been removed from the plastic bags and sleeping bag. Jenkins pointed out how the ropes had been tied around her in a manner that would choke her if she moved too much, leading him to believe she had been tied up by someone other than herself.

The last set of photos was of a demonstration staged using a crime scene technician who was about the same height and weight as Kathy Powell. The woman was dressed in protective clothing and had been placed inside the refrigerator to show the position of Kathy Powell's body as determined by matching her injuries to the corresponding blood and skin samples taken from the refrigerator walls and door. The technician's body was twisted in a grotesque position, and a murmur went through the crowd as they realized this was how Kathy Powell spent the last days of her life.

The photos had a devastating effect on everyone in the room, with the exception of one man. As Jenkins got back into the witness chair, he looked at Middleton and saw he was staring straight ahead as if the photos were not even in the room. Middleton had disassociated himself from the crime in the way only a true sociopath could.

At precisely 11:30 A.M., Viloria said he had no further questions for Jenkins but would be recalling him for additional testimony at a later time. The defense deferred cross-examination until Jenkins' testimony was completed and Judge Salcido recessed the courtroom for lunch. Middleton was led from the room, followed by his attorneys. Once he was gone, the press people rushed out to start their bi-lines. They'd been given a glimpse of life through the eyes of a madman, and the story would definitely lead off the evening news.

Jenkins and Viloria had a brief discussion about the day's events, and they were both pleased with how the testimony went. They were by no means out of the woods yet because they still had to deal with the major hurdle in their case. There was no doubt that Middleton was evil and had been murdered in the past, but that was not what they were here to prove. They had to show that Kathy Powell and Thelma Davilla died at his hands, and one single word hung over the case like a black cloud waiting to burst over their heads. *Undetermined.*

C.S.I. technician reenacting Kathy Powell's body placement while she was stored inside of the refrigerator in Middleton's storage shed.

Eddie Dixon and Steve Pitts standing in front of Middleton's "Torture Chamber" storage shed before it was searched. The refrigerator is in the left corner with the drum of souvenirs on top of it.

Cut out in the refrigerator that allowed Middleton to place Kathy Powell's head in the freezer portion.

Ropes and pulleys rigged inside of Middleton's storage shed.

Middleton's 1972 International truck that first drew attention to him as a suspect in Kathy Powell's murder.

Voodoo machete used by Middleton in the Santeria ritualistic rape in Florida.

Middleton's Miami P.D. .357 Magnum
service revolver located inside
of his storage unit.

Portion of the skeletal remains of
Thelma Davilla located in a
shallow grave North of Reno.

Middleton's Boston P.D. badge
and I.D. card located inside of
his storage shed.

Middleton's T.C.I. Cable Company
truck still held in storage
as evidence.

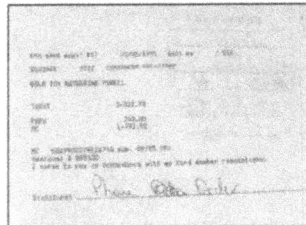

Credit card receipt from the
Good Guys purchase that
broke the case open.

Chapter 46:
Rocky

Testimony resumed at 2:00 in the afternoon when the prosecution called Detective Larry Canfield to the stand. Canfield testified to the facts surrounding the discovery of Thelma Davilla's decomposed remains and how Middleton was linked to the crime. He introduced into evidence hair samples matched to Davilla through DNA, the blanket she had been wrapped in when her sister last saw her, and some of the clothing she had been wearing. Canfield testified that all of these items had been in the possession of the Reno Police when Davilla was found, and the items had come from Middleton's shed.

Canfield then detailed the formation of the task force and their investigative efforts that led to charging Middleton with the murder. No mention of the Florida trip or anything they learned there about Middleton's past was brought up. Viloria was still uncertain if he would be able to get any of that information into evidence, but if he could, he would save it for trial.

Speccio asked only two questions of Canfield during cross examination. The first question was if Canfield had ever investigated a homicide case where the cause of death was undetermined. The second question was whether Thelma Davilla's cause of death had ever been determined. The detective quietly answered no to both questions.

Sparks Police Detective Dave Adams was the next to take the stand. He testified to the facts surrounding Thelma Davilla's disappearance and how the police initially handled the case. He then said the case was put in the opened and unsolved file until the discovery of her body. After that, he was brought back into the case since he was the lead detective when she initially disappeared.

Adams testified to the many man-hours the task force detectives put into interviewing known associates of Davilla. At least three of those people established possible links between Middleton and Davilla before her disappearance. Adams then testified to the service calls performed by T.C.I. Cable Company at Davilla's apartment and the possible link to Middleton.

He also testified that he and Canfield spent several hours doing interviews at the legal brothels east of Reno. Middleton was a frequent patron in two of the houses of prostitution, but they found a common theme throughout their interviews. Middleton never engaged in any sexual activity with the prostitutes when he visited the brothels. He would sit at the bar and drink with the girls, then try to get them to go out on dates with him. The word *stalker* surfaced several times during their investigative interviews.

Upon cross-examination, Speccio asked Adams the same two questions he asked Canfield. Had he ever investigated a homicide with no known cause of death, and had a cause of death been established in the Thelma Davilla case? Like Canfield, Adams answered no to both questions.

The fourth and final witness of the day was by far the most compelling. Dora Valverde took the stand and broke down in tears twice during her testimony. She described her sister as a hardworking and caring person who loved living in the United States and never caused anyone any harm during her entire life. She recounted her story of leaving for work on August 8, 1994—the last day she saw her sister alive. She also identified the blanket found in Middleton's storage shed as the same one her sister had been sleeping in when she last saw her.

Speccio did not cross examine Ms. Valverde and Judge Salcido dismissed everyone for the weekend after she was through testifying. Court was due to reconvene Monday morning and that was when Viloria planned to address the issue of cause of death.

Much of the morning of Monday, June 17, 2008, was spent with the defense team reviewing documents. It was common practice for documentation to be admitted into evidence without testimony to support it if the defense and prosecution both stipulated to the fact it would happen anyway if the person who prepared them actually testified in court. This was a time-saving practice at the preliminary hearing stages of a criminal case, but the actual experts would be called to testify if the case was bound over for trial.

Viloria decided not to call Dr. Roger Ritzlin or Dr. Frederick Laubscher to the stand at this point to testify regarding the autopsy of Kathy Powell or the examination of Thelma Davilla's remains. Speccio agreed to have the reports prepared by both doctors and the death certificates issued for both women entered into evidence without testimony. All documentation listed the causes of death as undetermined, so the defense had nothing to gain by having the doctors testify.

It was 1:00 P.M. by the time Viloria called his first witness of the day. Deputy Chuck Lowe testified to gathering evidence at both crime scenes, Middleton's storage shed and apartment, and finally at the homes of Kathy Powell and Thelma Davilla. He authenticated the photos on display in the courtroom as ones he had taken and testified to noticing similarities in how the victims in both cases were dumped.

Viloria next asked Lowe if during the hundreds of deaths he had responded to as a forensic technician, had he ever seen one where the death resulted from natural causes and the decedent was bound in the manner Kathy Powell was. Lowe answered no, and it was his opinion no one would willingly want to be bound in the manner Kathy Powell was.

Speccio objected to this last statement as conjecture, but Judge Salcido allowed the answer to remain on record since Lowe was testifying to his expert observations. Viloria felt he had just taken a very big step in proving criminal agency in the case.

The next witness was Richard Berger, the Sheriff's Department criminalist who examined the rope, fiber, and hair evidence in the case. Berger testified that the rope found in Middleton's storage shed was similar and consistent with the rope taken from the bodies of Kathy Powell and Thelma Davilla. Mr. Berger next said the blue fibers found on Kathy Powell's neck and body were virtually indistinguishable from the fibers found in the refrigerator in Middleton's storage shed.

During cross-examination, Speccio asked Mr. Berger if the rope used on either Powell or Davilla was a 100% match to the rope found in Middleton's shed. Berger said that it was impossible to get a 100% match with rope unless the two ends of a cut rope were present for comparison. Speccio asked no further questions, leaving the possibility that the ropes were unrelated hanging in the air for consideration.

Dr. Berch Henry, also a Sheriff's Department criminalist, took the stand next. Henry was a DNA specialist and had done the DNA testing in both cases. He testified that the hair recovered from the bondage clamps in Middleton's shed was Kathy Powell's. He also said the DNA samples taken from the foam rubber ball gag and from the inside of the refrigerator all matched Kathy Powell.

Dr. Henry said he tested the hair found inside the barrel and on the Mexican blanket found inside Middleton's shed. He testified that those hair samples matched DNA evidence he had retrieved from inside of the skull cap of Thelma Davilla.

When it was Speccio's turn to question the witness, he asked if the hair sample matches were determined to be 100% accurate. Dr. Henry answered the hair sample matched Powell's and had an assigned population frequency of one in 24,000 for Caucasian donors. In Ms. Davilla's case, the frequency was one in 17,000 for Hispanics.

Even though these numbers were well above what was considered a positive match, the fact that the comparisons were not an exact match might be enough to cast a shadow of doubt on the evidence if it were presented to a jury. Viloria made a mental note to do a better job laying the groundwork for the expert testimony at trial because Speccio was obviously doing his homework.

The last prosecution witness of the afternoon was Gary Cable, the Good Guys salesperson who had taken the phone order from the person identifying themselves as Kathy Powell. This part of the case presentation was tricky since Cable would also be called to testify against Evonne Haley when she was eventually charged with her part in the crime.

Viloria decided it was best to put only Cable on the stand during the preliminary hearing and save the testimony of his coworker Mike Serrateo for trial. Evonne Haley was once again in the courtroom, and if Serrateo saw her it might lessen his credibility when he identified her in later court proceedings. Since Haley refused to testify in the Middleton case, there was no reason not to charge her for her part in the Good Guys case now.

Cable testified that he took the phone order for the stereo equipment and his first impression of the caller was it was a man disguising his voice as a woman. He identified the sales receipt found in Middleton's shed as the one he made for the phone sale and authenticated his handwriting on the bottom where the words "phone order" were written. He also identified the stereo equipment found in Middleton's shed as the same merchandise purchased during the phone order.

Speccio asked only one question of the witness during cross-examination. He asked Cable if he had ever received any training on voice identification. Cable said no, but he usually talks to hundreds of people a week while performing his job and has become quite good at matching people to their voices. Viloria liked the answer and Speccio seemed angry that he had asked the question.

There still was no solid evidence to show cause of death or criminal agency, but Viloria was pleased with the groundwork he'd laid with circumstantial evidence throughout the day. He wished he had more, but he'd play with what was dealt him. Rocky Balboa always fought harder when he was against the ropes with the cards stacked against him, and so would he.

Chapter 47:
Great Expectations

There was only one prosecution witness left when the court reconvened at 9:00 the next morning. Viloria called Detective Dave Jenkins to the stand, to sum up the case. The courtroom was once again crowded with spectators and reporters, but Jenkins picked out Bonnie and Walt Rice, sitting in their reserved seats as he made his way to the witness stand. They pledged to remain in town until the end of the proceedings and had kept their word. They also still wore their buttons with Buffy's photo on them pinned to their shirts.

Judge Salcido reminded Jenkins he was still under oath from his prior testimony, and Viloria began the questioning as soon as the detective was seated in the witness chair. This line of questioning was concerning statements Middleton made to Jenkins during some of his interviews.

Jenkins recounted the statement Middleton made to him during their first contact while they were walking to the Records section at the Reno Police Department. He said this was the first time he was inclined to believe Middleton had something to do with Kathy Powell's death because he said he had knowledge of it but then recanted the statement when Detective Douglas joined them.

He next went on to inform about the bizarre explanation Middleton gave him regarding the circumstances of Kathy Powell's death. Middleton originally denied knowing her but then admitted to having consensual sex with her. Finally, he said she was alive and well when he left to go to the store but dead and tied up when he returned. Jenkins also told the judge about Middleton's "Pig in a Poke" offer to the District Attorney in order to gain clemency from prosecution.

Viloria asked Jenkins if, in his professional opinion, these were the actions of an innocent man. Speccio objected, but the judge overruled him since Jenkins was considered an expert in the areas of interview and interrogation. Jenkins did not go into the pathological liar theory since that, too, would be saved for trial. He did say that based on his training and experience, there was no way an innocent person would answer questions in the manner Middleton had.

Viloria was feeling good about the testimony until it was time for cross-examination. Speccio hit Jenkins hard about the marathon interview and asked if he had ever come upon an instance where a suspect told the police what they wanted to hear just to put an end to the questioning. Jenkins reluctantly agreed he had heard of such incidents, but it had never happened to him and assuredly was not the case with this interview.

Speccio stood up and said, "I just have a couple more questions for you, detective. Have you ever investigated a homicide where there was an undetermined cause of death?"

Jenkins took a deep breath and replied, "Yes, I have. Three cases come immediately to mind, but there may have been more."

"OK," Speccio said. "Let's just talk about these three that you can remember. Were they all adult victims?"

Viloria stood up and objected to the line of questioning based on relevance to the current case. Speccio asked for the court's indulgence, saying he would show relevance with the next couple of questions. The objection was overruled, and Judge Salcido instructed Jenkins to answer the question.

Jenkins said, "Of the three cases, two of the victims were infants in what initially appeared to be S.I.D.S. deaths but were later proven to be intentional acts by the parents. Only one case of undetermined death where the victim was an adult immediately comes to mind."

Speccio remained standing and said, "And who was the victim in that one case you investigated, detective?"

Jenkins paused and then answered, "A thirty-eight-year-old woman who was found deceased in a downtown Reno motel room on August 4, 1993. The coroner was unable to establish cause or manner of death during her autopsy, but we subsequently arrested and convicted her boyfriend for her murder."

"And what is the current status of that case?" Speccio asked.

"It is currently in front of the Nevada State Supreme Court on appeal from your office," Jenkins replied.

Speccio stepped closer to the witness stand and inquired, "And do you know the basis for that appeal, Detective Jenkins?"

Jenkins smiled and answered, "I'm certain we both know the answer to that question, Mr. Speccio. The conviction is being appealed because your office feels the state did not accurately prove the corpus delecti for the crime of murder since the coroner could not rule criminal agency was involved in the death."

"Thank you, detective," Speccio said. "No further questions."

Viloria chose not to ask Jenkins any questions on re-direct examination, and the judge told him he could step down from the witness stand. Since there were no other witnesses scheduled to testify, Jenkins was allowed to remain in the courtroom to listen to the closing arguments. He stood in the back of the room next to Douglas, who had come to court to listen to the last of the testimony.

Speccio hadn't called any witnesses for the defense during the proceedings, and he certainly wasn't going to put Middleton on the stand to testify in his own defense. Viloria would have loved to get a chance at picking Middleton's story apart under oath, but unfortunately that would probably never happen. People like Middleton were the reason the Constitution guaranteed a person the right not to testify in their own trial. He wouldn't be able to keep himself from lying, and those lies would never stand up against a skilled attorney like Viloria.

Middleton sat erect and stared straight ahead as Viloria began his closing arguments. Viloria remained standing behind the prosecution table as he spoke and kept his summation brief. A link had been established between Middleton and both victims. DNA evidence from both women was found inside Middleton's makeshift torture chamber, meaning they were both alive at some point when they entered the shed. Both women were found dead after their bodies were dumped, which meant their lives ended while Middleton held them in captivity. Kidnap, torture, rape, and murder were the common theme in both cases. Viloria ended by saying the prosecution more than proved there was enough probable cause to bind Middleton over for the crimes he was charged with.

The closing arguments for the defense consisted of two statements. Speccio stood and said, "The prosecution has not shown a link between these two cases, nor have they proven criminal agency was involved in either death. At this time the defense moves that the charges against David Middleton be dropped."

Judge Salcido studied his notes for a moment and then announced that he found enough probable cause to bind Middleton over for District Court trial on all charges. A trial date would be set as soon as he could consult the court calendar.

There was a commotion in the room as the news reporters hurriedly left to start preparing their stories. A photo of a confused Middleton with the headline "EX-COP GOES TO TRIAL FOR THE CABLE GUY MURDERS" would be printed on the front page of the morning paper. The task force detectives lamenting about poor press coverage were pleasantly surprised the news didn't dub the case the "Ex-Cop Murders."

After Middleton had been led from the courtroom, Jenkins and Douglas stood in the hallway waiting for Viloria. They watched Bonnie and Walt Rice hugging the families of the other victims in celebration inside the emptying courtroom. These were people who hadn't known each other a few short days earlier but would now forever be kindred family.

Viloria walked up to the two detectives and said, "Well, we made it past the first step."

"We did," Jenkins agreed. "But Speccio brought up the Frutiger case, and that concerns me."

Viloria said, "Frutiger was guilty, and he got convicted of murder. We can't help what happens after that."

Douglas said, "The rumor I'm hearing is the State Supreme Court is about to reverse his conviction and set him free."

"That's a pretty credible rumor," Viloria said. "That means Speccio is already planning his appeal, and that's something an attorney does when he knows he has a guilty client who is going to be convicted."

"I still don't like it," Jenkins said. "I'd feel a lot better if we had a solid cause of death to base our case on. Like Charles Dickens said in *Great Expectations*, 'Take nothing on its looks but take everything on evidence.' Our case is a little short on evidence for my liking."

Viloria rolled his eyes and said, "What they say about you is true. You really do know too much shit for a cop. We'll worry about the Frutiger case and the causes of death later. Middleton is guilty, and we're gonna send him back to hell where he belongs, so let's go celebrate with a nice lunch."

Chapter 48:
Frutiger

On August 4, 1993, the manager of the Regency Hotel in a seedy part of downtown Reno sent a maintenance man to investigate a putrid smell possibly coming from a broken sewer line under one of the buildings. The custodian crawled under the hotel and found the sewer lines intact but determined the foul odor was originating from room thirty-five.

The manager knocked on the door to room thirty-five, which was answered by a man named Clinton Frutiger, who rented the room with his girlfriend, Peggy Poulter. Frutiger told the manager he was just about to call her to report the odor but was waiting for Peggy to get out of the shower. He asked the manager to return in about ten minutes, and he would allow her to come inside to check for the source of the smell.

While the manager waited inside her office, she was surprised to see Frutiger hurry from the hotel room alone and speed out of the parking lot, driving Peggy Poulter's beige 1985 Oldsmobile Cutlass. The manager went back to room thirty-five. She could hear the shower running, but there was no answer when she knocked on the door. She entered the room and found there was no one in the shower, but the room was swarming with flies, and there were towels stuffed under the closet door.

The manager fought her way through the flies and pulled open the closet door. She found Peggy Poulter wrapped in plastic lying on the closet floor in a puddle of dried blood. She was the source of the foul odor, and judging from the amount of maggots crawling over her body, she had been dead for quite some time.

Reno Police Detective Dave Jenkins was assigned the case, and he responded to the hotel with his partner, Detective John Douglas. After their initial investigation was completed, Poulter's body was removed from the closet. With the assistance of the coroner, they removed the plastic bag that was covering her head and some of the plastic wrapping from her body. There were no immediate signs of trauma, but there was a suspicious-looking bulge in the plastic that remained wrapped around her body.

The detectives carefully unwrapped more plastic and then found what was causing the protuberance. The killer had wrapped Ms. Poulter's cat inside the plastic so she could take her beloved pet with her into the afterlife. Unlike Poulter, the cat's cause of death was immediately distinguishable since its head was grotesquely twisted 180 degrees from its natural position. Killing the cat showed aggression associated with someone close to the victim, so Clinton Frutiger became the likely suspect in what certainly appeared to be a murder. An attempt to locate was broadcast for Poulter's Oldsmobile, but by then Frutiger had a four-hour head start and was not located.

An autopsy was performed on Ms. Poulter the next day by Dr. Roger Ritzlin—the same doctor who would perform the autopsy on Kathy Powell six months later. Dr. Ritzlin observed Poulter's body was severely decomposed and estimated she had been dead for about a week. He said he could not determine a cause of death due to the decomposition but found her liver was enlarged, and her blood alcohol level at the time of her death was a .341.

Dr. Ritzlin determined Poulter could have died from heart disease, a cirrhotic liver, alcohol consumption at a lethal level, or strangulation. He found bleeding in Poulter's neck area but said it was a small amount and not consistent with trauma caused by strangulation. The plastic bag covering Poulter's head was described as being "draped over her head and not wrapped in a way that would cause suffocation," so that was also ruled out as a cause of death.

After completion of Peggy Poulter's autopsy, Dr. Ritzlin listed the cause and manner of her death as *undetermined.* The case was reclassified as a *suspicious death,* with Clinton Frutiger listed as a person of interest. Since Frutiger had unrelated outstanding warrants, Jenkins and Douglas went in search of him to see what he knew about the death of Peggy Poulter *and* her cat.

The next day, Poulter's car was located in the parking lot of a casino in Carson City, thirty miles south of Reno. The detectives staked out the car and took Frutiger into custody when he returned to it. In his wallet, they found Peggy Poulter's ATM card and two of her credit cards. Subsequent investigation showed Frutiger had been withdrawing the maximum amount from Poulter's bank account since July 1, 1993, and had made several charges on her credit cards after the time of her death. Inside the car, they also found a briefcase loaded with personal papers belonging to Ms. Poulter.

Based on the circumstances, the case was upgraded to a homicide, and Clinton Frutiger was arrested for the murder of Peggy Poulter.

Throughout his trial, his defense stuck to the story that Ms. Poulter had died of natural causes, and Frutiger hid her body because he was afraid to call the police. They explained the cat had been hit by a car, and Frutiger thought it was humane to bury the cat with its owner. He was subsequently convicted of murder and sentenced to life in prison.

An appeal was immediately filed by the Public Defender's office. The basis for the appeal was the State did not adequately prove criminal agency was involved in the death of Peggy Poulter when they presented their case to the grand jury. Since the cause and manner of death were never determined and there was a possibility Poulter died of natural causes, the defense argued the case should never have reached trial in District Court. Criminal agency was the *corpus delicti* in the charge of murder, so it was now up to the State Supreme Court to determine if the prosecution had met its burden of proof.

The Nevada Supreme Court was in the process of reviewing the Frutiger case at the time David Middleton was bound over for trial. Three murder cases being tried in different parts of Nevada could possibly be affected by the Nevada Supreme Court ruling in the Frutiger case. One of them had been officially dubbed "The Cable Guy Murders."

Chapter 49:
Habeas Corpus

Middleton's murder trial was scheduled to be heard in the Washoe County Courtroom of District Court Judge Peter Breen on November 13, 1995. As soon as Middleton's defense attorneys were notified of the date, they requested a continuance of at least ninety days in order to prepare their appeal of Judge Salcido's decision in the preliminary hearing.

Since Middleton was being held in custody and it was his own decision to forfeit his right to a speedy trial, the request for continuance was granted. A new trial date was set for Monday, February 12, 1996. The State Supreme Court would certainly rule on the Frutiger case before they recessed for the Christmas holidays, so the prosecution knew the defense had an ulterior motive for their continuance request.

Middleton's attorneys went to work on their appeal almost immediately after he was bound over for trial at his preliminary hearing. On August 30, 1995, Public Defender Mike Speccio and his Chief Appellate Deputy Attorney John Reese Petty filed a nineteen-page Writ of Habeas Corpus with Judge Breen seeking a reversal of Judge Salcido's decision.

Habeas corpus is a Latin term that translates to *you should have the body*. A Writ of Habeas Corpus is a legal document filed by a detainee seeking relief from unlawful imprisonment due to insufficient evidence against him. In Nevada these writs are heard *ex parte*—another Latin term that means *from or for one party*. It would be up to Judge Breen alone to decide on the Writ of Habeas Corpus without any involvement of the prosecution. This would be the first test of the strength of the prosecution's case against Middleton.

The main argument in the writ was that there was insufficient evidence presented to the Justice Of The Peace at the time of the preliminary hearing to establish the corpus delicti of murder. The writ read in part:

"Notwithstanding the substantial amount of time spent in the preliminary hearing held below, it is significant, for purposes of this petition, that the State failed to produce any evidence as to the cause of death for either Ms. Davilla or Ms. Powell. Indeed, according to the death certificates admitted into evidence, Ms. Davilla's cause of death could not be determined, and as to Ms. Powell, the cause of death could not be determined "after autopsy."

In this case, in order to establish the requisite probable cause to support a belief that crimes of murder had been committed and that Mr. Middleton had committed the crimes, the prosecution was obliged to prove the corpus delicti of the alleged crimes. To establish the corpus delicti of murder, two elements must be proven: (1) the fact of death; and (2) the criminal agency of another responsible for the death (Hooker v. Sheriff, NV. 506-1262 1973).

Here, there was no evidence, direct or circumstantial, showing criminal agency as the cause of either Ms. Davilla's or Ms. Powell's deaths nor was their evidence, direct or circumstantial, that Mr. Middleton was involved in the cause of either death.

Simply put, this is a case where the Justice Of The Peace was presented with no evidence to support the corpus delicti of murder—yet without so much as an explanation—bound Mr. Middleton over to the district court on both counts of murder. The Justice Of The Peace simply said, 'In this case, the State has brought a lot of evidence before the court, and I'm not going to try to even near elaborate over all of it. I'm not going to even try to do that...' and then bound Mr. Middleton over for trial. But the fact of the matter was that there was no evidence showing criminal agency as the cause of either death.

We are a nation that prides itself on following the rules of law. Thus, the rule of law applies equally to both citizens and governments in our constitutional scheme. Under the rule of law, Mr. Middleton should not have been bound over on the two counts of murder because the State failed to offer any evidence supporting the criminal agency prong of the corpus delicti of the crime.

For the reasons and authorities set forth above, it is respectfully submitted that the State failed to establish the corpus delicti of murder in the case of either Ms. Davilla or Ms. Powell. Accordingly, Mr. Middleton respectfully requests that this court grant the Writ of Habeas Corpus and discharge the two counts of murder."

Judge Breen took the writ under advisement and eventually gave both the defense and prosecution a chance to argue their cases. On Wednesday, October 18, 1995, Judge Breen called the attorneys into his chambers and issued his ruling. He rejected the Writ of Habeas Corpus and ruled the murder charges against David Middleton would not be dismissed. He also rejected the defense motion to have both murders tried separately so the cases would stay joindered for purposes of prosecution. Middleton's trial date remained February 12, 1996.

The ruling was a major victory for the prosecution, and Viloria met with Jenkins and Douglas later that evening for a celebration dinner of burgers and beers at a local pub. While they were waiting for their dinners, Jenkins asked, "What do you think their next move will be?"

Viloria replied, "Whatever it is, I'm sure it won't happen till the Supreme Court gets off their asses and rules on Frutiger. We're not out of the woods yet, but I'll be ready for them when we get to trial."

Douglas said, "Since it looks like we're gonna have some downtime in the case, I say we go out and arrest the devil's disciple. We may never tie her to the murders, but we've got her solid on the Good Guys case."

"I agree," said Jenkins. "But I'm not sure whether she's the devil's disciple or an unwitting angel of mercy. After going through everything we've got on her involvement with Middleton, I think she might have actually chased away a couple of his potential victims with her jealousy."

"I almost forgot about Suzy, the bartender," Douglas said. "I wonder how many other girls out there are alive today because Middleton's girlfriend is a raving bitch."

Viloria finished his beer and said, "I'm betting on the devil's disciple angle. Anyway, there's no reason to leave Haley running free anymore. She's not gonna do us any good testifying against Middleton, and the statute of limitations is ticking on her involvement at Good Guys. Bring me the case when you get it wrapped up, and I'll get you an arrest warrant."

Douglas said, "If nobody ends up killing anybody tonight, we'll be able to jump on this first thing in the morning. The sad part about this is we have a stronger case against Haley than we do against Middleton. It's gonna be a bitch if she ends up doing time, and he walks on a technicality."

Jenkins slowly rapped his knuckles three times on the wooden tabletop and then threw some grains of salt that had spilled on the table over his right shoulder. He said, "It's a good thing I'm not a superstitious man, or else I might think my partner just jinxed us. Is anyone up for another beer?"

Chapter 50:
For Whom The Bell Tolls

Three uniformed Washoe County Sheriff's deputies accompanied Jenkins and Douglas when they went to Evonne Haley's trailer at 10:00 in the morning on Friday, October 27, 1995. She initially would not open her door for them, but she acquiesced after Jenkins used his cell phone to call inside and calmly explained they had a warrant for her arrest and weren't leaving without her.

The arrest warrant signed an hour earlier by Judge Salcido charged Evonne Haley with one count each of burglary, fraudulent use of a credit card, and possession of stolen property—all related to her involvement in the Good Guys case. To say Haley was a bit upset when she learned she was being arrested would be like saying the sinking of the Titanic was a minor boating accident.

Haley appeared extremely disheveled in the booking photo that was printed on the front page of the Reno Gazette-Journal the next morning, but much to her credit, she learned a valuable lesson during her arrest. She now knew that punching a uniformed deputy in the mouth would earn her a quick trip to the carpet, a patch of rug burn on her face, and an added charge of obstructing an officer.

Haley's arrest warrant carried a one hundred thousand dollar cash-only bail since she was considered a flight risk with no roots in the community. She could not come up with this amount, so she remained in custody until her arraignment on Wednesday, November 1, 1995. Standing in front of Judge Salcido, Haley said she understood the charges against her and entered a plea of not guilty. Haley's court-appointed public defender requested a bail reduction since she had a teenage daughter at home and was a responsible member of the community.

Prosecutor Tom Viloria pointed out to the court that Haley's daughter was now in the care and custody of relatives in Colorado, which is most likely where Haley herself would head if she were to be let out on bail. After hearing both arguments, Judge Salcido denied the bail reduction and set a trial date for Evonne Haley on May 30, 1996, in the District Courtroom of the Honorable Judge Deborah Agosti.

With both Middleton and Haley now in custody, there was not much more work for the detectives assigned to the case to do. They had exhausted every investigative tool they could think of attempting to tie Haley to the two Reno murders. There was no doubt in anyone's mind that Haley at least had knowledge of the murders, even if she wasn't an active participant in them, but proving it was another matter. Chasing a weak case could ruin the strong one they already had against her, so they decided to cut their losses and take what they could get.

The task force was disbanded, and the detectives moved on to other cases. On Friday, November 3, 1995, the investigation into the murders of Kathy Powell and Thelma Davilla was officially listed as closed by arrest and pending prosecution. The detectives who worked the two cases had expended a tremendous amount of effort and displayed extraordinary investigative talents in order to solve the murders. They were proud of their accomplishments, but each of them knew a piece of the investigation would remain with them forever. They say when you look into the eyes of the devil, part of the devil will stare into your soul forever. None of them would ever forget the face of David Middleton.

Tom Viloria busied himself preparing for the upcoming trials of Middleton and Haley. Prosecuting Haley would be a fairly easy process since there was so much physical evidence against her. The evidence against Middleton was mainly circumstantial, but Viloria remained confident he could win a conviction against him. His flair for courtroom dramatics would allow him to present what evidence they did have in front of the jury in a way that would maximize its impact.

During his case preparation Viloria was contacted several times by the prosecutor's office from Montrose, Colorado. They were following the progress of the case with great interest, and Viloria hoped they would eventually decide to prosecute Middleton for the murder of Buffy Rice-Donohue. At one point, Viloria told the Montrose District Attorney he was convinced Middleton had murdered Buffy and would assist in any way possible with prosecution in Colorado after the Reno case was finished. The District Attorney told Viloria that no decision had been made yet on whether they would be seeking an arrest warrant for Middleton in the Buffy Rice-Donohue case, and that was where the discussion ended.

On November 30, 1995 the prosecution was dealt their first major blow in the David Middleton case. The Nevada Supreme Court issued a decision to reverse the murder conviction of Clinton Frutiger. They agreed with the Public Defender's office that probable cause for the involvement of the criminal agency involved in the death of Peggy Poulter had not been established at the grand jury phase, so the case should never have gone to trial. Clinton Frutiger was now a free man, and the popular opinion was that David Middleton would not be far behind.

Tom Viloria took the Supreme Court decision in stride. He expected it, so he was prepared. Viloria went into action before Mike Speccio could file another writ based on the Frutiger decision. On Friday, December 1, 1995, Viloria filed a motion with Judge Breen requesting the Public Defender's office be removed from Middleton's defense based on a conflict of interest. Evonne Haley was also being represented by that office, and she and Middleton were being tried on a case where they were co-conspirators. Viloria requested that an attorney not associated with the Public Defender's office be appointed by the court to represent Middleton.

Speccio argued that his office had more time invested in Middleton's defense than Haley's, so they should remain on the Middleton case and appoint another attorney for Haley. Since Viloria's ex-parte motion was already filed, Judge Breen could not take Speccio's arguments under consideration. He would have to rule on the prosecution's motion as it stood, and the defense would not be able to take any further action until he did so.

Viloria beat Speccio to the punch, but he knew his preemptive strike was nothing more than a delay tactic. It would buy him time, and time was the one thing he needed most in order to prepare for the inevitable appeal that would be filed on Middleton's behalf based on the Frutiger decision. Rocky won round one, but the fight wasn't over until the final bell rang.

Chapter 51:
Outside The Box

The day after Viloria filed his motion, he went to work with a vengeance, trying to find evidence that would strengthen his criminal agency argument in the murders of Kathy Powell and Thelma Davilla. Jenkins and Douglas were unofficially put back on the case with instructions to help Viloria in any way possible.

In a murder trial, the defense has the leeway to bring in as much expert testimony as the defendant can afford in order to prove his innocence. Nowhere was this better illustrated than in the acquittal of O.J. Simpson two months earlier. The prosecution in that case had more than enough evidence to convict Simpson of a double homicide, but his money bought him his freedom. David Middleton didn't have O.J.'s money, but the notoriety his attorneys would gain by getting him acquitted would be an investment in their future.

Viloria was well aware of the tactics utilized by Simpson's "Dream Team" defense and the furor still raging over the racial overtones resonating from that case. It was big news, and he was certain Middleton's defense team would try to capitalize on the tidal wave of press the case generated. He needed to line up expert witnesses to bolster his own case, but he didn't have the assets available to the defense.

The main problem for the prosecution in the Middleton case would be proving criminal agency was involved in the deaths of Powell and Davilla. The first step in doing this would be dealing with the coroner's ruling of undetermined cause of death. Reasonable doubt that Kathy Powell could have died of natural causes would blow both cases out of the water. Viloria needed to convince a jury that Kathy Powell had been murdered in order to make criminal agency believable in the Davilla case. Without Powell, he would lose Davilla, so that was where he started with his preparations.

After lengthy research, Viloria located someone who might be able to help him. Dr. Vincent Di Maio was the Chief Medical Examiner in San Antonio, Texas, and was a certified expert witness in deaths by suffocation. Dr. Di Maio was fascinated by the Middleton case after Viloria called and asked him for help. He agreed to review the coroner's autopsy report pro bono and testify in any subsequent court proceedings if needed.

Viloria faxed all the documentation he had to Dr. Di Maio and heard back from him two days later. Dr. Di Maio first addressed the coroner's concerns about Kathy Powell possibly dying from a heart attack because she had been taking lithium. It was his expert opinion that even though Kathy Powell had some mild perivascular fibrosis in her heart, lithium use would not have caused heart failure. He said studies done in the 1990s showed long-term users of lithium did not die from heart disease at a rate greater than the general public.

Dr. Di Maio next addressed the bruises found on Kathy Powell's elbows and knees. He said these were the result of a struggle to free herself from a confined space—which, in this case, would have been the refrigerator. He said petechiae was only found in thirteen percent of the deaths caused by asphyxiation he had investigated, so the absence of it in Powell's case did not preclude this as the cause of death. Dr. Di Maio said he would gladly testify under oath that it was his opinion the circumstances of Powell's disappearance and the condition of her body when found, indicate that her death was a homicide. He also said the circumstances surrounding Thelma Davilla's disappearance and the discovery of her skeletal remains indicated her death was also a homicide.

The report by Dr. Di Maio was good news, but Viloria knew the defense could easily find an expert witness of their own to contradict that opinion. Such was the nature of expert testimony, so he needed more. It was only a matter of time before Judge Breen ruled on the motion to remove the Public Defender from Middleton's defense. Whoever ended up with the case would file a motion to drop the charges based on the Frutiger decision, so time was running out.

The National Homicide Investigators' conference takes place the first week of December every year. 1995 was Reno's turn to host the conference, and the Middleton case was a hot topic with the detectives in attendance. As with most police conferences, most of the meaningful discussions take place at bars after the classes. True to form, Jenkins and Douglas were sitting at a bar in the El Dorado Casino with a group of detectives from different agencies filling them in on the Middleton case on Tuesday evening, December 5, 1995.

Jenkins explained the problem they were having proving criminal agency and asked if anyone had any suggestions. A redheaded Irish

N.Y.P.D. detective with a ruddy complexion and too much Bushmills in him said, "You should check with the Canuks. I hear they are doing some weird shit with knot investigations up there."

The N.Y.P.D. detective's partner was slightly more sober. He said, "What Timmy meant to say is you might want to give the Royal Canadian Mounted Police a call. They have a guy in Vancouver who is a knot expert, and he might be able to take a look at your case."

The next morning, Jenkins called the North Vancouver office of the Royal Canadian Mounted Police and was put in touch with an investigator named John "J.J." Van Tassel. He was not only a knot expert; he was currently the *only* knot expert in modern law enforcement who had offered testimony in a court of law on the subject. He took an interest in the Middleton case and agreed to fly to Reno the next day to examine the ropes and knots that were used to bind the victims.

After a thorough examination of all the knots used in both cases, Van Tassel submitted a report that would greatly aid the prosecution. He could not say all of the knots were tied by the same person, but he could accurately say all of the knots were the same type. He said he could testify that in his experience, a killer in a frenzied state will use the same knot on every occasion as part of the modus operandi of his crime because his subconscious mind reverts back to the state of euphoria he experiences during his criminal acts.

More importantly, Van Tassel said the knots on both Powell and Davilla had tightened after they had been tied. He determined this after comparing the knots used to bind the bodies to the knots used on the ropes tied around the exterior of the sleeping bag Kathy Powell's body was secreted in. Even though these ropes were used as handles to lift the dead weight of her body, the knots did not tighten as much as those that were in the ropes used to bind her. That showed she must have struggled against the ropes for a prolonged period of time prior to her death. The knots found on the skeletal remains of Davilla were in the same strained condition.

They now had expert witnesses who could challenge the coroner's ruling and also say that Powell and Davilla were both alive when they were tied up. They still needed more, and another innocuous conversation was about to give it to them.

To show Van Tassel their appreciation Jenkins and Douglas took him out to dinner before his flight left for Vancouver. While discussing the case, Jenkins said, "I still have the feeling we're missing something with the cause of death, but I think we have to get outside of the box to find it."

Eddie Dixon had accompanied the detectives to dinner. He said, "I don't know much about thinking outside the box, but I do know I can't stop thinking about what was going through that poor lady's head while she was dying *inside* of that box. That shit is gonna creep me out forever!"

Jenkins smiled and said, "Once again Eddie, you have proven you are a genius of your own sorts. We'll never know what Kathy Powell's thoughts were while trapped inside of that refrigerator, but we certainly owe her an effort to find out how long she was thinking them."

Chapter 52:
The Geek Squad

An idea popped into Jenkins' head after Eddie Dixon made his innocent statement about Kathy Powell's thoughts while she was being held inside the refrigerator. They had proof she was alive at some point while being held inside the refrigerator, but if they could prove exactly how long she could remain alive, they might be able to establish her cause of death in spite of the coroner's ruling.

There had to be a way to calculate how much oxygen a person Kathy Powell's size needed to sustain life and just how much oxygen was available to her inside of the refrigerator. They already had expert witnesses and physical evidence to show she was held captive inside of the refrigerator with the door closed, so naturally, the air supply would be limited to what was flowing through the two small holes drilled into the sides of the refrigerator.

The detectives working the Middleton case were knowledgeable enough to solve almost any criminal or legal problem thrown at them, but they all agreed this one was out of their realm of expertise. Since it was Eddie Dixon who sparked the idea in the first place, he went to the crime lab with Jenkins the next morning to see if they could get an answer to their question.

The forensic investigators listened intently while Jenkins explained the information he was looking for. The refrigerator was wheeled out of the evidence room and into the crime lab, and they spent the next hour taking measurements and doing calculations. After several exhaustive attempts, the technicians relented that this type of problem was over their heads, too.

One of the crime scene investigators who had come into the room to see what was going on said she had taken some night courses at the University of Nevada Reno's Engineering School. She told the detectives what they were looking for seemed more of an engineering problem than a forensic one, so maybe they should check there for help. It was a long shot, but it was better than none at all.

Jenkins called the University and was put in touch with Dr. Tariq Ahmed, the assistant professor in charge of the Civil Engineering program. Dr. Ahmed agreed to see them, and an hour later, the two detectives were standing in his office waiting for him to return from instructing a morning class.

Dixon studied the framed certificates covering the office walls and remarked, "This guy has more degrees than a thermometer and enough letters behind his name to start his own alphabet. I always thought of engineers as geeks, but if he can help us put Middleton away, I'll trade in my holster for a pocket protector in a heartbeat."

Dr. Ahmed walked into the office and introduced himself to the detectives. He was tall and lean with a dark Middle Eastern complexion and curly black hair, and he wore black horn-rimmed glasses on his youthful-looking face. He looked more like a student than a professor, but Jenkins and Dixon both smiled when they spotted the telltale pocket protector holding three pens in the pocket of his white button-down shirt.

When Jenkins finished explaining what they needed, he expected to be told there was nothing the professor could do to help them. Instead, Dr. Ahmed calmly said, "This will be a very simple problem to solve. I will need to take a few measurements of my own, of course, but then all I will have to do is prepare an oxygen flow in a confined space for human respiration calculation. If you need this quickly, I can calculate the survivability time to fifteen minutes either way, but I can narrow that down to a more accurate time through further calculations."

Jenkins assured Dr. Ahmed that a fifteen-minute window of survivability would be more than adequate for what they needed. Dr. Ahmed opened his desk drawer and took out a common tape measure and a large calculator. He put them both into his briefcase and told the detectives he would be more than happy to accompany them right then to take the measurements. If the request surprised the doctor, he certainly did not show it. His demeanor was so calm that one would have thought the detectives had asked him to solve a simple multiplication problem instead of calculating how long it took a murder victim to breathe her last breaths.

The next day, Dr. Ahmed presented a twelve-page report containing his calculations to the detectives. After reading through it, they realized the only numbers they could understand in the report were the page numbers, but Dr. Ahmed agreed to explain his calculations in court if needed. The information the detectives needed the most was written in layman's terms on the cover page of the report. It read:

Subject: Oxygen Flow Calculation In A Confined Space For Human Respiration

Dear Ed. With reference to our discussion, I am writing this letter to inform you of the results of my analysis regarding the subject mentioned above. As shown in step 9 of my calculation, the oxygen utilization rate for human respiration is about 13.8 L/hr (liters per hour), which is about 180 times greater than the conservative estimate of oxygen flow through the two holes in the refrigerator (0.076 L/hr). Therefore, we can neglect this flow. So, my conclusion is that a person the size of your victim would die within about 5.5 hours. However, if oxygen partial pressure for human survivability is made available to me, I can calculate a more accurate time if you need it. Sincerely, Tariq Ahmed, Ph.D., P.E.

The detectives were elated by the report. They now had an expert witness who would testify that the maximum amount of time Kathy Powell could have survived inside that refrigerator was 5.5. hours. Jenkins pulled out the first murder book they'd prepared and flipped it open to the section detailing the times Middleton visited his storage shed after Kathy Powell first disappeared.

His first visit to the storage shed was at 5:47 A.M. on Saturday, February 4, 1995. This was when they theorized, he brought Kathy Powell to the shed and locked her in the refrigerator. Throughout that day, he made periodic visits to the storage unit, but there was only an hour or two between visits. They would never know what he did to Kathy Powell during those visits, but they were certain she was alive and held captive inside the refrigerator.

The timeline showed a gap of over twelve hours between Middleton's visit to the storage shed at 5:38 P.M. on Saturday, February 4th, and his next visit at 6:19 A.M. on Sunday, February 5th. All the evidence they had gathered thus far led them to believe Kathy Powell had been held captive inside the refrigerator whenever she was left alone in the storage shed. Based on the report from Dr. Ahmed, they could now say there was no way she could have survived inside the refrigerator during that twelve-hour time span between visits.

Even if Middleton hadn't planned to kill Kathy Powell, they could now prove she died at his hands during the commission of a felony. This was enough to prove criminal agency under the felony murder rule, and that was all they needed to get past any appeals based on the Frutiger decision. The only downside to the engineering report prepared by Dr. Ahmed was that word traveled fast in police circles, and the Major Crimes Unit quickly became known as *The Geek Squad.*

Chapter 53:
Justice

On Friday, January 5, 1996, Judge Breen issued his ruling on the removal of the Public Defender's office from Middleton's defense. He agreed with Viloria's motion and removed Mike Speccio and his staff from Middleton's defense.

A private attorney named Fred Pinkerton from Reno was appointed by the court to defend Middleton. Pinkerton was a skilled trial lawyer and would be a worthy adversary for the prosecution. His first act as Middleton's attorney was about as predictable as the January snow in the Sierra Nevada Mountains surrounding Reno.

On Wednesday, January 17, 1996, Pinkerton re-submitted Speccio's original Writ of Habeas Corpus to Judge Breen and asked him to take another look at it in light of the Frutiger decision. The gauntlet was thrown down, and the fight was now in Judge Breen's court.

The resubmission of the writ started a new media frenzy. The newspapers speculated that the murder charges against Middleton would be reversed just as they were in the Frutiger case. Interviews were done with the relatives of Kathy Powell and Thelma Davilla, and they all expressed their displeasure with the fact the court was even considering a reversal of the murder charges.

Kathy Powell's brother was quoted as saying, "I am very upset that there is even a remote possibility the court would reverse the murder charges against Middleton. If that decision is made, I think the people of Nevada have reason to be seriously concerned about their safety."

The television media also jumped on the case. The Maury Povich show televised taped interviews of the Rice family in Colorado and Middleton's Florida victim, Alyssa Cervantes, from her home in Miami. The interviews portrayed Middleton as a murdering predator who had been slipping through the cracks in the justice system his entire life, and it now appeared another chasm had just opened for him in Reno.

Tom Viloria seemed unfazed by the publicity or the possibility the murder charges might be reversed. Middleton's trial had once again been postponed until June 6, 1996, and Viloria had other matters to keep him occupied while he awaited Judge Breen's decision. Evonne Haley was set to go to trial soon and Viloria wouldn't allow anything to distract him from vigorously prosecuting her case.

Haley went to trial in Washoe County District Court on Monday, April 29, 1996. Her attorney filed a pre-trial motion that precluded the prosecution from mentioning anything about the Powell-Davilla murder investigations other than to say Haley was accused of using the credit card of a deceased person. Due to the publicity surrounding the case, it was ludicrous to think anyone on Haley's jury panel did not know about the murder investigation, but the fact Viloria could not mention it made his job more difficult.

Viloria presented the two Good Guys employees, Detective Dave Wood and Detective Dave Jenkins, as prosecution witnesses. He was allowed to introduce some photos of Middleton's storage unit into evidence, but only those that showed the location of evidence pertinent to the crimes Haley was charged with. The ominous refrigerator could be seen in the background of the photos, but no mention of it was made in court.

The stereo equipment, the red hand truck, the yellow messenger service windbreaker and the handwritten phone order receipt from Good Guys were also introduced into evidence. The last piece of evidence introduced was photos of Middleton's distinctive-looking International Harvester truck that started the initial chain of events in the case rolling.

The defense only called one witness to the stand. Haley's nineteen-year-old son had flown in from Colorado to testify in his mother's defense. He had no knowledge of the crime but testified to the fact his mother was an honest person who would never knowingly commit a crime. He said Middleton had manipulated Haley since she met him, and he believed his mother honestly thought she was picking up legitimately purchased items at the Good Guys store.

Viloria did not cross examine the witness because the teenager appeared to be the only person in the courtroom to actually believe his mother was an honest person. Proving him wrong would do nothing to help his case, but keeping him on the stand might provoke sympathy for Haley from the jury.

Haley did not take the witness stand in her own defense and never so much as looked at the jury throughout the two-day trial. She appeared nervous and jittery and spent her entire time in the courtroom staring down at the table in front of her. Closing arguments in the case concluded at 2:00 in the afternoon on Tuesday, April 30, 1996. At 2:30 the jury informed Judge Agosti they had reached a verdict. Evonne Haley was found guilty on all counts, and sentencing was set for May 31, 1996.

The pre-sentencing report prepared by the Nevada Department of Parole and Probation on Evonne Haley was favorable. They could not consider any other allegations of Haley's involvement in the Middleton case for their report since she wasn't charged in the murders. This was her first felony conviction, so they recommended she be given probation for the Good Guys case. Probation is the standard sentence in Nevada for a first-time offender in a property crime.

Fortunately, Judge Agosti was not bound by the report, and she knew Evonne Haley was very much involved in other aspects of the Kathy Powell murder case. Judge Agosti sentenced Evonne Haley to seven years in the Nevada State Prison based on her conviction in the Good Guys case. She also sentenced her to another three years in prison for her initial charge of being under the influence of methamphetamine when Jenkins arrested her at the beginning of the investigation. Even though the sentences would run concurrently, Evonne Haley would not be eligible for parole for at least three and a half years.

Viloria closed the book on the devil's disciple and hoped to never again set eyes on her. He was pleased with the sentence but not as much as the husband and wife from Colorado sitting in the spectators' section behind the prosecution table were. They still wore the buttons bearing their daughter's photo pinned to their shirts, and they prayed Buffy was smiling down from heaven as she watched a hysterical Evonne Haley being led from the courtroom in handcuffs.

Chapter 54:
I'm Ready For 'Em

On Monday, June 3, 1996, Judge Breen contacted all involved parties and advised them he had made a decision on the Writ of Habeas Corpus filed on Middleton's behalf. He scheduled a hearing in his courtroom at 9:00 A.M. on Thursday, June 6, 1996, to discuss his findings. The early rumors circulating from the courthouse were the news would not be good for the prosecution.

By 8:00 A.M. on the morning of the hearing, the white marble steps leading to the front entrance of the courthouse were crowded with spectators and news crews waiting to get inside. News trucks sporting satellite antennas were parked on side streets, and reporters were going over last-minute instructions with their camera crews. All the local networks, as well as FOX and CNN, were represented. The press smelled a story, and they were on it like sharks on chum.

Tom Viloria sat calmly in the District Attorney's office, discussing the prosecution's options with Dick Gammick and Chief Deputy District Attorney David Stanton. The unofficial word had already filtered down that Judge Breen would be reversing the murder charges against Middleton, but even without the murder charges, he would not walk away a free man like Clinton Frutiger had.

The prosecution still had two strong kidnap cases and credit card crimes to charge Middleton with. It was the District Attorney's opinion that they should move forward with prosecution on these charges and cut their losses on the murder charges. He was certain they could win a conviction resulting in life in prison for Middleton if they prosecuted him on these charges alone, but they might lose everything if they tried to fight the decision to drop the murder charges.

Viloria pointed out that a life sentence wouldn't really mean life because Middleton would have the possibility of parole. A more realistic timeframe for his prison sentence if he *was* convicted of these crimes would be twenty years. That would put him at fifty-five years old when he became eligible for parole, and that was definitely still young enough to kill again. Not fighting the ruling would also set a precedent for some very poor case law, and that was something Viloria wanted no part of.

The only way to possibly fight Judge Breen's inevitable ruling on the murder charges was to get the Nevada Supreme Court to reverse its own ruling in the Frutiger case. Court decisions often get reversed due to the interpretations of different judges looking into new and changing laws. But as District Attorney Gammick pointed out to his young prosecutor, *no one* had ever gone in front of a group of Supreme Court judges and asked them to reverse a decision they themselves had made less than six months prior.

Viloria shrugged his shoulders and simply said, "I'm ready for 'em."

Gammick gave Viloria the go-ahead to file an appeal as soon as Judge Breen announced his decision but made it perfectly clear that other employment options might be on the horizon for him if his plan backfired. Viloria already had most of the appellate paperwork prepared in anticipation of the decision, and he would spearhead the fight while Gammick and his chief assistant handled the press.

Viloria was seated at the prosecution table when Middleton was led into the courtroom at 8:45 A.M. Middleton was once again dressed in a blue jail jumpsuit with his hands cuffed to a belly chain. But this time, he was smiling like a kid at Christmas as he took a seat next to his attorney, Fred Pinkerton, at the defense table.

The second row of spectator seats behind the prosecution table had once again been reserved for the families of the victims. Bonnie and Walt Rice were in attendance and had been accepted into this group of survivors. They still wore their pins with Buffy's photo on them, but there was a new twist at this proceeding. The members of Powell's and Davilla's families had followed suit and made pins with photos of their own loved ones on them. They wore them on their shirts in plain view, so there was no doubt which side of the conflict that particular row of spectators was rooting for.

None of the task force detectives were in attendance. There would be no testimony offered in this proceeding, and they already were reasonably certain what Judge Breen's decision would be. They wanted to avoid the media circus that would certainly follow the proceeding and trusted Viloria to speak for them in the case.

At precisely 9:00, Judge Breen entered the courtroom through the door leading to his chambers behind the judge's dais. After everyone was seated, he addressed his audience. He said, "I have reached a decision in this matter, but I would first like to explain what the State law has given me to work with while reaching my conclusion.

240

Based on the recent Frutiger decision, I have had to divide the evidence in this case into two categories. The first is that the two victims were murdered, and the second is that it was the defendant who murdered them."

The courtroom was eerily quiet as Judge Breen continued. "Now the prosecution has assured this court they have plenty of evidence to prove the second category, but in light of the Frutiger decision, I am not allowed to consider any of that. The only thing I can focus on is the corpus delicti, which, in the case of murder, is the body. I can only ask myself one question, and that is, 'What does the body tell us?'

Viewed alone, the body of Ms. Davilla tells us nothing, and the body of Ms. Powell tells us very little. Based on the recent Supreme Court decision this is the only evidence I can consider, so I must rule in favor of the defense on their Writ of Habeas Corpus. Based on the new standards of evidence set forth by the State Supreme Court, I find the prosecution has not adequately shown criminal agency was involved in either of these deaths. The two counts of murder Mr. Middleton has been charged with will be dropped, but the other charges will remain."

There was an uproar in the courtroom, and Judge Breen banged his gavel to bring the crowd to order. Middleton smiled broadly and shook hands with his attorney. Pinkerton then stood up and asked Judge Breen to set bail in the amount of ten thousand dollars for his client since this was now not a murder case.

Viloria stood and objected to bail in any amount. He reminded Judge Breen that Middleton was still being charged with two kidnaps, one of which involved torture. He also informed the judge he would be filing an appeal to the State Supreme Court on his decision before the end of the work day.

Judge Breen sided with the prosecution and ruled Middleton would be held in custody without bail until trial. The date of that trial would be set after the State Supreme Court ruled on the prosecution's appeal. The judge then adjourned the proceeding, and the reporters rushed outside to begin their interviews with people as they left.

Viloria left the courthouse undetected through a side door, but Gammick met with the press on the front steps of the courthouse to give a statement. He said, "The dismissal of Middleton's murder charges shows me the justice system is broken, and it is up to us to fix it."

Chief Deputy District Attorney Dave Stanton added, "There are some very savvy criminals out there, and I think this gives them a recipe for how to commit murder and not be held responsible."

A reporter shouted out a question asking Gammick what he thought of Judge Breen and the Frutiger decision in general. Gammick answered, "I hate to seem like I'm ducking and dodging you, but we're just not ready to comment on anything in that area. All I can tell you is we're going to put this right back on the Supreme Court. They can let Middleton go on these murders if they want, but I'm sure as hell not gonna."

The attorneys for the defense had a different view of Judge Breen's decision when they were interviewed. Fred Pinkerton said, "Frankly, I'm proud. It's good to see that the system is working, and we're dealing with the law instead of popular opinion."

Attorney John Petty, who wrote the original writ, said, "We don't want judges who make decisions based on what's politically popular; we want them to make decisions on the law. That is what Judge Breen did here today."

The reporters then moved on to interview some of the victim's family members. Kathy Powell's brother Jeff said, "Naturally, I'm very upset with the decision. I was kind of expecting it, but now the reality is sinking in. I think Middleton's background as a police officer gives him knowledge a lot of people wouldn't have and helps him manipulate the system. I just hope we can turn this around."

Walt Rice said, "It really sinks hard in my heart that this can happen. I have a lot of faith in the District Attorney's office in Reno, so I don't think this is the end of the line for Middleton. But still, I'd like to see Montrose file murder charges against him in case he gets away with it here."

Dave Jenkins had a different opinion than those being interviewed, perhaps because he was looking at a bigger picture. Privately, he said, "Judge Breen made the only decision he could, based on what he had to work with. He dropped the charges against Middleton so we could go after the Supreme Court on Frutiger. If he had let the murder charges stand at the District Court level, Middleton would have beat his conviction on appeal. Then we'd never get him because of double jeopardy. Judge Breen is a stud, and we now have more work to do in order to take advantage of the gift he just gave us."

Chapter 55:
Rock And Roll Time

It is said that the wheels of justice turn slowly, but this was not the case in the Nevada State Supreme Court ruling on the appeal of Judge Breen's decision to dismiss the murder charges against David Middleton. With speed that even surprised the District Attorney's office, the court ruled in favor of the prosecution and reinstated the murder charges against Middleton on July 25, 1996.

Some attribute the speedy decision to Viloria's gathering of expert witnesses and his excellent documentation of facts related to the involvement of criminal agencies in the deaths. Others say the court anticipated the appeal, and they were waiting to overturn what they knew to be a bad decision in the first place. Whatever the reason, Middleton was once again facing murder charges.

The State Supreme Court stopped short of reversing their entire decision on the Frutiger appeal, but they did say every case needed to be looked at on its own merit and corpus delicti should be based on any relevant evidence available. In the Frutiger case, the Court said the evidence used by the prosecution linked the suspect to the victim but not to his involvement in her death. They specifically cited that even though he was driving Peggy Poulter's car and using her credit cards, it did nothing to establish criminal agency being involved in her death.

The Court also cited the medical evidence presented by the defense in the Frutiger case. Peggy Poulter did have identifiable medical problems that could have caused death by natural causes. This was not the case with either Kathy Powel or Thelma Davilla because both women were reasonably healthy.

The State Supreme Court decision also clarified Judge Breen's opinion that he could not look at any evidence not offered by the bodies themselves in determining criminal agency. The Supreme Court decision read in part:

This conclusion is not mandated by our decision in Frutiger. The court must consider and weigh all evidence offered that bears on the question of death by the criminal agency. In this case, the circumstances of the disappearance of the women, the discoveries of their bodies in remote locations, tied with ropes, wrapped in garbage bags and bitten severely, clearly create a reasonable inference of criminal agency. Furthermore, unlike in Frutiger, where the weight of medical evidence indicated a likelihood of death by natural causes, in this case, there is no evidence to rebut the inference of death by criminal agency. The District Court erred in not considering at least the circumstances of the disappearances of the women and the discoveries of their bodies. There is ample evidence by those circumstances alone tending to prove that Powell and Davilla died by the criminal agency.

With respect to the question of the felony murder charges, we conclude that at the preliminary hearing, the State met its burden of proving corpus delicti for the two felony counts of kidnapping and murder during the commission of a felony.

We reverse the District Court's order granting the respondent's pretrial petition for a Writ of Habeas Corpus, and we remand this matter to the District Court for further proceedings. It will be up to the trial jury to weigh all relevant evidence presented and then conclude if corpus delicti has been met beyond a reasonable doubt.

Nev. 1996

Sheriff, Washoe County v. Middleton

112 Nev. 956, 921 P.2d 282

With that decision, the State Supreme Court was able to save face by not admitting they had erred in the Frutiger case while at the same time clarifying the facts of their ruling so they did not hinder future murder prosecutions. Also important was the State Supreme Court did not refer to any of the expert witness documentation Viloria had gathered for his appellate motion. They simply ruled that only probable cause of criminal agency and not proof beyond a reasonable doubt was needed at the preliminary hearing, and the State had met this burden of proof.

Since the expert witness evidence wasn't referenced in the decision, it was not yet divulged to the defense. Viloria could now keep that information to himself and bring it out only when needed. This was a major victory for the prosecution in general but especially for Tom Viloria. Not only did he go into the ring, the underdog, he beat the odds and came out on top.

It was a very happy Dick Gammick who called a press conference that afternoon to announce murder charges against David Middleton were being reinstated. He said, "We're back in business, and it's rock and roll time!"

Fred Pinkerton was much more subdued during his interview regarding the State Supreme Court decision. He said, "I try not to act emotionally in these things. My own reaction is the Supreme Court's decision is its decision, so now it's time to go to work." Pinkerton acknowledged his client might now face the death penalty but said he probably wouldn't go to trial for at least a year, and a lot could happen in that time.

Kathy Powell's brother Jeff acted as spokesperson to the press for his family and the family of Thelma Davilla. He said the families were elated the murder charges had been reinstated, and they were happy with the State Supreme Court ruling.

Bonnie and Walt Rice also expressed similar sentiments during a telephone interview. Bonnie added the only downside to the decision was now that Middleton was back on trial for murder in Reno, she feared the Montrose District Attorney would not file charges against him for murdering their daughter in Colorado. The authorities in Montrose were still taking a wait-and-see approach on the Buffy Rice-Donohue case.

The most moving interview came when a reporter from the *Reno Gazette-Journal* called Florida victim Alyssa Cervantes and asked her what she thought of the latest development. She said, "I feel a little bit more at ease. I was a little bit edgy when I found out they could drop the charges, and he could just walk away from everything. He ruined my life, and he practically walked away from what he did to me. It's really scary if you think about it. I thank God every day for the detectives in Reno who took that monster off the street, and I also pray to Him to give attorney Tom Viloria the strength and courage to make sure Middleton never goes free again."

The detectives and the prosecutor felt a bit guilty when they read that quote in the paper the next day. While Alyssa Cervantes was thanking God and praying for them, they were in various states of inebriation, sitting at a bar celebrating while they discussed how nice it would be if the court ruled Middleton could get death by suffocating inside of a refrigerator instead of by lethal injection. Then they thought about it and stopped feeling guilty at all. Like Douglas said, "Even the Big Man would understand that one."

Chapter 56:
Invisible Victims

At a hearing on Friday, August 30, 1996, Dick Gammick advised Judge Breen that the District Attorney's office would be seeking the death penalty for David Middleton. He based this decision on the aggravating circumstances of torture and depravity of mind.

Judge Breen set a trial date of May 5, 1997, but everyone knew this was not a realistic timeframe for the defense case preparation. They were now facing a capital murder case, and nine months would not be enough time to mount a defense in a case such as this. The police murder book alone totaled in excess of 2,500 pages, and that did not include evidentiary reports or expert witness testimony.

The prosecution's case was built mainly on circumstantial evidence, so the job of the defense would be to prevent as much of that as they could from being introduced in court. The way to do that was through pre-trial motions, and those took time. It was said from the start that this case would be won or lost long before the jury heard the first witness, so the pre-trial motions were the most important job of the defense and the prosecution.

Fred Pinkerton was one of Reno's top defense attorneys and no stranger to murder trials built on circumstantial evidence. In 1985, he represented former world-class skier Craig Holliday in a Reno case where he was accused of murdering his mother for her estate. The Holliday case was based largely on circumstantial evidence, and Pinkerton gained an acquittal for his client.

Pinkerton told a reporter, "I'm a trial lawyer, and a circumstantial case is a trial lawyer's dream. After you go through a couple of them, you learn a lot about presentation and analysis of evidence."

Pinkerton went back to the beginning of the case and started taking apart the prosecution's arguments one piece at a time. This meant Viloria would also have to go back to the beginning to defend the State's case. It was a time consuming process, but one that needed to be done in order to get a conviction.

The first motion Pinkerton submitted to the court was to sever the Davilla case from the Powell one and try them separately. He argued the joinder of the cases could prejudice his client, because the jury might cumulate the various crimes charged and find guilt when they might not do so if the crimes were tried separately. There was also a possibility the jury might develop feelings of hostility toward Middleton since they were hearing testimony about several crimes he was being charged with instead of one crime.

Even though this argument had been made at the Justice Court level, Judge Breen had to rule on it again for the trial court. After reading Viloria's briefs and hearing lengthy discussions from both sides, he ruled the joinder of the two cases was proper. The cases would be tried together and any further discussion on the matter could be taken up in appeals court should the case get to that level.

The next defense motion requested a change of venue for the trial based on pre-trial publicity. Pinkerton cited interviews done with the victim's families as well as the Maury Povich interviews done with the Rice's and Alyssa Cervantes. Viloria pointed out that Middleton himself had done a television interview with *Inside Addition* proclaiming his innocence, and a large part of the pre-trial publicity had come from his former defense attorney, Mike Speccio. The case already had achieved national news coverage, so moving it out of Reno would have no effect on the outcome whatsoever.

Judge Breen denied the change of venue request citing the fact modern electronic media would expose potential jurors to pre-trial publicity no matter where they moved the case. They would have to rely on their voir dire of the jurors and jury instruction to keep the publicity from having an effect on the trial.

The process dragged on at a snail's pace until the defense and prosecution found themselves still doing battle outside of the courtroom as the court date approached. On April 9, 1997, Pinkerton went to Judge Breen and asked for an extension on the trial date. There had been so many pre-trial motions that he and his staff were not prepared to go to trial in April. He blamed this partially on the fact that the District Attorney's office had just turned over an abundance of documentation that they allegedly *forgot* to give the defense during the initial discovery phase of the proceedings.

Judge Breen was not happy about the request, but he set a new trial date for August 11, 1997. He cautioned both the defense and the prosecution that this would be the last extension he would give, and the trial would start on that date regardless of whether or not they were ready.

The new court date was more than two years after the initial discovery of Kathy Powell's body. Witness testimony could be unreliable even if the events were fresh in their minds, but time caused people to forget certain things. A good defense attorney could make a witness who was completely credible right after an incident look like he was a liar in front of a jury if he became confused. Any contradiction in witness testimony, no matter how slight, could cause a reasonable doubt in the mind of a juror and end up with an acquittal or hung jury. Viloria was ready to go to trial, and he was even less happy with the postponement than the judge was.

He also wasn't happy with some of Judge Breen's rulings on the defense pre-trial motions. The court ruled the prosecution could not introduce any of Middleton's prior acts from his conviction in Florida or any of his allegations of police on-duty misconduct during the case-in-chief. This included the Santeria priest testimony and the ritualistic rape of the civilian police employee. The prior acts might be brought in during the penalty phase, but Judge Breen ruled Santeria was a religion protected under the First Amendment so Middleton's involvement in it could not be used against him.

Viloria moved to introduce the animal head voodoo dagger since it had been found in Middleton's storage shed and was possibly used in the commission of the crimes he was being charged with. Pinkerton objected, saying this was a tool used in the Santeria religion, so it was also protected by the First Amendment. After more lengthy debate, Judge Breen ruled a photo of the dagger could be introduced into evidence, but the longhorn at the end of the animal skull handle would have to be cut from the photo.

Viloria relented to the judge's decision, but the horn was what he wanted to get in front of the jury since this is what Middleton allegedly used to anally rape his victim in Florida. He was confident he would have been able to steer the testimony about the dagger to that crime if he could get in front of the jury, but he now lost that option.

Judge Breen also ruled that no testimony or evidence related to the Buffy Rice-Donohue murder could be introduced during the trial. Since Middleton had been neither charged nor convicted in that crime, anything related to it could not be used against him. If the Montrose Police had at least charged him with the murder, Viloria might have been able to introduce evidence showing prior bad acts. Middleton was not even listed as a suspect in that case, so he had the right to claim innocence until proven guilty.

The one major battle Viloria won was Pinkerton's motion to deny Bonnie and Walt Rice access to the court proceedings. They still wore the buttons with Buffy's photo on them every time they showed up in court, and Pinkerton said this would prejudice the jury since Middleton had not been charged in that crime. Judge Breen had already denied a defense motion to keep the press out of the courtroom since this was an open proceeding. He cited the same precedent and denied the request to keep the Rice's out of the courtroom. As long as they did not disrupt the proceedings, they had the right to be there.

Viloria wasn't concerned with the presence of Bonnie and Walt Rice influencing the jury because he knew it wouldn't. He knew he was going to get a guilty verdict no matter who was sitting in the courtroom. He wanted Bonnie and Walt Rice in that courtroom because, in their eyes, David Middleton was being tried for three murders—not two. The third victim Middleton was on trial for murdering would be invisible to the jurors, but would be seen clearly through the eyes of her family, and the man who was prosecuting her killer.

Chapter 57:
Squeak

Jury selection began at precisely 9:00 A.M. on the morning of Monday, August 11, 1997. During the trial phase, a defendant is allowed to dress in a manner that does not make him look guilty in the eyes of the jury, so Middleton's attorney supplied him with an appropriate outfit. He wore a dark blue suit, white shirt, and blue and red striped tie. His curly hair was pulled into a ponytail, and he wore gold wire-rimmed glasses. He looked more like an attorney than a murderer as he sat at the defense table—except very few attorneys wore a belly chain and handcuffs under their suit coats.

Webster defined the word *peer* as a person of equal standing, so to say Middleton would be tried by a jury of his peers would be a euphemism. In order to make the statement correct, the jury would have to be made up of twelve sociopath serial killers who just happened to be pathological liars in addition to their other attributes.

Nevertheless, by the end of the day, a jury agreed upon by both the defense and the prosecution had been selected to hear the case. The panel consisted of six males and six females. Two of the women were African American, and one of the males was Hispanic. An African American male and an Asian female were also selected as alternates. This diverse group proportionately reflected the demographics of the area.

Before jury selection began Judge Breen cautioned the prospective jurors that the case would probably last at least two weeks, and much of the testimony and evidence offered during the trial would be graphic. He also informed them the District Attorney's office had filed an intent to seek the death penalty if Middleton was convicted, so the jurors would be ruling on that issue, too. The fourteen people ultimately selected as jurors agreed to stay in for the long run.

The trial began at 9:00 the next morning when Viloria presented his opening arguments to the jury. Dressed in an impeccably pressed grey pinstriped suit and crisp white shirt, Viloria stood in front of the jury box and outlined the prosecution's case for the twelve people who would ultimately decide David Middleton's fate.

He told the jurors the defense would be trying to convince them Kathy Powell and Thelma Davilla both died of natural causes that had

250

nothing to do with David Middleton. He then assured them that by the time the prosecution completed its case, there would be no doubt in any of their minds that both women would be alive and well had Middleton never crossed their paths.

Viloria admitted the prosecution's case was made up of mainly circumstantial and forensic evidence. He said the reason for this was the only other type of evidence available was eyewitness testimony, and Middleton had made sure none of that existed. There were only three people who knew exactly what happened to Kathy Powell and Thelma Davilla. Two of them were dead, and the other wasn't talking. Viloria assured the jurors that by the time he finished laying out all of the State's evidence, there would be no doubt in their minds David Middleton caused the deaths of Kathy Powell and Thelma Davilla.

When it was Pinkerton's turn to address the jury, he told them the State built their case on nothing but pure conjecture in an attempt to pin two unsolved deaths on Middleton. He said they would hear testimony backed up by expert witnesses that Kathy Powell's death wasn't a homicide. And no one had *any* idea how Thelma Davilla died because her body yielded no evidence.

Pinkerton said the defense did not condone the actions Middleton took after discovering Kathy Powell had died, and they would stipulate to the fact he made a mistake by disposing of her body in the manner he did. But that mistake did not constitute the crime of murder or any other crime currently written into statute. He then alleged the charges related to Davilla's death were nothing more than a matter of the police finding a scapegoat already in custody to close the case with.

As to the charges relating to the Good Guys case, Pinkerton told the jurors the police already had a suspect in custody for that. He said the defense would show Middleton was guilty of nothing more than using poor judgment and putting trust in the woman he loved. Pinkerton's last statement caused Bonnie Rice to grimace as if a foul odor just entered the room.

At 10:00 A.M., Viloria called Officer Pat Dreelan as the first witness for the prosecution. Dreelan described in great detail every aspect of his dumpster-diving adventure the night Kathy Powell's body was discovered. Viloria asked his witness how he could so vividly remember the incident in such great detail more than two years after the fact. Officer Dreelan stated under oath that he still had nightmares about finding Kathy Powell, so remembering that night was all too easy for him. The defense declined to cross-examine.

Detective Dave Jenkins was the next witness to take the stand. The jury did not get to hear testimony regarding the original incriminating statement Middleton made to Jenkins during his first interview. The defense had won a motion to keep the spontaneous statement Middleton made about possibly having knowledge of Kathy Powell's death out of court since it was their opinion Miranda Rights should have been given to him before he was physically taken to the Police Records section that day.

But Jenkins *was* allowed to testify to everything else he did during the investigation, and his testimony alone seemed like it would be enough to convict Middleton. Several jurors shook their heads in disgust when Jenkins told of Middleton's statement that he found Kathy Powell bound and dead when he returned to her apartment after going to the store to buy liquor. Middleton didn't seem to notice the jurors' looks of disbelief because he never made eye contact with them throughout the proceedings.

Viloria led Jenkins' testimony to the discovery of the storage shed just before court was about to recess for the day. The timing of the testimony relating to the discovery of the torture chamber and the refrigerator was carefully planned by the prosecutor so the imagery would remain with the jurors throughout the night and become ingrained in their subconscious. What happened next was *not* planned, but since Viloria was known to have a flare for dramatics at trial, everyone who knew him swore it was.

The Judge ruled that the prosecution could have the refrigerator brought into the courtroom so Viloria could show it to the jury. The photos introduced at the preliminary hearing of the demonstration using the forensic investigator inside of the refrigerator to reenact Kathy Powell's body position were already on display in the courtroom along with the other crime scene photos. But the refrigerator itself would be the most compelling piece of evidence introduced by the prosecution.

An evidence technician was standing by in a storage room down the hall from the courtroom with the refrigerator loaded onto a wooden dolly. The dolly was the type used by furniture movers and was nothing more than a carpeted wooden rectangle with a plastic coaster-type wheel mounted on each corner. The bailiff phoned the evidence technician to tell him they were ready for the refrigerator, and the courtroom was deathly quiet as everyone waited for its arrival.

An eerie sound could be heard in the distance as everyone in the courtroom turned their attention to the doors leading to the hallway. The sound was faint at first but grew steadily louder by the second. It was a rhythmic staccato sound of *eak, eak, eak.* Ordinarily, the sound probably wouldn't have attracted much attention, but in a silent courtroom filled with murder photos and stories of death, the noise was almost as frightening as the man seated at the defense table himself.

The noise seemed almost deafening by the time the evidence technician wheeled the refrigerator into the courtroom, and it was then the origin of the sound was discovered. One of the wheels on the dolly was badly in need of lubrication, and the steady squeaking noise drew even more attention to the refrigerator of death as it was brought to the front of the courtroom.

One of the jurors later said the most memorable part of the trial for him was that steady *eak, eak, eak* as the refrigerator was wheeled into the courtroom. He said it was almost as if Kathy Powell was calling to them from her place in the afterlife.

The squeaky wheel was probably nothing more than a coincidence, but unfortunately, cops don't believe in coincidences. Tom Viloria became a legend in police folklore that day, because by the time the story made its way to the cop watering holes that night there was no coincidence about it. The story of a young prosecutor sitting in a darkened aisle of a Home Depot the night before trial, searching through racks of wooden dollies until he found one with just the right squeak would live forever. Viloria never admitted having anything to do with the squeaky wheel—but he never denied it either.

Chapter 58:
Don't Cheat The Hangman

The prosecution finished the direct examination of Dave Jenkins at 10:00 A.M. on Thursday, August 14, 1997. After hearing two full days of testimony from Jenkins, the jury had a good understanding of why the deaths of Kathy Powell and Thelma Davilla were investigated as homicides, how they were linked together and attributed to one suspect, and how that suspect came to be identified as David Middleton.

During cross-examination, the defense hammered Jenkins on the marathon interview and made allegations that the only reason Middleton talked to the police at all was that he was promised he would not be charged with murder. Jenkins remained poised and confident during this cross-examination. He assured the court the interview was purely voluntary, no promises were made and it was ended as soon as Middleton said he didn't want to talk to them anymore. He then added that Middleton really didn't tell them anything helpful to the investigation during the interview anyway.

The defense then changed course and asked Jenkins if the police had ever explored the possibility that a third person was involved in the murder of Kathy Powell. The inference was that Middleton was telling the truth about returning to Powell's apartment and finding her dead, but the police were so focused on him that they did not investigate the involvement of another person in the murder.

Jenkins simply stated that once they identified Middleton as a suspect, the evidence they gathered was so overwhelming that it would have been a waste of resources to look anywhere else. There were no further questions, and Jenkins was excused from the witness stand.

Viloria spent the next day and a half bringing detectives, crime scene technicians, and forensic investigators to the stand to testify about their involvement in the investigation. By the time court recessed for the weekend at 4:30 P.M. on Friday, August 15, 1997, all of the forensic evidence linking Middleton to the two murders had been introduced.

The jury was not sequestered, but Judge Breen instructed them not to talk about the case or pay attention to any publicity generated by it. Given the amount of news coverage the trial was getting, that was akin to telling a child not to look under the tree on Christmas morning.

The court reconvened at 9:00 in the morning on Monday, August 18, 1997. The jury first heard testimony from the two Good Guys employees who completed the transaction where Kathy Powell's credit card was used. The fact that Evonne Haley had already been found guilty of using Middleton's truck to pick up the stereo equipment was allowed into testimony since her case was already adjudicated. Pinkerton also did not fall prey to the trap his predecessor landed in by questioning whether a salesperson who talks to hundreds of people a day on the phone could tell whether the caller was a man or a woman, so neither witness was cross-examined.

Viloria then began calling his expert witnesses to the stand. The first to testify was John "J.J." Van Tassel of the Royal Canadian Mounted Police. None of the jurors had ever seen a Mounty in person, and they seemed a bit disappointed when Van Tassel walked into court wearing a dark blue business suit instead of a red serge uniform and black riding boots. Their disappointment ended after Van Tassel took the stand and recited his resume to the court.

In addition to offering testimony on knots in several Canadian cases, Van Tassel had just returned from Boulder, Colorado, where he assisted investigators by examining knots in the John Bennett Ramsey murder case. That case was at the forefront of every American newspaper, so the fact Van Tassel had been called in to help on it lent more credence to his testimony in the Middleton trial.

Viloria used a PowerPoint projector to display photos of the knots tied in the ropes used to bind Kathy Powell and the ropes found on the remains of Thelma Davilla. Van Tassel patiently explained the similarities in all of the knots and how he could tell the victims had been struggling against the ropes. The jury seemed mesmerized by the testimony as Van Tassel's explanation made the knots almost seem to come alive before them. The effective display of knot imagery was more Viloria theatrics—and it worked.

Pinkerton only asked Van Tassel two questions during cross-examination. Could Van Tassel tell if all the knots he examined were tied by the same person, and could he tell if any of the knots were tied by David Middleton? Van Tassel answered no to both questions and Pinkerton said he had nothing further for the witness.

Since Viloria had anticipated this line of questioning, he asked Van Tassel on re-direct questioning just what he could tell about the person who tied the knots. It was then that Van Tassel introduced his testimony about a person's frenzied state of mind reverting to the knot he was most familiar with and the feelings of euphoria a killer might get each time he tied that knot. These statements coming from the world's foremost and possibly *only* knot expert were damaging to Middleton, and the look on Pinkerton's face said he knew he'd made a mistake by opening the line of questioning.

The next witness called to the stand by the prosecution was Dr. Vincent Di Maio. After being sworn in, Dr. Di Maio told the jury that in addition to being the Chief Medical Examiner in San Antonio, Texas, he was also a consultant in forensic pathology. Dr. Di Maio said he had personally performed roughly two thousand autopsies and had been offering expert testimony in cause-of-death cases for five years.

Viloria then asked Dr. Di Maio what his opinion was on the cause and manner of the deaths of Kathy Powell and Thelma Davilla. Dr. Di Maio said, "Based on all the evidence I have examined in these two cases, if the deaths would have occurred in my jurisdiction, the causes of death would have been listed as undetermined, and the manner of death would be a homicide. I feel the method of death for Ms. Powell was asphyxia, most probably due to suffocation."

When asked about the method of death for Thelma Davilla, Dr. Di Maio said, "In view of the circumstance surrounding her death and the fashion in which her body was found, it is my opinion this death was also a homicide. Due to the condition of the body, I could not go any further with the manner of death. Knowing what happened to Ms. Powell suggests that Ms. Davilla was also asphyxiated, but I would not be able to rule out shooting or stabbing either."

Dr. Di Maio's last statement weighed heavily on the jurors. They had already been shown photos of two guns and the voodoo machete—minus the menacing horn, of course—that were taken from Middleton's storage shed. Viloria didn't have to convince the jurors *how* Middleton killed his victims, only that he *did* kill them. The fact he had now shown the jurors three possible scenarios involving the manner of Thelma Davilla's death greatly strengthened his case.

The defense elected not to cross-examine Dr. Di Maio since they would be calling expert witnesses of their own to refute his testimony. Judge Breen then recessed the court for lunch, but before the trial resumed in the afternoon, the bailiff brought him a note from the jury foreman. The note said the jurors were somewhat confused by the description of the area where Thelma Davilla's remains were found, and they requested a site visit before they heard any further testimony.

The judge granted the request, but since Middleton and his attorneys had the right to be present during the site survey, it would take time to put the trip together. The court was adjourned for the day, and all parties were told to meet at the courthouse at 9:00 the next morning for the trip to the site. Due to safety concerns, he advised the attorneys of this in his chambers so the press and public would not know about it. He also placed a gag order on this particular part of the proceedings until the trip was completed.

At 9:00 A.M. on Tuesday, August 19, 1997, the twelve jurors and two alternates were loaded onto a chartered bus for their twenty-five-mile ride to the gravesite. Armed deputies were placed in the seats directly in front of and behind the jurors for security. Judge Breen, along with the defense and prosecution attorneys, rode in the front of the bus. Two marked sheriff's cars, each carrying four heavily armed S.W.A.T. officers, were used as escorts in front of and behind the bus.

A sheriff's van with blacked-out windows and a heavy mesh screen separating the driver and passenger compartments trailed the motorcade. The van was driven by another S.W.A.T. officer, and his partner sat in the passenger seat with a twelve-gauge shotgun cradled in his lap. Middleton rode in the back seat of the van with Dave Jenkins and John Douglas sitting on either side of him. Sitting in the seat directly behind Middleton was Eddie Dixon, dressed in black Reno P.D. S.W.A.T. fatigues with a C.A.R.- 15 assault rifle hanging from his neck in a tactical sling.

Detective Larry Canfield was waiting for the jurors when the bus and escort vehicles pulled up Dog Valley Road and stopped at the location where Thelma Davilla was found. It was a bright, sunny morning, and the temperature was already hovering around ninety degrees. The Sheriff's S.W.A.T. team ringed the perimeter of the area for security as Detective Canfield led the judge and jurors on a tour of the site.

Middleton stood in the shade underneath a group of trees with Jenkins, Douglas, and Dixon, watching the jurors examine the area. Middleton was allowed to dress in a suit for the trip since he would be visible to the jurors. His hands were cuffed to the belly chain under his jacket, but the judge agreed with the defense team that, for appearance reasons, the police could not use ankle cuffs on him.

257

At one point, Middleton looked over his left shoulder away from the activity and toward the glistening Truckee River running through the valley below them. Eddie Dixon patted his C.A.R.-15 and said, "Please don't think about running, Mr. Middleton. I'm too old and out of shape to chase you, and I'd hate to cheat the hangman."

Middleton turned and smiled his evil grin at Dixon, but the smile quickly faded when he saw Evidence Eddie had a look in his eyes that scared even the devil himself. There was no doubt in his mind a morning run would not be in his plans for the day.

Chapter 59:
Rest

The field trip to the Verdi dump site set the trial back one full day. When the court reconvened at 9:00 A.M. on Wednesday, August 20, 1997, Viloria told Judge Breen the prosecution had only four witnesses left to testify. He then called Dr. Louis Patetta as his first witness of the day.

Dr. Patetta was the orthodontist who took the dental impression of Middleton. He testified that he took the mold after Detectives Jenkins and Douglas brought Middleton to his Reno office with a seizure order. He said he personally took the impression and subsequently turned it over to Forensic Dentist Raymond Rawson.

The only questions the defense had for Dr. Patetta were regarding the chain of custody for the dental impression. Once that was established, the witness was excused.

The next prosecution witness was Dr. Rawson, who testified that he examined the bite marks found on Kathy Powell's torso and later matched them to the dental impression taken from David Middleton. Viloria used his PowerPoint projector to display a large color photo of the bite mark to Kathy Powell's left breast on the screen in front of the courtroom. Blood and bruising could be clearly seen in and around the teeth marks in the photo.

Because of the bleeding Dr. Rawson said he could tell the victim was still alive when she was bitten. He then told the jury that the depth of the teeth marks and the bruising meant the victim would have been in a great deal of pain when she was bitten.

Viloria asked Dr. Rawson if in his opinion a bite such as that would have caused a person to scream in pain. The defense objection to the question was overruled, and Dr. Rawson said a person would definitely scream in pain if they were bitten with the force used to cause the bite mark in question.

Viloria then asked Dr. Rawson if in his opinion a scream such as that would be stifled if the victim had been gagged with a rubber ball in her mouth. This time Judge Breen sustained the defense objection to the question being speculative. Viloria withdrew the question, but it still hung in the air as plain as the blue rubber ball gag displayed on the evidence table.

Dr. Rawson next testified that when he examined the bite he could tell it was caused by a person with a distinctive under bite. He was provided with a dental X-ray from Middleton and noted he did in fact have a distinctive under bite. When he was subsequently provided Middleton's dental impression he matched it to the bite and concluded it was caused by David Middleton. He said his observations were further confirmed through the DNA match to Middleton based on the saliva found around the bite mark.

What the prosecutor did next was the epitome of Tom Viloria's theatrical productions. With the push of a button on the PowerPoint remote, a set of winged teeth came flying slowly into the photo displayed on the screen. The teeth made chomping motions as the red wings mounted on them quickly fluttered and carried them toward their final destination. The last chomp was when the teeth bit down firmly on Kathy Powell's left breast and came to rest perfectly, matching the bite mark. Viloria simply said, "I have no further questions for this witness."

An act like that would be impossible to follow, so the defense declined to cross-examine Dr. Rawson, and he was excused. The next witness called by the prosecution was Professor Tariq Ahmed from the U.N.R. Engineering School. Professor Ahmed cut an impressive figure as he strode through the crowded courtroom toward the witness stand. He was dressed in a grey pinstriped suit, and his curly hair was trimmed short and impeccably groomed.

After Professor Ahmed was sworn in, he walked the jurors through his calculations on oxygen flow and human respiration. Viloria displayed PowerPoint photos of the calculations as the witness spoke, and Dr. Ahmed was able to break everything down into layman's terms for them. He finalized the report with the most important calculation of all—Kathy Powell would suffocate if held in that refrigerator for more than five and one-half hours.

On cross-examination, Pinkerton asked the professor how accurate his estimation of five and one-half hours was. Professor Ahmed's answer was honest and genuine. He said he was one hundred percent certain this estimate was correct because he believed the victim would have actually died within three and one-half hours since the holes drilled in the refrigerator were so small. He said he calculated the equations based on the best-case scenario in order to give Mr. Middleton the benefit of the doubt, but since Ms. Powell was obviously struggling to get out of the refrigerator, her oxygen use would have been greatly increased.

Middleton had just been shot down by a round fired from an engineer's calculator—not from a cop's gun. Every juror now had the picture of Kathy Powell desperately trying to scratch and kick her way out of the refrigerator while gulping down the last precious breaths of fetid air available to her inside of the coffin Middleton placed her in. It was a gruesome image, but exactly the one Viloria wanted them to take into deliberations with them.

Professor Ahmed was excused, and Viloria called his last witness to the stand. Detective John Douglas testified to the dates and times Middleton visited his storage shed after Kathy Powell disappeared. Using the timeline retrieved from the storage facility security system, they determined there was a twelve-hour gap between Middleton's visits to the shed from Saturday, February 4, 1995, to Sunday, February 5, 1995. It had been proven that Kathy Powell was alive inside the refrigerator at some point, so based on Dr. Ahmed's calculations, there was no way she could have survived that twelve-hour time span.

Having Douglas testify to this instead of one of the other detectives was another calculated decision by Viloria. Not only was Douglas a believable and likable witness, but he was also an African American. Since the summation witness for the prosecution was the same race as the defendant, the defense would look foolish if they tried to insinuate racial issues were involved in the case.

The defense asked Douglas some perfunctory questions about the accuracy of the security clock, but since the self-calibrating system proved to be functioning properly, this was a moot issue. After Douglas was excused Viloria told Judge Breen the prosecution was resting their case. But the case was the only thing that rested that night because the trial was far from over.

Chapter 60:
House Of Cards

The prosecution had done a good job laying a nasty trail of evidence leading toward Middleton's involvement in the deaths of Kathy Powell and Thelma Davilla. Pinkerton had only one option available to him when it came time to present his case. He had to attack the manner of death because if he could raise doubt about criminal agency, all the evidence the prosecution had presented would be meaningless.

The court was back in session at 9:00 A.M. on Thursday, August 21, 1997. Middleton himself was not on the defense witness list as testifying on his own behalf. Before the jury was brought into the courtroom, Judge Breen asked him if he wished to testify.

Middleton replied, "I really do want to testify, but just on the Davilla case part of it. But I guess I can't because the cases are joined. I can't testify to one without looking bad on the other, so I guess I just can't testify at all."

With Middleton's response read into the record, Judge Breen had the jury come in and ask the defense to call their first witness. Pinkerton called Dr. Robert Bucklin to the stand. Dr. Bucklin was a deputy medical examiner for Clark County, Nevada, and an expert in forensic pathology. He testified that after examining Powell's autopsy results, he found she suffered from heart disease, and this could have contributed to her death. He said he did not think she died of asphyxiation.

On cross-examination, Viloria asked Dr. Bucklin if he was one hundred percent certain Kathy Powell did not die from asphyxiation. He answered no, but it was his opinion the chances were extremely remote. Viloria next asked if struggling to get free from a confined space while gasping for air in an environment with limited oxygen could exacerbate a person's heart condition. The witness answered in that scenario, a heart condition could definitely be worsened, but he could not say if that was actually what happened.

The next witness called by the defense was a psychiatrist named Dr. Jerry Howle. He testified that since lithium was found in Kathy Powell's system during autopsy, it could have been a contributing factor in her death. He said lithium could cause cardiac arrhythmia and carried some risk of sudden death.

When it was Viloria's turn to question the witness, he asked Dr. Howle if he was familiar with a 1991 study by the American Heart Association that found long-term users of lithium did not die from heart disease at a greater rate than the general public. Dr. Howle said he was familiar with that study, but it was his experience a person should get an E.K.G. test done before they started taking lithium. Since Kathy Powell did not do this, there was still a possibility that taking lithium contributed to her death.

After Dr. Howle was finished testifying the defense rested their case. Judge Breen recessed the court for lunch and told the attorneys to be ready to present their closing arguments to the jury at 2:00 that afternoon.

Viloria thought it was a good move on Pinkerton's part to keep his defense simple. Manner of death had been the weak point of the case from its inception, so attacking that was a sound course of action. All the defense needed to do was raise doubt about the manner of Kathy Powell's death to have them find Middleton not guilty on the murder charge.

Viloria knew all along if he lost Powell the rest of the case would come tumbling down like a house made of playing cards. He rolled the dice when he decided to fight the manner of death issue, and now he stood a good chance of losing everything. He always had the Good Guys case to fall back on so Middleton wouldn't walk away totally free, but the most he'd get for that crime was five years in prison.

There was no time to think about that because, in two hours, he would have to present a summation of the most important case he had ever been involved in to the twelve people who would decide Middleton's fate. As he read through his notes one last time, the photo of Buffy Rice-Donohue propped up on his cluttered desk reminded him there were more people depending on him than just those in the courtroom. It was time to head back into the ring for the final round.

Chapter 61:
Stringing Pearls

Prosecuting a case built almost entirely on circumstantial evidence is akin to a jeweler crafting a fine necklace out of individual pearls. Each piece of evidence laid out in front of the jury is like a pearl gently placed on the black felt covering the jeweler's work table. The closing argument is the braided gold strand that runs through the pearls and pulls them all together to form the finished product.

When Viloria finished his closing arguments at 4:00 that afternoon, everyone in the courtroom could see that he was the equivalent of a master jeweler. He took each piece of evidence in chronological order and pulled them together in a way that convinced his listeners there was no way the deaths of Kathy Powell and Thelma Davilla were anything *but* brutally sadistic murders.

Viloria's last statement to the jurors was the gold clasp that would hold his necklace in place, and hopefully win a guilty verdict for Middleton. He said, "Kathy Powell did not tie herself up and place herself in that refrigerator, just like Thelma Davilla did not bind and bury herself in that field you walked through. The manner in which these women died would suggest the involvement of criminal agency to any reasonable person, and I see twelve reasonable persons seated before me.

Your job is to decide proof beyond a reasonable doubt of criminal agency—not what the exact means of that criminal agency was. Kathy Powell and Thelma Davilla call to you from their graves with that proof, and with the proof of who that criminal agent was. Thank you."

After Viloria took his seat at the prosecution table, his most memorable event of the trial occurred. Middleton turned and looked at Viloria from his seat at the defense table and gave him the thumbs-up sign. He then mouthed the words, "You got me."

There was not enough time left in the day for the defense to present their closing arguments, so Judge Breen recessed the court for the day. At 9:00 A.M. on Friday, August 22, 1997, Fred Pinkerton took his turn summing up the defense case for the jury. It was his job to pull apart the necklace Viloria built the day before and send the pearls scattering in different directions before the jury left for deliberations. It was a job he had done many times before and one he did very well.

Pinkerton started out with the Thelma Davilla case. He said the prosecution did not present one single witness at trial who could positively establish a link between David Middleton and Thelma Davilla. He reminded the jurors they heard testimony from two witnesses who said they had seen Davilla with a woman who resembled Middleton's girlfriend, and there was possibly an African American man with her on one of these occasions. But at no time did anyone ever point a finger at Middleton and say, "I saw *that* man with *that* woman."

As to the cause and manner of death for Thelma Davilla, Pinkerton emphasized there was none—because there was no way to determine it. There were several explanations on how Thelma Davilla could have died and came to be buried in that field, but the police did not explore any of them. Likewise, the police did not explore any of the myriad possibilities about how evidence from Thelma Davilla ended up in Middleton's storage shed.

The reason for this was the police had already focused on Middleton because of his involvement with Kathy Powell. They became oblivious to the fact they were dealing with two separate cases and made the mistake of investigating them as one case with two victims. Because of this, they possibly missed important clues and evidence that would have led them to the real story behind Thelma Davilla's death.

Pinkerton then moved on to Kathy Powell. He said there was a very simple solution for how Kathy Powell ended up inside that dumpster on the night of February 11, 1995. He said the reason it was simple was that Middleton himself already told it to the police.

Pinkerton said, "Mr. Middleton admitted to having kinky sex with Kathy Powell, but the sex was consensual. We've already heard testimony that Ms. Powell was not a well-woman, and we know that at some time, while she was with Mr. Middleton, she expired.

"The defense does not condone the fact that Mr. Middleton admittedly panicked and hid Kathy Powell's body. We certainly do not agree with his decision to eventually dispose of her body in a dumpster either. But you are here to decide whether Mr. Middleton is guilty of *murder*, not to judge the sexual acts of two consenting adults or the poor decision Mr. Middleton made after Kathy Powell expired."

In his summation, Pinkerton told the jurors that without the Kathy Powell case being classified as a murder, the Thelma Davilla case would have been listed as nothing more than a suspicious death. He said the prosecution did not establish proof beyond a reasonable doubt that Kathy Powell's death was a murder, and their entire theory in the Davilla case was built around the fact that it was. Lastly, he reminded the jurors it wasn't the defense's job to prove a murder didn't occur—it was the prosecution's job to prove one *did* occur. Pinkerton then thanked the jury and took his seat next to Middleton.

After a fifteen-minute recess, Judge Breen began his jury instructions. He told the jury it was now time for them to review all of the supporting evidence presented in this case and make their determination whether guilt beyond a reasonable doubt had been proven by the prosecution. Since there were multiple charges stemming from two different cases, it was their responsibility to address them separately and determine guilt or innocence for each crime charged.

The judge also reminded the jurors they had heard much conflicting testimony during the trial and gave them instructions on how to deal with this. Citing a Nevada Supreme Court ruling titled *Bolden v. State,* he told the jurors it is up to them to determine the credibility of the evidence and what weight to give it when deciding on guilt or innocence. When Judge Breen was through with his instructions, he excused the jury to begin their deliberations and adjourned the court for the day.

Viloria stopped to talk to Bonnie and Walt Rice before leaving the courtroom. They told him he was doing a great job, and they were confident the jury would rule in favor of the prosecution. They said they were remaining in Reno until the verdict was reached and asked Viloria if he would call them if he heard anything.

Walt Rice then told him a prosecutor from Montrose had sat through his closing arguments, but they didn't want to distract him by telling him sooner. There was still no word about whether Middleton would be charged in Colorado for Buffy's murder, but they weren't holding much hope the authorities in Montrose would change their minds.

As Viloria walked to his office, he wished he was as confident as the Rice's that the jury would find Middleton guilty. Pinkerton had fought a clean fight while defending Middleton, but he also put up some good arguments that might interject reasonable doubt into the jury's thought process. It only took one juror to wreak havoc during deliberations, and a hung jury was just as good as a not-guilty verdict for the defense.

Prosecuting the case for a second time due to a hung jury would be far too costly, so the charges would have to be amended to exclude murder if that were to happen. Viloria would consider anything less than a guilty verdict a loss, and he'd already decided to walk away from the case if that were to happen.

Although the jury was not sequestered during the trial, they would be during the deliberation phase. Deliberations would go through the weekend if needed, but Viloria and everyone else following the case hoped it wouldn't go that long. The common rule of thumb was the longer the jury deliberated, the better the charge of acquittal. As Viloria locked up his office for the day, he had the feeling it was going to be a long weekend.

Chapter 62:
The Knockout Punch

Deliberations went on through the weekend as the jurors quietly discussed the case inside a locked conference room on the second floor of the Washoe County Courthouse. On four different occasions during their first day of deliberations, they sent the bailiff to retrieve articles of evidence and evidentiary photos related to the case so they could review them.

On the second day they sent word to Judge Breen asking him to clarify a point of law dealing with the two-pronged test for criminal agency. When Viloria heard that, he became even more nervous than he had been at the beginning of deliberations. The fact the jury needed clarification on *any* point of law was never a good sign for the prosecution.

Each day, lunch and dinner were brought to the jurors in the conference room, and they deliberated straight through until 8:00 P.M. At that time, they were escorted to their rooms at a local hotel and then returned to the jury room at 9:00 the following morning.

By Sunday night, Viloria heard unofficially that the jurors were close to a decision. They had nearly deadlocked at one point but had now apparently worked through their problems and supposedly would have a decision sometime the next morning. Viloria shared the news with the task force detectives, and they all spent their third long sleepless night since the trial had ended.

On Monday, August 26, 1997, at 9:00 A.M., Jenkins and Douglas joined Viloria in his office and anxiously awaited news of the jury's verdict. They all cleared their calendars for the day so they would be free to go to the courtroom when the jury announced they were ready. On the outside, the three men appeared calm and collected as they waited for the news, but every time Viloria's phone rang they all practically jumped out of their chairs with anticipation.

At 11:00 the call came through that the jury had reached a decision. Judge Breen would convene court at 2:00 in the afternoon so the jury could announce their verdict. Calls were made to the other task force members as well as the victim's families to tell them the verdict had been reached. They did not have to call the Rice's because they were patiently waiting in the courtroom cafeteria for word about the jury deliberations.

The courtroom was packed with spectators and reporters by 2:00, and everyone rose to their feet when Judge Breen entered the room. After he took his seat at the bench and everyone else was seated, the jury was led into the courtroom. The calmest person in the room appeared to be David Middleton as he smiled and nodded at the jurors. He looked more like a man greeting people at a social function than someone who was waiting to hear his fate.

Judge Breen looked at the jurors and asked, "Mr. Foreman, has the jury reached a verdict?"

The jury foreman was a forty-six-year-old postal worker who looked much more pale and tired than he did when he was last in court the previous Friday. He stood and answered, "Yes, Your Honor, we have."

The foreman gave a sealed envelope to the bailiff, who then walked to the bench and handed it to Judge Breen. The courtroom was silent as the judge tore open the envelope and quietly read the paper inside of it. After a moment, he looked at Middleton and said, "Will the defendant please rise?"

Middleton and Pinkerton slowly stood up and faced the judge's bench. It was so quiet Viloria swore he could hear his heart pounding as he waited for the judge to announce the verdict. Finally, Judge Breen said, "In regard to count number one, this jury has found the defendant, David Stephen Middleton, *guilty* of the first-degree murder of Katherine Powell."

A loud chorus of cheers erupted from the courtroom, and Judge Breen waited until the crowd quieted before continuing. Viloria's head was spinning, and he almost didn't hear the judge say, "Regarding count number two, this jury also finds the defendant *guilty* of the first-degree murder of Thelma Davilla."

And that was the last thing Viloria heard. Judge Breen had to quiet the crowd by threatening to clear the courtroom, but even after the noise settled, Viloria could only hear two things in his head. *The jury finds the Defendant guilty of the first-degree murder of Katherine Powell and guilty of the first-degree murder of Thelma Davilla.*

When all was said and done the jury had found Middleton guilty of every crime he was charged with. He now faced sentencing on two counts of first-degree murder, two counts of first-degree kidnapping, one count of grand larceny, and one count of fraudulent use of a credit card. Viloria had won the fight with a knockout.

Middleton remained standing and showed no emotion as the judge polled the jurors to make sure the verdicts he read were correct. After the polling was complete, he dismissed the jury and told them to return at 9:00 the next morning for the penalty phase. He thanked them for what was certainly a difficult job and told them he would not keep them sequestered during the penalty phase.

Judge Breen then dismissed the court, and the escort deputies flanked Middleton as he stood motionless with his head held low at the defense table. He was then led out of the courtroom, looking more like a beaten dog than the devil incarnate.

The families of Kathy Powell, Thelma Davilla, and Buffy Rice-Donohue stood silently with their heads bowed while they thanked whatever God they prayed to that Middleton had been found guilty. Viloria was swarmed by the task force detectives who congratulated him while escorting him through the group of reporters waiting for interviews. He wasn't in this for the glory, so the interviews would be left up to the district attorney.

When Douglas suggested a celebration was in order, Viloria replied, "Maybe just a small one. The hard part starts tomorrow, and I've still got work to do."

Chapter 63:
The Old Rag

During the penalty phase the prosecution would be able to introduce some of Middleton's prior criminal acts and put family members on the stand to testify to victim impact. Viloria planned to put relatives of both Kathy Powell and Thelma Davilla on the stand. He also made arrangements for Alyssa Cervantes to fly to Reno from Florida to testify about the crimes Middleton committed against her when she was sixteen.

Viloria also petitioned the court to allow him to introduce evidence from the Colorado investigation of Middleton's involvement in the Buffy Rice-Donohue case and his alleged rape of the civilian employee when he was a Miami cop. The witness lists for the prosecution and the defense, as well as any motions before the court, would have to be discussed outside the presence of the jury. Even though the jurors reported at 9:00 A.M. on Tuesday, August 27, 1997, it was highly doubtful they would hear a word of testimony until later that afternoon.

Since this was a death penalty hearing, Pinkerton relinquished the lead of Middleton's defense to another attorney from his office who had more experience in this area. Attorney Patrick Flannigan took over the case and immediately began making motions to the court against Viloria's planned strategy for the penalty hearing.

Outside the presence of the jury, Flannigan moved to preclude evidence that Middleton had been charged with sexual assault and kidnapping in Florida in 1990. The Florida case resulted in the conviction of one count of aggravated battery and one count of false imprisonment, so it was Flannigan's opinion that any mention of sexual assault would violate Middleton's constitutional rights. He also argued there was no reason for the victim in that crime to testify since only the fact Middleton had been convicted was relevant to the penalty hearing.

Viloria objected to this, but Judge Breen sided with the defense. He said, "I'm not going to allow testimony concerning sexual assault in the State's case. However, I warn defense counsel that any explanation of this conviction is going to open up the door to Mr. Viloria's ability to explain what he perceives as the facts of this case."

The defense then motioned that no mention of the Buffy Rice-Donohue case or the alleged rape in Florida could be made during the penalty hearing. Middleton was not charged in the Colorado case and the victim could not be called as a witness to testify to Middleton's criminal behavior. Even though the alleged victim in the Florida case could testify about what Middleton did to her, she believed it was a Santeria religious ritual, so testimony was precluded by the First Amendment.

Viloria argued that the defense was hiding behind the Constitution, but Judge Breen again sided with the defense. No mention of either incident could be made in front of the jury, and Viloria's strategy to argue for the death penalty was slowly being chipped away.

The next defense motion concerned testimony by the victim's families. Flannigan voiced concern that members of Powell's family might get on the stand and ask for the death penalty, which in turn might influence the jury's decision.

Viloria said he would instruct the family members not to specifically ask for the death sentence but argued that they could ask for the maximum sentence. He then argued that if defense witnesses asked for a penalty less than death, he could recall the family members to ask for the death sentence.

Judge Breen asked Viloria if it was his interpretation of the Constitution that he could do that. Viloria had heard enough about the protection the Constitution was giving Middleton and flew into a lengthy tirade about it. He said, "The rights of the defendant have wallowed the Constitution, making it meaningless. I would submit that it is just that, an old rag that needs to be modified. It has no meaning."

Judge Breen ruled for the defense, and the reporters listening to the arguments had a field day with Viloria's comment about the Constitution. He meant it in the context that the Constitution was now being used to protect the criminal and not the victim, but that was not how it read in the morning papers.

Even if Reno wasn't a fairly conservative town, the headline "PROSECUTOR CALLS CONSTITUTION AN OLD RAG" was never a good thing to read. It was the first bad press Viloria had during the case, but it was bad press that would stay with him for a long time.

Chapter 64:
Going Home

The Jury was led into the courtroom at 1:00 in the afternoon, and the proceedings began. Since this was the same jury that had already heard the case at trial, Viloria dispensed with a lengthy opening statement. He told the jury that in considering the death sentence for the two murders, there were four aggravating circumstances in the Davilla case and five in the Powell case.

In Davilla, they could consider that Middleton had two prior felony convictions—one in Florida and his weapons conviction in Reno. One of those convictions involved the use of threats of violence. The murder was also committed in the commission of or the attempt to commit first-degree kidnap, and Middleton was convicted of more than one murder during the proceeding.

In the Powell case, the same four aggravating circumstances were present, but there was also a fifth they could consider. Powell's murder involved torture and depravity of mind. Viloria was reasonably confident that he could win a death sentence based just on these aggravators, but he wished the judge would have ruled in his favor on introducing Middleton's past criminal history.

When it was Flannigan's turn to address the jury, he reminded them that even though the death penalty was an option, they were under no obligation to use it when sentencing Middleton for the crimes he had been convicted of. He said he would be calling a character witness in support of Middleton and offering testimony from the Board of Pardons.

Viloria kept his case simple since he had to alter his original strategy. The first witness he called to the stand was Kathy Powell's brother, Jeff. He testified to the fact his sister was a good and caring person, and the lives of her family members had been devastated by her murder.

Viloria was not allowed to ask Mr. Powell what his opinion was of the proper sentence for Middleton. He did ask the witness, "How do you think a person who took someone like your sister from the world should be treated?"

Powell said, "I can't see giving that person any more respect, dignity, or mercy than he showed Kathy."

The defense objected, but Judge Breen overruled and allowed the statement to remain on record. Flannigan did not cross-examine.

The second and last witness Viloria called was Thelma Davilla's sister, Dora Valverde. Ms. Valverde broke down in tears on the witness stand. She said all her sister ever wanted was to live free in this great country, but now she would never live anywhere again because of David Middleton. Once again, the defense did not cross-examine.

When it was Flannigan's turn, he called only one character witness to the stand for Middleton. His step-mother Margaret* had married Middleton's natural father, and had known Middleton since he was ten years old. She testified that Middleton was always a good and caring person and that something must have gone terribly wrong in his life for him to have become involved in crimes such as these. She said she believed Middleton could become a functioning member of society again if he were allowed to do so.

Flannigan then asked, "And did you know he got in trouble in Miami?"

The woman answered, "Oh yes, but that was a long time ago."

Viloria saw this as his opening. On cross-examination, he asked, "So you are aware then, ma'am, that your stepson took a sixteen-year-old girl to a remote area, kept her in his car, and engaged in sexual activity with her?"

Flannigan sprang to his feet and immediately objected to Viloria's question. He was red-faced with anger and moved for a mistrial. The aggravation showed on Judge Breen's face as he ordered the bailiff to remove the jury from the courtroom.

When the jury was gone, Judge Breen asked, "Why now, Mr. Viloria? Why now without my advanced permission?"

Viloria argued that the defense opened the door for the question by asking an explosive question about Middleton getting in trouble in Florida. Judge Breen didn't buy his explanation. He said, "I'm questioning your motives here. You are precluded from asking any questions, any further questions of this witness or you'll pack this to the ninth circuit on your back."

When the jurors returned to the courtroom, Judge Breen admonished them that Middleton's prior conviction did not relate to sexual activity and asked if anyone would have trouble disregarding Viloria's question. None of them indicated they would.

Viloria's tactics earned him a complaint to the State Bar's ethics review board, but it was worth it. Were it not for a 1990 plea bargain resulting from a sloppy investigation in Florida, the jury would have gotten to hear from the victim herself. At least he got the gist of the case out in front of them. The jurors could say they'd have no trouble disregarding the question—but there was no doubt they'd heard it.

Flannigan then called Susan McCurdy, Executive Secretary of the Parole and Pardons Board, to the stand. He asked Ms. McCurdy, "If Middleton were sentenced to life imprisonment without the possibility of parole, could that sentence ever be commuted to parole?"

"No, it could not," she replied.

On cross-examination, Viloria asked, "Ma'am, that assumes that the legislature doesn't change the law during the next session, or the next session after that, or the next session after that, doesn't it?"

"That is correct," she answered.

Viloria asked, "They are always free to change the law as they do every year, right?"

"That is also correct," she said.

"So there is no guarantee that life without won't be subjected to change and no longer be life without. Is that also correct, Ms. McCurdy?"

"Yes," she replied, "that is also correct."

"No further questions," Viloria said.

The defense made no objections, and both sides rested their cases. Judge Breen adjourned the court for the day and said they would reconvene at 9:00 A.M. the next morning for jury instructions.

At precisely 9:00 A.M. on Thursday, August 28, 1997, the jury was led into the courtroom to hear their sentencing instructions from Judge Breen. Guilt or innocence was no longer an issue. The only thing the jurors were to discuss was what sentence David Middleton would get for each of the crimes he was convicted of. Judge Breen told the jurors the latitude of sentencing and the guidelines for issuing those sentences and then excused them for deliberations.

This time, there was no need to sequester the jury. At 10:30 A.M., the jury foreman advised the bailiff they had reached their decision, and all parties were ordered back into the courtroom.

Judge Breen took the sealed envelope containing the sentences from the bailiff. He opened the envelope, read the sentences to himself, and then had the defendant stand to hear them.

Judge Breen said, "Mr. Middleton, for both murders, the jury found no mitigating circumstances sufficient to outweigh the aggravators. You are hereby sentenced to death for the murders of Kathy Powell and Thelma Davilla.

"For the two counts of first-degree kidnapping, one count of grand larceny, and one count of fraudulent use of a credit card, you are sentenced to the following prison terms: life without the possibility of parole, life without the possibility of parole, ten years and ten years. May God have mercy on your soul, Mr. Middleton. This court is dismissed."

A Nevada State Appellate Court was asked to review the death penalty ruling based on prosecutorial misconduct on the part of Tom Viloria. On November 28, 1997, the Appellate Court issued its ruling. The conclusion of the appellate decision reads, "*We find Middleton's claims to lack merit. We therefore affirm his judgment of conviction and sentence of death.*"

It was time for the devil to return to hell...maybe.

Chapter 65:
Jabba

It takes at least fifteen years to kill a person in the state of Nevada once they've been given the death sentence, and David Middleton is no exception. As of the writing of this book, David Middleton is still very much alive and heavily involved in scripting the continuing appeals of both his conviction and death sentence.

After Middleton's conviction, Judge Breen ruled there was no longer a conflict of interest and moved the responsibilities for the appeal process back to the Public Defender's Office. Middleton's string of appeals has addressed issues such as ineffective counsel, prosecutorial misconduct, Miranda rights, improper evidence handling, search and seizure, and the wrongful joinder of the cases. He's gone through several attorneys on his quest to beat his charges and the death sentence, but so far, all of his appeals have been denied.

As soon as Middleton lost his last appeal in August of 2007, his newest and most current appeal was filed. This will be his last appeal at the State level, but then the arduous process of Federal Court appeals begins. The one avenue of appeal that worries everyone associated with the case is the same one that worried Dave Jenkins the first time he heard it—*undetermined cause and manner of death.*

Case law changes often, and all it will take is one ruling like the Frutiger decision to cast a shadow of doubt over Middleton's murder conviction. There will be no guarantees that Middleton won't win an appeal until the day an executioner injects him with a lethal cocktail. And for some of the people whose lives Middleton has destroyed—that day can't come soon enough.

Until then, Middleton has found a new home on Death Row in the Ely Nevada State Prison. He has become what is described as a model prisoner with a charismatic charm that has made more than one prison guard wonder if maybe he really *didn't* kill those two women in Reno. One female prison guard said she was actually relieved when she was moved off of her assignment on Death Row because she felt herself getting a little *too* close to David Middleton. After all, as Middleton often reminded the guards, he used to be *one of them.*

During Middleton's last appearance at the Washoe County Courthouse in August of 2007, one of the jail deputies working the transport van was also working in the courthouse during the trial in 1997. He said he almost didn't recognize Middleton, who now went by the moniker of "Big Dave."

The deputy said, "He was so fat we had to give him his own row of seats on the bus. If it wasn't for Middleton's name on the paperwork, I wouldn't have even known it was him. Big Dave, my ass. He looked more like Jabba the Hut!"

Middleton had his first federal appeal overturned by the Nevada State Supreme Court in January 2013. His petition, filed by the Federal Public Defender's Office in Las Vegas contained a long list of claims charging that his trial counsel was ineffective, resulting in important evidence being left out of the trial and they failed to object to repeated prosecutorial misconduct.

In ruling against the appeal, the six justices ruled there was considerable evidence that Middleton was guilty of kidnapping and murdering Kathy Powell and Thelma Davilla. His appeals will continue at the federal level, but not forever...

Chapter 66:
The Matron

Evonne Haley also appealed her conviction on the charges from the Good Guys case. The Nevada State Supreme Court affirmed her conviction in a proceeding titled Haley v. State on July 28, 1998. She was then returned to the Southern Nevada Women's Correctional Institute in Las Vegas to serve the remainder of her seven-year sentence.

On July 23, 1999, Haley received news that she was going to be released from prison early. Before she could celebrate the good news, she was told the reason she was being released from her sentence early was that she was being extradited to Colorado on charges related to her part in the murder of Buffy Rice-Donohue.

The Rice's at first were ecstatic when they found out Haley was being returned for prosecution. But then they learned through their attorney, Keith Killian, that Montrose District Attorney Wyatt Angelo had cut a deal with Haley. If she took the stand and told the truth about what happened to Buffy, Angelo would only charge her with four felony counts of being an accessory to murder after the fact. She would be sentenced to eleven years in prison, but the District Attorney would stipulate she would be released no later than November 15, 2003.

A tearful Haley took the stand in Montrose, Colorado, on September 10, 1999. The prison had not been good to Evonne Haley. The words pretty or even good-looking had probably never been used to describe her, but a reporter for the *Denver Post* described her as looking "frumpish and matronly" at her trial.

Haley described herself as being like an older sister to Buffy. She said she did pick Buffy up the last day she was seen alive and drove her to the apartment she shared with Middleton because Buffy wanted to buy cocaine.

Haley said Buffy left the apartment alone with Middleton, and she stayed behind. She said two hours later, a distraught Middleton returned to the apartment and said he had accidentally killed Buffy during an argument in a wooded area near Colona, approximately twenty miles from the apartment.

Haley said Middleton begged her to keep quiet about the murder because, as a black man in a white town, he would never get a fair trial. Haley said she believed Buffy's death was an accident and helped Middleton dispose of the body because she feared she would lose her daughter if anyone found out about the killing.

District Attorney Angelo never addressed the facts that Buffy had been beaten badly, her body was bound with rope, or that the duct tape gag over her mouth when she was found had teeth marks in it to show she was alive when she had been gagged.

And then there was the matter of the witness who saw Middleton carrying what looked like Buffy's body out of his apartment—not out of a wooded area twenty miles away. Angelo accepted Haley's story as the truth and told the judge the State was willing to abide by the plea bargain.

Bonnie Rice was incensed. She stepped in front of the defense table, pointed a finger at Evonne Haley, and shouted, "That is an outright lie! I condemn you for the murder of my daughter!"

Bonnie Rice was forcibly removed from the courtroom by two deputies. Evonne Haley walked out of the courtroom on her own to begin serving her token sentence for what she said was her part in the death of Buffy Rice-Donohue.

Attorney Keith Killian was quoted in the *Denver Post* as saying it was routine to have a forty-five-day span between a trial and the acceptance of a plea bargain in order to examine a pre-sentencing report and to consult with the victim's family regarding the sentence. In this case, Evonne Haley was sentenced on the same day she testified. No one ever asked the Rice's or Mason Donohue how they felt about the plea bargain.

The Rice's had requested through an appellate court that a special prosecutor try Haley in this case. The court was supposed to rule on their request the following Monday, but Angelo took Haley to court on a Wednesday.

Killian told the *Denver Post* he couldn't help but wonder if Angelo purposely hustled the case through court before the appellate court could rule on Rice's request. He said by entering into a plea agreement that resulted in a conviction, Angelo took the pressure off the Montrose Police Department for doing an inept investigation of Buffy's death in the first place.

Whatever the reason for offering Haley the plea bargain, Angelo now had co-conspirator testimony that Middleton killed Buffy Rice-Donohue. This testimony could be used against Middleton because it could be corroborated by a veritable mountain of independent evidence.

And yet, Angelo refused to file charges on Middleton. He said, "You can't kill a man twice, so why waste good money prosecuting someone who is already on Death Row in Nevada?"

Lieutenant Tom Chinn would eventually become Chief of Police for the Montrose Police Department. District Attorney Wyatt Angelo would later become an Assistant U.S. Attorney in Colorado.

Evonne Haley was released from prison in November of 2003 after serving her four-year sentence for Accessory to the Murder of Buffy Rice-Donohue. She is now a free woman and reportedly moved in with relatives in Grand Junction, Colorado, after her release from prison. A reporter from the *Denver Post* went to Haley's house shortly after she was released from prison to try to interview her. Haley's aunt answered the door and said, "Oh, that thing. That happened so long ago that we try not to talk about it."

She then closed the door and the reporter never got her interview. It seems Evonne Haley didn't have as much trouble forgetting about the Buffy Rice-Donohue case as everyone else did. Haley could not be located for an interview for the updates to this book, so her current location is unknown.

Chapter 67:
Moving On

No one will ever know what caused David Middleton to change from being a respected member of the law enforcement community to a convicted serial killer. The reason for this is the killer himself is not talking. To this day David Middleton proclaims his innocence to anyone who will listen. Well, not just anyone. He declined to be interviewed for this book, so maybe he only proclaims his innocence to those who might actually believe him—or those he can intimidate. He did write a few letters from prison to his old Miami P.D. partner, Paul Kuiper. He said he was innocent of any crimes in those letters, but he said a lot of other things over the years the veteran Miami cop didn't believe either.

There are a lot of questions surrounding the murders committed by David Middleton that will forever go unanswered. One of those questions is just how many people he has killed over the years. Law enforcement knows of three, but they speculate there are more. There is one fact the law enforcement officers close to this investigation are certain of. Big Dave wore a badge at one time, but he was never *one of us.*

Middleton still has not been charged with the murder of Buffy Rice-Donohue, and according to the District Attorney's Office in Montrose, he probably never will. But as the saying goes, never say never. Perhaps the Colorado authorities might change their mind about prosecuting Middleton someday.

It appears they may have missed their chance to do so at one point without using the "can't kill a dead man twice" reason for not doing so. The Nevada murder charges against Middleton were dropped on June 6, 1996, based on the Frutiger decision referenced in Chapter 48 of this book. The charges weren't re-instated by the State Supreme Court until July 25, 1996, and it wasn't a given those charges would ever be brought back.

This was a window of opportunity where murder charges could have been brought against Middleton while he was in custody on the kidnap charges in Nevada. The San Miguel County Sheriff's Office in Colorado had already submitted their murder investigation naming Middleton as a suspect in Buffy's death to the District Attorney, so it would have been a simple matter of issuing the charging document. At least that way, there would have been another murder case hanging over Middleton's head if another court reversed this decision, and he would have been charged with the murder he committed. Why this wasn't done is a question that remains unanswered.

Many people's lives have been dramatically changed because David Middleton's path crossed theirs. His victim's lives ended, but their loved ones continued with theirs and had to adjust to the horrific tragedies he inflicted on them.

Mason Donohue spent many years alone and lonely after Buffy's murder. She was his first and only love, and he has never truly moved on after losing her. Eventually, he earned his Master's Degree in education, and in 2005, he married and moved to a small town in Wyoming to start a family. They say there is a difference between moving away and moving on, though.

Bonnie and Walt Rice spent everything they had trying to get the Montrose authorities to investigate the murder of their daughter and prosecute her killer. They sued the Montrose Police Department and District Attorney Wyatt Angelo. Even though the court found evidence of malfeasance in some of their claims, they were forced to issue summary judgment due to the statute of limitations and issues of clemency.

Losing a child is every parent's worst nightmare, but the living hell the Rice's went through is unfathomable. But true to the words carved on Buffy's gravestone—they will never stop fighting for her.

Bonnie Rice was instrumental in starting the First Victim Advocate Group in Montrose. She said she never wanted to think of another victim's family being treated the way they were and wanted to see at least one good thing come from Buffy's death. After all was said and done, Bonnie took the time to sit down and have coffee with Lieutenant Tom Chinn from the Montrose Police Department. She said she would never forget, but she was not above forgiving.

Tom Viloria continued on with a successful career in the Washoe County District Attorney's office before moving on to an even more successful private practice. His law offices in downtown Reno are the most prestigious in the city. But of all the cases he's been involved in, it is the Buffy Rice-Donohue case that still haunts him.

After Middleton was sentenced in the Powell and Davilla cases, Viloria felt so strongly about his guilt in the Buffy Rice-Donohue case that he called the Montrose District Attorney's Office and offered to prosecute

Middleton *pro bono.* He said the entire Middleton prosecution in Reno only cost $400,000, so if Colorado swore him in as a special prosecutor and he gave his services for free, the prosecution would be more than affordable.

Sheriff Bill Masters from San Miguel County, Colorado, heard about Viloria's offer and donated $50,000 from asset forfeiture funds to the Montrose district Attorney's Office to help with the costs of prosecuting Middleton should they wish to do so. The money was spent elsewhere, and Viloria's offer was declined. Viloria said he never could figure that out and it will always bother him. District Attorney Wyatt Angelo did not give a reason to Viloria for declining his offer to prosecute the case.

John Douglas left the Reno Police Department shortly after the Middleton case was adjudicated. He took a job with the Nevada Division of Parole and Probation and quickly worked his way into an upper management position. He retired from that position, and law enforcement in general, in May of 2008. His hair was grayer than the day he booked David Middleton for the murders of Kathy Powell and Thelma Davilla, but Eddie Murphy still would have envied his smile when he announced his retirement. Rumor has it that smile gets a little bigger when he's cruising the scenic Nevada roads on his highly-polished black Harley trike, not thinking about the evil he's seen in his career.

All of the other detectives who worked the Middleton case have also since retired as of the first release of this book—except one. Dave Jenkins continued slaying dragons, fighting evil, and speaking for those victims who could no longer speak for themselves long after he played a major role in taking the devil out of the free society in 1995.

In 2008, Dave Jenkins briefly hung up his trademark suit and tie and donned his blue dress uniform to attend his daughter Ali's graduation from the Reno Police Department Academy. Jenkins' daughter was twelve years old the night he was called away from his family to the scene where Kathy Powell's body was discovered. He was an integral part of taking David Middleton and so many other animals off the street, and these are cases he'll never forget. But pinning the shiny new seven-point star badge of the Reno Police Department on his daughter's crisp, blue uniform shirt at her academy graduation thirteen years after he became a dumpster diver was by far one of the most memorable and much more pleasant high points of his career.

As of the completion of this book, Detective Ali Jenkins was a well-respected member of the Reno Police Department's Robbery-Homicide Division. Not only is she carrying on her father's legacy as a "corpse cop," she's doing it from the same battered gunmetal grey desk her dad occupied and solved so many cases from during his career. The irony here is unmistakable.

Dave's son Adam was nine years old the night Kathy Powell's body was discovered. Adam also eventually migrated to police work with the Reno Police Department, and there's a good chance that the desk in the Robbery Homicide Division will stay in the Jenkins family for a long time.

If a person is known and remembered for what they leave behind as they pass through life, it appears Detective Dave Jenkins has achieved the same success rate in his personal life as he did in solving cases in his professional life. Dave retired from the Reno Police Department in 2010 after serving thirty-four years, seven months, and thirteen days. But like he says, who's counting…

Chapter 68:
Updates And New Information

Until this point, this book has been written in the third-person point of view. We'll now switch to first-person, as this is the only way I can properly update the narrative with new information that has come forth since the first writing of the book. As I mentioned in the Author's Note at the beginning of this book, a lot of new information came my way after the release of the first edition. I will source references where applicable, but all of the information here was obtained personally by me through either direct contact or further research by myself and my team.

When I retired from the Reno Police Department in 2006, I took a position as Director of Public Safety for a large K-12 school district in Southern California. Cops have means available to them to protect their identities and contact information, but when I took a position with a public agency, I gave up a lot of those protections. My office contact information was easy to find with a simple Google search, and people found me with information about the Middleton case.

I received a phone call in my office on an afternoon in July of 2009 from a woman who said she had information about the Middleton case. This was about eight months after the first edition of this book was originally released. The caller was the woman referred to in this book by the pseudonym of Alyssa Cervantes. This was the then sixteen-year-old victim Middleton kidnapped and sexually assaulted in Miami, which was the case that ended his law enforcement career and sent him to prison for the first time. Through subsequent conversations and interviews with Ms. Cervantes, she approved my use of her real name in any further work done with this book. I have declined to do so out of respect for her privacy and will continue to use the aforementioned pseudonym when referring to her.

Ms. Cervantes was able to confirm with me all the information regarding her case and her exposure to David Middleton, referenced in this book. She was a young teenager in the wrong place at the wrong time, and she put her *trust* in a Police Officer in uniform when David Middleton stopped her on the street. She was kidnapped, sexually assaulted, and then dropped on the side of the road, an act akin to dumping roadside trash. The crimes took place in Middleton's police car during what must have been a hellish experience for the young woman. The nightmare continued for her when authorities initially didn't believe her and then again when she had to relive this harrowing experience during courtroom testimony in front of the devil himself, David Middleton.

Among the other scars carried throughout life by this sexual assault survivor is the fact she still blames herself for the victims that Middleton killed after getting out of prison for the assault on her. Ms. Cervantes calmly described to me how Middleton stared at her in court throughout her testimony, and she knew then that he would never allow another victim to live to tell their stories about their encounter with the devil. He's allowed her to live and would now pay the price by going to prison. Ms. Cervantes had read about the murders of Buffy, Kathy, and Thelma in my book. The stories were very similar to her own, right up until the point where they were murdered in order to take their courtroom testimony to the grave with him.

This brave young woman contacted me to tell her story, as I was unable to locate her during my original research and used police reports, court records, and news articles to source reference these terrible crimes committed against her. She wanted me to hear this directly from her, and I have a great deal of respect for her for this. Ms. Cervantes appeared in an interview for a documentary in 2015. The documentary was done by a video company independent of my work but based on my book and the Middleton case. She appeared in the documentary using her real name on camera and told her story.

She told me she was doing this to help other victims and, hopefully, to keep other women from being victims. Watching Ms. Cervantes's interview was an emotional time for all of us, as is the fact that she will carry this weight with her for the rest of her life. This documentary was the last contact I had with Ms. Cervantes, and we were unable to locate her for the re-write of this book. If she is reading this, we wish her our best, wherever she may be.

Three weeks after my initial phone call from Ms. Cervantes, I was again sitting in my office when I got a call from another woman who said she wanted to talk about the Middleton case. The caller told me she was the woman who was dating David Middleton in Reno at the time he kidnapped and killed Kathy Powell. She is referenced in the case book for the Reno murder investigations, so I was able to confirm through the investigative details that she was who she claimed to be. Her name was not released during courtroom testimony and is, therefore, not public information, so out of respect for her privacy, I will not reference it here.

The caller told me she had been dating Middleton for about two months at the time he was arrested for Kathy Powell's murder. She had a hard time believing this, as she described Middleton as her "knight in shining armor." She had met Middleton when he was installing cable T.V. in her apartment, and they started a dating relationship after he returned to install an additional free cable box in her apartment. I knew from the police reports that this scenario was the same we saw with Kathy Powell, and most probably with Thelma Davilla.

This woman had been interviewed by detectives in the Powell investigation, so I know from her background information and physical description that she shared several similarities with Kathy Powell. I also knew detectives had found a list in Middleton's possession with her name on it and that I was now talking on the phone to his next intended victim. I'm not a believer in the supernatural, but I knew this call was the closest I would probably ever come to talking to a ghost if they actually do exist.

The caller told me she had a dinner date with Middleton the night he discarded Kathy Powell's body in the dumpster. They were supposed to go to a Mexican restaurant in southwest Reno called Los Tres Hombres. Middleton called her about an hour before he was supposed to pick her up for dinner and told her he could not make it and would call her later in the week to reschedule. We know from the time stamp on the surveillance tapes at Middleton's storage shed that he loaded Kathy Powell's body in his truck during the time frame he would have made this phone call. He knew he would be dumping the body when he canceled the dinner date and most likely had the body in his truck when he made that call. Los Tres Hombres was about two blocks from the dumpster Kathy Powell's body was found in and in the same area of the caller's apartment. Any good cop will tell you there is no such thing as coincidence. Middleton had staked his turf, and was circling his next victim like a shark on the scent of blood.

Before ending the call, the woman told me she never heard back from Middleton after the night he broke the date because he was arrested before they were supposed to meet again. She told me she didn't initially believe he killed anyone until after she read about the discovery of Middleton's storage shed torture chamber and the bite mark on Kathy Powell. She bore a scar from a similar bite mark on her breast, and it was inflicted by David Middleton during consensual sex. She next calmly told me she was certain Middleton removed Kathy Powell's body from his storage shed in order to make room for her own body sometime in the near future. Every one of us who looked at that case believed she was right. I now knew from this phone call that their next date had been scheduled for Friday, February 24, 1995. This was the day after Jenkins and Douglas removed Middleton from society, an act which almost certainly extended the life expectancy of the woman I was currently on the phone with.

As eerie as this phone call was, the twelve-page handwritten letter I received from the caller several days later was even more bizarre. She began by saying she didn't have a computer and didn't use email, so she sent the information via "snail mail." She went on to describe how she met Middleton and the fact he told her he was both a former NFL player and a former cop from Miami. He told her she could *trust* him, and she did.

She trusted him enough to leave him alone in her apartment to babysit her two children multiple times during the period they were dating, but she said, in retrospect, she probably should not have done that. She also said Middleton did not want to meet any of her friends or family and did not want her to tell them she was dating him. He told her his reason for this was he did not want her to be negatively judged for an interracial relationship, but she now understood he didn't want anyone to know about him since he was planning to kill her.

The last thing this woman wrote in the letter was that she loved David Middleton and hoped to someday see him again as a free man. It takes a good understanding of victimology to even begin to understand this last statement, and it takes an even better understanding of the workings of the mind of a psychopath to begin to understand how manipulative Middleton was and probably still is. One person's devil is another person's knight in shining armor, and that can be mindboggling to most people. This type of naiveté and blind trust from a victim being manipulated by a person with psychopathic tendencies is seen often in criminal investigations and was a commonality in Middleton's prior victims. The sad and scary fact is Middleton is not the only one out there like this.

Cops can become jaded after a period of time because they have difficulty trusting anyone when they first meet them and tend to see the bad in people before they see the good. I never figured out if this is a blessing or a curse, but it's a learned skill I would never trade. Trust is a gift that should be earned, not given. There is evil in this world. We can't fear it, but we must be aware of its existence among us.

These two initial contacts from Middleton's former and potentially future victims showed me the story did not end with the release of my book and that I needed to continue to gather data whenever I could. I did not intend to write an updated version of this book when it was first released and did not go out to actively do research, but the information just kept finding me, and I collected it all. It seemed wherever I went, someone either knew about the case or knew someone who was involved in the case.

On one occasion, I called the prison in Lovelock, N.V., to get some information on another project I was working on. The female Correction Officer who was helping me recognized my name and knew about my book. She told me she had initially been assigned to Middleton's cell block after he was first sent to prison at another facility. She asked me if she could call me when she was off duty to give me some information, as she did not want to talk on the recorded phone line from prison. I gave her my number, and she called me later that evening.

The Correction Officer told me she knew Middleton was a convicted murderer and knew the specifics of the case, but through interactions with him, he had her convinced he was innocent. Middleton told her he used to be a cop, so he was *"one of them."* He also told her he was wrongly convicted because they were trying to pin the murders on a black man. He said his attorney was convinced he would beat the case on appeal and he'd be out of prison soon. She said Middleton started talking to her about the possibility of getting into a dating relationship with her after he got out and suggested they could possibly start that relationship while he was still in prison and she was working on his cell block.

The officer described Middleton as the "most charismatic man she had ever met." She told me she started to believe his innocence and have thoughts about a dating relationship with him. She eventually asked for a transfer before she "did anything stupid" and moved to another facility to get away from Middleton. She said she was in therapy because of this, and she realized how close she had come to making a very big mistake.

So even in prison, staring down the possibility of death by lethal injection, Big Dave was still working it. After hearing this story, I could almost hear Middleton inviting this woman back to his cell for a little quality time and maybe some cable T.V. while she was on break. I never met the Correction Officer in person, but if I were a gambling man, I'd bet she bore a resemblance to the other female victims who had the misfortune of crossing paths with the devil. This Correction Officer gave me permission to use this story but requested her name not be used. I will honor that request here. I've confirmed she is still working in the prisons and doing well today.

I've met other people in social or public gatherings who found out I wrote this book and offered information about Middleton. I met one of the female jurors from Middleton's trial at a gathering unrelated to my work at a wine bar event in Reno my wife and I were attending. She told me he was the most evil person she'd ever seen, and the way he stared at her in the courtroom made her feel like he was not only trying to get inside her head but all the way inside her soul. I asked her to describe Middleton in one word, but I already knew the answer. She called him the *"devil."* She also told me the death penalty was never off the table during deliberations, and the jurors were *"terrified"* of Middleton as he looked at them in the courtroom.

A female deputy for the Washoe County Sheriff's Office who was a bailiff in Judge Breen's courtroom during the murder trial also offered me some good insight. It seemed Middleton had an evil aura around him that trained cops picked up on. Even in his blue suit and horn-rimmed glasses, they knew not to turn their backs on him as he sat at the courtroom defense table.

When asked twenty years later to use one word to describe David Middleton, this veteran Deputy replied without hesitation with the single word, *"terrifying."* She went on to say there was enough concern about Middleton that the Sheriff assigned an extra bailiff and the Detention Response Team, which is the jail equivalent to a S.W.A.T. unit, to the courtroom at all times during the trial. This Deputy also accompanied the judge, jury, and defendant on the field trip to view the gravesite where Thelma Devilla's remains were found. She confirmed Detective Ed Dixon's information referenced in Chapter 58 of this book that this was a tense situation where there were safety concerns related to Middleton being out in the open.

I also ran into a Nevada District Court Judge who sat as an appellate judge on the appeal of Middleton's death sentence. I'd been in front of this judge several times in court cases during my career and knew him as a fair and honest jurist. We talked briefly about the Middleton case and the death sentence appeal. The judge told me, "There was no way I was going to reverse the death sentence on that son-of-a-bitch. Some people just deserve to die." I had to smile at that one. Although I have mixed feelings about the death penalty in certain cases, I agree with the judge on this one. Some people just do deserve to die, and Middleton is the poster child for that group of folks...

Perhaps the most informative person I met after the release of the first edition of this book was Middleton's former partner in the Warrants Division of Florida's Miami Police Department. Paul Kuiper reached out to me after he read my book shortly after its release, and I've had the pleasure of sharing some good conversation and a couple of good bottles of wine with him over the last few years as we discussed this case. I've grown to know Paul as a good and honest cop who retired with his ethics and morals intact, and that means a lot to me when talking to those in our profession. This gave his interviews with me and his stories about Middleton credibility, and he also gained my trust.

I needed a better understanding of what happened in Miami when Middleton was a cop there, how he got away with what he did to allow him to leave Florida and get to Colorado, and then eventually arrive in Reno to kill. Paul helped me immensely to get that understanding. Paul also confirmed everything in prior chapters written in this book concerning events in Florida. He did this through either firsthand knowledge of the incidents or conversations he had with persons who had firsthand knowledge of them.

When David Middleton was hired in Miami in 1982, the department was called the Miami-Dade Police Department. That changed to the Metro-Dade Police Department in about 1983 and then again to the Miami Police Department in about 1988. This type of change is common when consolidation of law enforcement services due to growth in an area occurs. It is also common for some sub-standard police officers to get lost in the chaos of the change, and some questionable behavior could go unnoticed. It appears David Middleton was a master of staying below the radar during those times of often chaotic change in the department.

Paul Kuiper was Middleton's partner in the Warrants Division, but he didn't know a lot about him prior to getting to that division. Middleton only worked uniform patrol for about two years prior to his detective assignment, and Paul never heard anything good or bad about him. Uniform patrol is when a lot of cops get weeded out of the profession because sub-standard or unethical behavior is likely to be discovered in those assignments due to more structured duties and close supervision. This is the reason most departments require rookie officers to do a certain amount of time in uniform patrol before being assigned to a position like a detective, where there is limited supervision and more of a chance for bad or unethical behavior to go unnoticed.

According to Paul, there was a lot of out-of-town travel on extraditions involved with the duties in the Warrants Division, and that type of travel could be a recipe for disaster for a cop prone to unethical behavior. Perhaps the rapid growth of the department contributed to Middleton being able to move to a detective position so early in his career, but one needs to ask if there is a possibility his behavior would have been noticed had he been left in a position where there was more direct supervision and less time to get into trouble. As the saying goes, you can't un-ring a bell, so this is a moot issue.

During my conversations with Paul, he described an escalating pattern of behavior with Middleton becoming obsessed with women, sex, and drinking throughout their partnership. Paul referenced several stories where he was out of town with Middleton on extraditions, and they'd share a hotel room. On several of these occasions, Middleton would take the company car and not return to the room all night. Paul would find him in the morning passed out drunk in the car or in the hotel stairway. He had no idea where Middleton had disappeared, but the behavior was getting worse, and Paul had had enough. He eventually told his supervisor about this and requested a new partner.

I asked Paul what the final straw to break their partnership was. I knew from reading the initial investigative reports he'd eventually asked for a new partner, but I didn't know why. Paul relayed a story about an extradition he and Middleton were on in New Jersey in about 1988. Paul had grown up in New Jersey, and during the extradition, he met up with some old friends for dinner at the Brass Rail Bar in Hoboken, N.J. This is an upscale pub-type restaurant, and Middleton accompanied Paul to dinner. Paul told me they met two women at the bar and asked them to join the group for drinks. Paul was single, and according to him, he was getting friendly with one of the women. He remembered she worked for the County Prosecutors Office, was very nice, and was dressed professionally.

At some point, the woman Paul was talking to excused herself to go to the restroom. Middleton also excused himself to go to the restroom, and Paul didn't think anything of this. A couple of minutes later, the woman returned to the table looking very angry. She grabbed her purse and told Paul, "I don't know what kind of sick shit you and your partner are into, but I'm not into it. I'm leaving."

Paul told me he tried to catch up to the woman to find out what happened, but she yelled at him to leave her alone. When he asked

Middleton what he had said, Middleton laughed and said, "I said something pretty nasty to her, but I was just joking around." Paul didn't think Middleton was joking and asked for a new partner when they got back to Miami. The incident left a lasting impression on Paul, and he still remembers the exact words exchanged that night. In light of what we now know about Middleton, one can only imagine what he said to the woman in the restroom to cause her reaction.

Shortly after the end of their partnership, the Internal Affairs Division began an investigation into Middleton for consorting with the known felons Gerrilyn Smith and Jabir Mohammand, referenced earlier in this book. They were also looking into money laundering related to his side business, Total Concept Cleaning. They removed Middleton from his duties in the Warrants Section and assigned him to desk duty during the course of the investigation. He remained on desk duty for over a year and was still on that assignment when he dressed up in his uniform off-duty and, after hours, got into an unmarked police car and kidnapped the sixteen-year-old girl he would later sexually assault.

Paul said he believes someone inside the department tipped Middleton off that he was being looked at for the kidnap and sexual assault. He said one day, Middleton just didn't show up for work, and then he was gone. It seems he rented a U-Haul Truck, loaded up all of his belongings, and fled town in the middle of the night. The truck was discovered abandoned in another state, and Middleton was nowhere to be found.

I was aware that Middleton was later located living in an apartment in Greenville, Mississippi, and extradited back to Miami for the kidnap and sexual assault charges, but Paul filled in one fact I was not aware of. The apartment complex Middleton moved into with Evonne Haley in order to hide out and lay low in Greenville was one known to be inhabited largely by local cops. Middleton ingratiated himself with the local cops in the complex, and they accepted him after he told them he was a former cop from Miami. He was *"one of them."*

When the wanted fliers for Middleton on the Florida sexual assault charges went out to police departments, one of the local cops recognized him as his neighbor at the apartment complex and went there to arrest him. As Paul Kuiper put it, "We never catch the smart ones…"

Chapter 69:
Questions Re-Visited

Even with all the new information that came our way after the initial release of this book, two facts remain unchanged. The first is the disappearance of Buffy Rice-Donohue is still listed with the Montrose Police Department as an open, unsolved, and ongoing investigation twenty-five years after she was abducted. In spite of the fact Evonne Haley admitted under oath she assisted David Middleton in loading Buffy's body into her car, driving it to Norwood, CO., and burying the body in the shallow grave she was later found in off of Mountain View Lane, the case is still listed as open as far as the Montrose Police Department is concerned.

Haley testified under oath in her deposition and gave the details of how Middleton killed Buffy accidentally in a cocaine binge, but the coroner's evidence shows otherwise. In her testimony, Haley denied taking part in killing Buffy but admitted to helping dispose of her body and also helping Middleton get out of town. Evidence shows Buffy was possibly still alive during her final trip to her grave, and this would refute Haley's denial of being involved in the murder. According to courtroom testimony, this evidence was never brought up at the proceedings, so Haley was taken at her word.

Evonne Haley was charged with twelve counts of Accessory to Murder, but she was allowed to plead to four of those counts based on the plea agreement made with District Attorney Wyatt Angelo. That agreement stated she would serve no more than four years for her crimes. Colorado Revised Statues (CRS) 18-8-105 define the elements of the crime of Accessory. The statute also says the maximum sentence for the crime of Accessory is the same as for the crime itself. CRS 18-3-102 defines the elements of the crime of murder and states the penalty for the crime is life in prison or, in certain cases, death.

A four-year sentence for a person convicted for crimes that carry the possibility of life in prison seems pretty light. Especially if the person convicted of the crime happens to have a prior felony conviction related to the murder of a school teacher in Nevada less than a year after Buffy's murder. The reason for this sweetheart deal has always been a source of question and concern to those familiar with the case, including Buffy's family. Wyatt Angelo ignored my repeated and documented requests to talk about this during the first writing of this book. He had moved from his position as District Attorney for the 7th District Court to a position as an Assistant U.S. Attorney for the Federal Court in Grand Junction, CO., in 2002, but my questions were about how the Middleton case was handled and the deal given to Evonne Haley. Those questions remain unanswered.

Wyatt Angelo moved on and is no longer available to answer those questions, but persons interviewed for this book have their opinions about this. Some people feel Haley was given a light sentence to keep her quiet about some elements of the handling of Buffy's case by the Montrose P.D. and the District Attorney's Office. I am by no means making any allegations of misconduct by these or any other agencies related to this case; I am just stating facts from my interviews with people familiar with these circumstances.

In courtroom testimony under oath, Haley stated Lt. Tom Chinn told Middleton to get out of town after Buffy's disappearance, and this is why they fled Montrose. I have nothing to confirm this, other than Haley's testimony in the civil case Donohue v. Hoey (source referenced earlier in this book), but the statement was left hanging out there in the case and never explored any further. Haley is a liar, amongst many other negative attributes, so I do not give her statements a lot of credibility. But Lt. Chinn also ignored repeated and documented requests for an interview during the first writing of this book, so I have no source references to refute Haley's statements. Lt. Chinn, who later became Chief Chinn, was no longer with the Montrose P.D. when we were researching this updated edition of the book, and we were unable to locate him for additional requests for interviews.

Only three people know the truth about Evonne Haley's involvement in Buffy's murder. One of them is dead, one of them is on death row in Nevada, and one of them is living as a free woman somewhere in Colorado after serving her four-year prison sentence. None of the three will ever talk about the crime again.

Evonne Haley walked out of prison in November of 2003 after completing her sentence at the age of 46. Wyatt Angelo was no longer the District Attorney, but the current District Attorney, Thomas Raynes, was forced to abide by the agreement made by Angelo. His statement regarding Haley's parole after only four years was, "It's always frustrating to have your hands tied with that type of case, but having said that, I respect the decision made by my predecessor."[7] San Miguel County District Court Judge Dennis Friedrich was also not happy about Haley's parole and said as much in court documents. Since the agreement had already been made, he had no choice but to grant Haley parole.

The second fact that has not changed is Buffy's killer is alive and living in a prison outside of the small town of Ely, NV., and he has not been charged with the murder. Although he received the death sentence for his crimes in Nevada, he is still playing out his appeals. Middleton was fifty-seven years old as of the writing of this book, so he will more than likely die of natural causes than he will of lethal injection. Prison life just isn't known to be conducive to a long and healthy life. Even though David Middleton is on death row for the murders of Kathy Powell and Thelma Davilla, and he'll spend the rest of his living days in captivity, he spends them knowing he got away with murder. At least one we know of, but it is one that can be easily proved.

Why hasn't Middleton been charged with Buffy's murder, why is the case of her disappearance still listed as open with no suspect, and why is no one speaking on behalf of a victim who can no longer speak for herself? These were questions raised at the end of this book when it was first released, and they will be raised again here. Maybe taking a fresh look at these questions will bring some answers and some closure to Buffy's story.

I will note here that the San Miguel County Sheriff's Office, under the direction of Sheriff Bill Masters, completed a comprehensive criminal investigation into the Buffy Rice-Donohue murder. Buffy's body was found in their jurisdiction, and the Sheriff's Office investigation will be referenced later in this book. The location where Buffy's body was discovered was what is known in criminal investigations as a "dump site." She was obviously not killed there, and all indications are she was kidnapped from Montrose. There is a high probability she was also killed in Montrose, as Middleton and Haley were seen carrying a large garbage bag similar to the one Buffy's body was discovered in out of their Montrose apartment.

I have been involved in many murder investigations where the original crime occurred in one jurisdiction, and the dump site is in another. The typical method of investigating these types of crimes, especially when the exact murder scene cannot be determined, is the agency having

---

[7] Montrose Press, October 24, 2003

jurisdiction over where the crime originated, maintains the primary investigative responsibilities, and is assisted by the agency where the body was discovered. This was the procedure with the Thelma Davilla case in Nevada. She went missing from the jurisdiction of the city of Sparks Police Department and was discovered in the jurisdiction of the Washoe County Sheriff's Office. The Sparks Detectives took the lead on the case and were assisted by the Sheriff's Office detectives. Both agencies contributed investigative efforts documents in reports contained in the Murder Book.

Murder is a capital crime that is tried in a state District Court, so it doesn't matter that multiple agencies are contributing to the investigative efforts, as it all goes to the same judge and jury. The exception to this investigative procedure is if a victim is transported across state lines, and then the F.B.I. gets involved and can take over as the primary investigative agency due to the involvement of federal laws pertaining to interstate crimes. The local agencies would still contribute to the investigation, and that is usually done through the formation of a task force.

My questions about the handling of the Buffy Rice-Donohue case had to do with the initial handling of the case prior to the discovery of her body in the jurisdiction of the Sheriff's Office. These were questions I had when writing the original book, and my goal was to clear them up as best as I could prior to releasing the second edition. In order to do this, I needed assistance in researching the Montrose case involving Buffy's disappearance.

Several people assisted me with research for the re-writing of this book, as I wanted to ensure all information contained in it was factual. I employed the services of a skilled private investigator from Reno named Curtiss Kull to assist with interviews, background information, and document retrieval related to the Buffy Rice-Donohue case. Curtiss is a thirty-plus-year lawman who went into private practice after retirement. I'd worked with Curtiss over the years and knew him to be an excellent investigator with morals and ethics beyond reproach. He also had a connection with the Middleton case, as he was on the undercover team that used to follow Middleton prior to his arrest while detectives were building their Reno case on him.

I received little assistance from the police department and courts in Montrose when I wrote the original book. This is the reason I used a licensed private investigator for the follow-up information needed for the second edition of the book. I wanted to ensure all information I used was factual and that Curtiss was the right person to get this job done. He spent most of his career investigating the worst of the worst criminals, completed a lot of major cases, and put a whole lot of bad guys in jail over the years. The remainder of the information in this book is either source referenced through open source documentation, my own personal interviews with persons involved in this case, or investigative efforts documented in Curtiss' information reports.

Court documents from cases that have been adjudicated become public information and are kept in the custody of the records section in the court of jurisdiction. My investigative team made phone contact with the records section of the San Miguel County Courthouse on March 14, 2019, to request records related to Yvonne Haley's Accessory To Murder court transcripts. Our investigator was directed to the court website to fill out the request for information paperwork, which was done on March 19, 2019.

The Colorado Open Records Law (CRS 24-72-201) states the agency the request is made to has three days to respond to the records request. Our request stated we were on a timeline where the records were needed by April 1, 2019. We next heard back from the court records section via email on March 27, 2019. The email from C. McKinney stated the documents we requested would take a minimum of thirty to forty-five days to compile. As much as we appreciated their offers for assistance, this was not in our time frame, so we did not use those specific court records. I was able to locate sufficient information in open source research, particularly information from Evonne Haley's deposition, to complete sections of this book I required the documentation for.

Phone contact was also made with the records section of the Montrose Police Department on March 27, 2019, in an attempt to learn the current status of the Buffy Rice-Donohue case with their department. I was specifically looking for investigative efforts between Buffy's disappearance on November 21, 1993, and the time her body was discovered on May 24, 1995. This eighteen-month time period would be crucial to any investigation, especially since the Sheriff's Office investigation did not start until after the discovery of Buffy's body in their jurisdiction.

Middleton and Haley left Montrose in April of 1994 and moved to Reno, NV. This was five months after Buffy's disappearance. I was looking for records on any investigation into Buffy's disappearance that may have focused on Middleton and Haley as suspects. By the time the pair left

Montrose, it was obvious Buffy wasn't coming home. Her car, purse, and all her belongings had been left behind, and no one had any contact with her. She was last seen with Haley, and the investigation would have certainly pointed to her and Middleton. The main question was if an investigation into Middleton and Haley would have prevented them from leaving Montrose for Reno, and if so, was that investigation done by the Montrose P.D.

It is a common investigative fact that the longer an investigation goes on, the more difficult it is to solve a crime such as this. Witnesses forget facts, move on, or, in some cases, pass away. Crime scenes that were not originally located are nearly impossible to find due to changes related to the passage of time. Witnesses familiar with this case had told me there were very few investigative efforts done by the Montrose P.D. during the time when she disappeared and the time her body was discovered, and the only way I could confirm or disprove that information was through research of the initial investigative reports.

The records clerk answering Curtiss' call to the Montrose P.D. was initially very helpful, but upon re-contact, he advised us he was told by his supervisor not to release any information without the proper records request being filed. Curtiss filed that request online, but we were never re-contacted regarding the request. Several phone calls to the Montrose P.D. Detective Division were also made, and messages were left requesting information, but the calls were not returned. All requested information was considered public information related to the case, and we were not requesting anything that would be considered classified or law enforcement sensitive.

Based on the lack of cooperation from the Montrose Police Department when I wrote the original book and the problems we were having with re-contact on our recent requests for assistance, we did not feel we were going to get any further cooperation from them. I still considered this information crucial to the factual completion of the updated edition of this book, so we made our request more official.

On April 12, 2019, I filed a Colorado Freedom Of Information Act (FOIA) Request with Chief Blaine Hall of the Montrose Police Department. In order to ensure there is no misunderstanding of the requested information and for use as a source reference, I will include the FOIA request here for the reader's information. Some personal contact information has been removed, but the document is otherwise verbatim to the one submitted to the Montrose P.D.

Colorado Freedom Of Information Act Request

April 12, 2019

Blaine Hall

Police Chief and Custodian of Records

Montrose, Colorado Police Department

Chief Hall,

Under the Colorado Open Records Law, C.R.S. 24-72-201 et seq., I am requesting an opportunity to inspect or obtain copies of public records that your agency is in custody of. The following are the records and/or documentation covered under this request:

1. *The investigative report of the disappearance of Ms. Buffy Rice-Donohue from Montrose, CO., on November 21, 1993. Should portions of the investigative report be exempt from C.R.S. 24-72-201 et seq., we request documentation stating the date the initial police report was taken and the classification of crime listed on the initial report when it was first taken.*

2. *Documentation of the number of follow-up investigative reports completed by the Montrose Police Department between the date of Ms. Buffy Rice-Donohue's disappearance and the date her remains were discovered in the area of Norwood, CO., on May 25, 1995.*

3. *Documentation of the date the classification of the investigative report regarding the disappearance of Ms. Buffy Rice-Donohue was changed after the discovery of her remains on May 25, 1995, and what the new classification was changed to (i.e., Suspicious Death, Homicide, etc.)*

4. *If this classification was not changed to Criminal Homicide upon the discovery of Ms. Buffy Rice-Donohue's remains on May 25, 1995, we request the date the classification was changed to Criminal Homicide and the number of investigative follow-up*

reports completed by the Montrose Police Department during that timeframe.

5. *Documentation stating the current status of the Homicide investigation into the death of Ms. Buffy Rice-Donohue as of the date of this request (i.e., Open and Unsolved kidnapping and Homicide, Closed by Exceptional Clearance, etc.).*

6. *Documentation of the circumstances of the discovery of a roll of film containing nude photos of Ms. Buffy-Rice Donohue by private citizen Nelson Jennett on 01/02/94. Of particular interest in this request is how this roll of film came into the custody of the Montrose Police Department, who in that department took custody of the film, how it came to be developed (i.e., crime lab, private photo lab, etc.), what evidentiary value these photos had to the Buffy Rice-Donohue case if there was a follow-up report completed on the discovery of these photos, and if they were subsequently booked into police evidence.*

7. *Documentation of the current location of these photos. Please note that we will not be requesting any copies of these photos due to their content and personal value to the owners, but their current location is of importance to this request.*

8. *Documentation of any internal personnel investigations regarding the police handling of the aforementioned photos or possible 4th Amendment Rights violations involved in the police seizure of these photos. We will not be asking for any type of personnel investigative reports or disciplinary records related to this request at this time. Simple documentation advising if this incident was investigated and, if so, whether allegations of any misconduct were determined to be founded or unfounded will suffice at this time for the purposes of this request. Source reference here is the court records and depositions involved in the civil case titled Donohue v. Hoey (No. -2-1405, District of Colorado, D.C. No. 97-M-2595).*

9. *Any records or documentation of the arrest or citation for criminal trespass (Montrose City Code 6-1-11 (A) (1)) of Ms. Bonnie Rice at the Montrose, CO. apartment complex of David Middleton and Evonne Haley on 02/01/94 (case has been adjudicated and is no longer an active investigation).*

10. *Any documentation or follow-up police reports regarding the decision to drop the aforementioned criminal trespass charges against Ms. Bonnie Rice on 05/11/94.*

302

11. *Any correspondence, electronic or otherwise, between the Montrose, CO. Police Department and the Washoe County, NV. Sheriff's Office between May of 2015 and July of 2017 regarding additional DNA testing of evidentiary items currently in the custody of the Washoe County Sheriff's Department that were located in the searches of property leased by David Middleton during the Kathy Powell Homicide Investigation.*

12. *Any email correspondence on the Montrose, CO. Police Department email system between the dates of March 1, 2019, and the date of this request that mentions the names David Middleton, Evonne Haley, Private Investigator Curtiss Kull, or the requestor of this information, Jeff Kaye.*

If there are any fees for searching or copying these records, please inform me if the cost will exceed $250.00. The statute requires a response to this request within three days following receipt of this letter. If access to the records I am requesting will take longer, please contact me with information about when I might expect copies or the ability to inspect the requested records.

If you deny any or all of this request, please cite each specific exemption you feel justifies the refusal to release the information and notify me of the appeal procedures available to me under the law. My contact information is listed below the signatory line in this request. My preferred method of contact regarding the status of this request is by phone or email in order to expedite this process.

Thank you for your time and consideration of my request.

Sincerely, Jeff Kaye

The registered letter containing the FOIA request was received by the Montrose Police Department on April 17, 2019. On April 18, 2019, I received a phone call from Commander Matt Smith from the Montrose Police Department regarding my FOIA request.

Commander Smith was extremely professional and said they would cooperate with the request in areas they could, but part of the case was still an ongoing and open investigation. Colorado Public Records Request laws say a law enforcement agency is under no obligation to release a report on an open investigation. The fact the Buffy Rice-Donohue case is still open, answered the question I had as to the case status. To this day, the case is still listed as open and unsolved, with no suspect listed. Commander Smith confirmed this was the current case status, and this was due to no new information coming through to investigators.

But new information on the case did come through. It came from Evonne Haley during her sworn testimony in court in San Miguel County, Colorado, six years after Buffy was murdered. Haley told them in sworn testimony who killed Buffy and how he did it. But apparently this information was not added to the case after she gave it to them, and this is why Middleton was not listed as a suspect.

I do not have the Montrose P.D. investigative reports and probably never will. But open source research, interviews with people familiar with the case who were willing to talk to me, and lack of answers from the Montrose Police Department are enough to lead me to believe the case was never updated to name David Middleton as a suspect. Haley's statements put the origin of the case back in the jurisdiction of the Montrose PD, but there is no way to know if that information was added to the case without the ability to review it. Open and unsolved only has one meaning to a trained investigator…

I agree that co-conspirator testimony alone is not enough to be considered probable cause for arrest, and there is plenty of case law to support that. But Haley's sworn testimony, coupled with trace and DNA evidence taken from Buffy's body and the coroner's report of injuries causing Buffy's death, is surely enough evidence to support Haley's details of Buffy's kidnap and murder at the hands of David Middleton. There was certainly enough probable cause to seek an arrest warrant for David Middleton or to at least list him as a suspect. Commander Smith was not with the department during Buffy's murder or the subsequent investigation, so he had no answers when I raised these questions.

The fact Middleton was not named or charged as a suspect in Buffy's case is important here for more than the obvious reasons. We researched murder cases throughout the United States in every way we could think of going back as far as records were kept. We were unable to locate a single murder case where there was a suspect charged and convicted for Accessory to Murder, but no principal suspect was ever charged with the actual murder.

Naturally, we found myriad open and unsolved murder cases in our research, but these were "cold cases" with no suspects. We found murder cases where the primary suspect was killed during the arrest or died of other causes during the investigation, and other suspects were listed either as accessories or co-conspirators. But in these cases, a primary suspect was listed and the case status was typically "closed by exceptional clearance without prosecution."

The only case we came across during research for this book where a suspect was arrested and found guilty of Accessory to Murder, but the case was still listed as open and unsolved with no suspect charged for the actual murder, was the murder of Buffy Rice-Donohue. By no means do I suggest here that we researched every murder case in the history of the U.S. because that would not be possible. I'm just saying we looked as hard as we could for a similar case, and we just couldn't find one.

I raised this question during my conversation with Commander Smith, and he was unaware this case status was the one anomaly we could find. I offered to update this information and source reference any similar cases if Commander Smith could locate any that had an arrest of an Accessory without naming a principle, and I will gladly do that if this information is discovered.

Colorado formed a "Cold Case Task Force" at the state level, so perhaps they have information I'm not privy to as a private citizen. Interestingly enough, San Miguel County Sheriff Bill Masters was named to head the task force when it was formed in 2015. Bill Masters is still Sheriff, and as mentioned in this book, he is more than familiar with Buffy's case. I interviewed Sheriff Masters by phone for this updated edition of my book. He was aware Haley had been charged as an Accessory to murder, and Middleton had not been charged but was unaware of any similar case in Colorado or anywhere else in the U.S. His direct quote was, "That was a strange one."

When the Cold Case Task Force was formed in 2015, the Montrose Press did an article on it. Tom Chinn was Chief of the Montrose Police Department at the time and is quoted in that article. He names three open and unsolved missing persons cases from Montrose in this article. There is Kenneth Chacon from 2005, Tony Bastion from 1994, and Ben Gray from 1978.[8] Lt. Chinn failed to mention the open and unsolved murder case of Buffy Rice-Donohue in this interview.

---

[8] Montrose Press, Article by Senior Writer Katharhynn Heidleberg, December 11, 2015

I had my reasons for asking for every item listed in our FOIA request as it relates to this book and the open case on the Murder of Buffy-Rice Donohue. Items six, seven, and eight in the FOIA request deal with the nude photos of Buffy that were discovered after her disappearance. This is a particularly sore spot with everyone who hears about it. As a matter of fact, if you ever get the chance to meet investigator Curtiss Kull and ask him about this aspect of the case, stand back because he breathes fire when talking about it. Not only is Curtiss a career lawman, he's a father. We all think of our own kids when dealing with investigations. We just can't help it.

How the roll of film was taken out of the mobile home Buffy, and her husband shared was a clear Fourth Amendment rights violation for unlawful search and seizure. The private investigator who entered the mobile home and seized the roll of film was acting as an agent of the police, so his actions fall under Fourth Amendment protections against warrantless searches and seizure of evidence. Buffy was not declared deceased at the time the film was seized, so she and her husband still had legal standing in the Mobile Home, which was considered a private residence.

If the film was needed for possible evidence, there should have been a search warrant, and law enforcement should have seized it. We know through the Donohue v. Hoey case that no search warrant was used for this seizure of private property from a private residence. Fourth Amendment violations are investigated at the Federal level, and a lot of cops have gone to jail for less than this.

Someone from the police department got those photos developed. Again, this was done without any type of court order or evidentiary chain of custody. We also know this from Donohue v. Hoey, and I was able to confirm this through interviews done with personnel familiar with this case while researching the update for this book.

It appears no evidence report was ever completed, and these photos never made it to the evidence vault. This was my reason for asking about documentation of the status of the photos. Still, that information was not provided to me, and Commander Smith had no independent knowledge of this aspect of the case during my conversation with him. Again, if documentation is provided to contradict this, I will gladly update this section of the book to reflect those source references.

There is only one word to describe how the nude photos of Buffy were handled after they were developed, and that word is *disgusting*. This was a clear act of disrespect and debasement to the victim and an affront to every one of us who wears a badge or has a child of their own.

Even though the photos were illegally seized and improperly developed, as soon as it was known they had no relevance to the case, they should have been either returned to Buffy's husband, or destroyed if he didn't want them. If there was any doubt they might have relevance to the case, they should have been booked into evidence.

The officer who is named in the Donohue v. Hoey case as a witness to these photos being passed around in Lt. Chinn's office was the evidence custodian at the time. He would know about the proper handling of evidence, and this is why he came forward to make the complaint about the handling of the nude photos of Buffy when he observed it. For purposes of this book, I was able to source reference the information regarding these photos documented in the Donohue v. Hoey case through interviews with persons named in that case as witnessing this conduct.

The passing around of the nude photos of Buffy without her permission, if it happened today, could be prosecuted as a felony crime under statutes present in all fifty states dealing with "sextortion" cases. These statutes also cover cases most commonly called "revenge nudity cases," where explicit photos are distributed for some type of retribution without consent. There are enhancements to penalties if these crimes are committed for purposes related to sexual gratification.

The fact the nude photos of Buffy were passed around, without consent or relevance to her case by on-duty law enforcement officers, some of them in uniform, could also pull this into the Federal Statutes covering Oppression Under Color of Authority. These are the same statutes David Middleton should have been charged under when he kidnapped and raped a sixteen-year-old girl in Miami while he was in uniform. There must be a line drawn between the predators and those charged with protecting society from them. If that line was not crossed in this case, it most certainly was stretched to the breaking point by some who were involved in it.

Crimes were possibly committed during the police handling of Buffy's photos, but they were not investigated. Even if they were not criminally investigated, there should have at least been a procedural investigation and an internal investigation for Conduct Unbecoming an Officer. This internal violation, affectionately known as "C.U.B.O." in police jargon, has ended more than one law enforcement career. Since this is not a criminal statute, there is no proof beyond a reasonable doubt standards or Fifth Amendment protections against self-incrimination. The standards of proof are a simple "Preponderance of Evidence."

But if no one looks at the evidence of misconduct, it is impossible to determine its weight in a violation of procedure or conduct. This was my reason for asking for item eight, the internal investigative information, in the FOIA request sent to the Chief of the Montrose Police Department. Internal Affairs investigative reports are stored forever, so if an investigation was done on the handling of these photos, the information would be available. I did not request the actual investigative report in the FOIA request. I only wanted to know if an investigation was done, and that information would not be exempt under Colorado law governing public records release since it is not an on-going investigation. I did not receive any information back from the Montrose P.D. regarding this section of the FOIA request.

Like any good investigator, I typically know the answer to a question before I ask it. I knew through interviews there was no Internal Affairs investigation into the handling of Buffy's photos before I made the FOIA request, but the fact there was no response to that portion of the request confirmed this.

There couldn't have been an investigation, because the photos were stored in the desk drawer of the person who would have conducted that investigation. This was also the same person showing the nude photos to other male officers, and the same person who later became Chief of Police, and neglected to mention Buffy's name in the article written on the Cold Case Task Force in 2015. Once again, if the Montrose Police can provide documentation to say there was an investigation into the handling of these photos by then Lt. Tom Chinn, or documentation to refute the claims about the display of the photos made in Donohoe v. Hoey which were supported by subsequent interviews for this book, I will gladly amend this section to reflect that information.

As an author, it is my job to get the facts right, and to be honest enough to go back and correct any mistakes I might have made while writing a book in order to make things right. This is an easy standard for me, because it is the same standard I used for my work during the thirty-three years I wore a badge. We are all human, and we all make mistakes at times. I know I've made my share, and sometimes they were during police investigations. Where ethics and morals come into play in that equation is the willingness to own a mistake, and then go back and correct it, regardless of how that makes you look.

Mistakes may have been made in the investigation of the disappearance and murder of Buffy Rice-Donohue. Nothing will ever bring her back, but it is never too late to own these mistakes and make them right.

Chapter 70:
The Book

Law enforcement reports regarding a murder case are typically put together in a binder, which is called the Murder Book. The reports are also stored electronically, but detectives like to look at the hard copy murder book when reviewing a case because all the information, crime scene photos, and evidence is there in front of them to see.

The first section of the murder book is the chronological time frame of the crime itself and the subsequent investigation of the crime. I've read my share of murder books during my career in law enforcement, and I was able to review the books on Kathy Powell and Thelma Davilla after I retired while researching this book.

I wrote this book as a private citizen after my retirement and did not use a badge to gain access to any records. I was able to review the Powell and Davilla murder books because the Reno Police Department and the Washoe County, NV. District Court complied with my Public Records request for information. In most of my research for this book, public information was given to me without a formal FOIA request. This is why it's called "Public Information."

Montrose Police Commander Matt Smith told me during our conversation on April 18, 2019, that I would be receiving a detailed email from Chief Hall addressing the items in my FOIA request. The time frame under Colorado law for response to a FOIA request is three days. I told Commander Smith I was on a deadline for submission of this manuscript and would look forward to the email so I could include any additional information in this book. This manuscript was submitted to my publisher on May 8, 2019, and I was still looking for that email.

Through research of open source data and multiple interviews with persons familiar with this case, I was able to put together the timeline used in this book outlining the murder of Buffy Rice-Donohue without a review of the murder book. I was also given the portion of the murder investigation completed by the San Miguel County Sheriff's Office, which contained a timeline for their investigation, and this was also helpful.

No interview information that I could not corroborate with an independent source has been included in this book in order to keep it factual to the best of my knowledge. I read enough about this case and talked to enough people familiar with it to come to one conclusion about Buffy's murder. She knew something about David Middleton; he took her, did something horrific to her, and then killed her to keep her quiet. Bonnie Rice is of the same opinion, and a mother's instincts are rarely wrong...

One possible motive for Buffy's murder is referenced in an Affidavit for a search warrant written by Deputy Michael Westcott of the San Miguel County Sheriff's Office written under Incident Case Number S95-0690. The search warrant requests medical records from Dr. Richard Gingerly of Montrose, who was Buffy's doctor. According to the affidavit, Buffy visited the doctor four days prior to her disappearance, complaining of injuries and symptoms that would be consistent with a forced sexual encounter. The affidavit also states Buffy told the doctor the injuries were a result of "problems she was having with her drug dealers." It was common knowledge and referenced elsewhere in this book that Middleton and Haley were supplying drugs to Buffy.

There is no indication that Buffy filed any type of sexual assault case with the police, but this information is pertinent. We know, in retrospect, that Middleton saw what happened in Miami when he left his sixteen-year-old sexual assault victim alive to testify against him. He changed his Modus Operandi when he got out of prison and never again left a victim of his depravity alive to testify in court again. Buffy told her mother she was terrified of Middleton when she moved back home, and perhaps she had good reason to be.

Some of the people I interviewed who are familiar with the Buffy Rice-Donohue case asked that I not use their names in this book when referencing the information they gave me. Reasons for this varied, but the overriding theme was fear of retaliation in the community. Regardless of the reasons, I will honor these requests for anonymity. The First Amendment gives an author a great deal of latitude in protecting sources who wish to remain anonymous.

I was able to locate and talk to some of the officers from the Montrose Police Department who were in the department when Buffy was murdered and were familiar with the case. One retired officer told me it was their opinion the reason the Montrose Police Department was not providing me with investigative records, was there were not many records to supply. The officer called this case a "Travesty of Justice" and said there really was no investigation done when Buffy disappeared. The officer's exact words were, "They treated that poor girl like a piece of shit because of who she was."

The reason the officer gave me for making this statement was that it was a well-known fact in the department that there was bad blood between an Assistant Chief and Buffy's dad, Walt Rice. I could not corroborate this with independent information, so I will not name that Assistant Chief in this book, and he is no longer with the department. The officer told me there was no real investigation into Buffy's disappearance and no investigative reporting done until after her body was discovered.

It was this retired officer's opinion this is the reason why the department wasn't releasing reports and why they were told not to discuss the investigation, or lack thereof, with the Reno detectives when they visited Montrose during the Middleton investigation. There is very little information in the Reno murder book that was obtained from the Montrose Police Department. Lt. Chinn was in Reno for much of the Middleton trial, and there is also no information from him in the Reno murder book related to the Buffy Rice-Donohue investigation. This lack of information would corroborate the statements to me from this officer.

The officer also described a split in the department, and the community in general over the handling of the case. In a small police department, that type of divisiveness is bad for morale. The officer subsequently retired over issues related to the handling of the Buffy Rice-Donohue case and what it did to the department. I was told there are still bad feelings in the community and the department about the case and that "people just don't like talking about it." The anger I heard in this officer's voice when talking about the case twenty-five years after Buffy's disappearance told my cop's sense I was hearing the truth.

The Montrose Police were called to the apartment of David Middleton and Evonne Haley by Bonnie Rice soon after the night Buffy disappeared. I knew that when first writing this book, and it is detailed in this revised edition as it was then. What I did not know when writing the original book was that Lt. Tom Chinn was called at home regarding Buffy's disappearance and advised of the suspicious circumstances by the on-duty patrol watch commander. This is also a fact I learned from officers who were working that night.

One of the officers who was at Middleton's apartment that night reported back to the watch commander about the encounter, as he thought the circumstances were suspicious. The officer said when they were outside of the apartment with Middleton and Haley, they were told no one else was inside the apartment. Middleton and Haley said they had been home when Mason Donohue and Bonnie Rice had been there earlier pounding on the door but didn't open the door for them. This was before Middleton and Haley were seen by witnesses carrying the large garbage bag out of the apartment.

Whether Buffy was inside of the apartment, alive or dead, is a fact that will never be known. This is because the officers did not check inside the apartment. Middleton was taken at his word when he told officers there was no one inside the apartment. Officers might have also located Middleton's shotgun inside the apartment had they entered to check the suspicious circumstances. The same shotgun he still had with him when he was arrested in Reno.

The watch commander thought the circumstances reported back to him were suspicious enough to place the afterhours call to Lt. Chinn and request either he or a detective come out to investigate. Lt. Chinn reportedly took the call from the watch commander, but he neither responded nor sent out a detective. These facts from that night were corroborated through several independent interviews.

By no means am I inferring that had a detective call out been done the night Buffy disappeared, and had Middleton's apartment been searched, that Buffy might be alive today. What I am saying is that since no detective call-out was done, no investigation was started that night, and no search of Middleton's apartment was conducted. For those reasons, the question of whether Buffy was still alive when officers went to Middleton's apartment will always remain unanswered.

Even if Buffy had already been murdered when the Watch Commander made the call to Lt. Chinn, a crime scene and evidence might have been located inside the apartment. Based on the witness statements from people who saw Middleton and Haley carrying out the large garbage bag similar to the one Buffy's body was found wrapped in, the evidence inside the apartment may have included her body itself. This evidence might have led to an early end to the investigation by the arrest that night, or at least shaping the direction the investigation went in terms of who kept jurisdiction of it and how much attention the case got from law enforcement.

Would the evidence inside that apartment have led to an arrest of Middleton and Haley that night? We'll never know. What we do know is an arrest of Middleton or even a focus of the investigation on him as the suspect in a kidnap or murder probably would have prevented him from ever getting to Reno, Nevada, to murder his victims there.

This case happened in Montrose, Colorado, in the jurisdiction of the Montrose Police Department. This same type of situation can and does happen in police departments all over the Country, including my own department. It happens, but not talking about it does not make the problem go away. If circumstances leading to a mistake in a law enforcement investigation are not corrected through internal investigations and subsequent training, they will happen again. I'm not saying nothing was done internally at the Montrose Police Department to look into this; I'm just saying I don't know and probably never will.

Humans run police departments. The officers responding to calls and making life-and-death decisions are also humans, and they don't have to opportunity to use hindsight when making decisions. But every cop knows hindsight will be used to judge the decisions we make. Law enforcement officers live in a world that is a grey area, but we're judged in black and white. Mistakes get made all the time. The difference is the way they are handled after the fact. Do we own them and go back to fix what we can, or do we bury them so they can become our dirty little secrets? That is a decision we have to live with...

Chapter 71:
Murder In Montrose

The Montrose Police Department might have made mistakes during the investigation into the disappearance and murder of Buffy Rice-Donohue, but there was also some fine police investigative work done by another local law enforcement agency after her body was discovered. The body dump site was just off of Mountain View Lane in a remote area of Norwood, Colorado. The location was sixty-five miles and a lifetime away from where Buffy was last seen with Evonne Haley. Witnesses saw her in the front seat of Haley's car, in a parking lot adjacent to David Middleton's apartment in Montrose, eighteen months and one day earlier.

The dump site was in the jurisdiction of the San Miguel County Sheriff's Office, an agency with eight deputies working under the direction of Sheriff Bill Masters at the time of the discovery. Deputy Michael Westcott was at home at 8:15 P.M. on May 24, 1995, when he received a call from a Norwood resident telling him his daughter and her boyfriend had found a human skull while on a fishing trip in a remote area of Norwood. The pair marked the location of the dump site with a broken fishing pole, wrapped the skull in newspaper, and placed it in an empty cooler to preserve it. They then brought it home to show authorities. The caller told Deputy Westcott it was obviously a human skull and a jawbone was also located at the site.

This call came into Deputy Westcott when he was at home and off-duty, much like a call had gone to Montrose P.D. Lieutenant Chinn eighteen months and one day earlier. Deputy Westcott left the comfort of his home and responded to the phone call requesting his service. He later learned the phone call he was responding to and the one made by a watch commander to Lieutenant Chinn eighteen months and one day earlier were about the same person. The late Buffy Rice-Donohue…

Deputy Westcott removed the skull from its wrapping and examined it. Deputies wear many hats in small law agencies, and examining bodies is one of the duties they are trained to do. Upon looking at the skull, Deputy Westcott saw it was from a small person, and there were signs of blunt force trauma to it. There were broken bones around the eye sockets to the point where they were no longer symmetric. There was a skull fracture on the right side of the skull in the area of the temple, and several of the upper teeth were missing. Since no obvious dental work was present in any of the other teeth, it appeared these missing teeth had been knocked out. The lower jawbone discovered at the dump site was detached, but it matched the upper jawbone that was still attached to the skull.

Deputy Westcott's experience told him these types of injuries were not consistent with a fall or any other natural cause, so he knew from the start he was probably dealing with a homicide, and he treated the case as such. His investigative observations were later confirmed when the cause of the death of Buffy Rice-Donohue was listed by the Medical Examiner as multiple blunt-force trauma strikes to the head at the hand of another. The fact Deputy Westcott handled this as the homicide he knew it to greatly assisted in maintaining the investigative integrity of the case.

At about 8:45 PM that same evening, the witnesses who discovered the skull directed Deputy Westcott to a remote area of Norwood about 2 ½ miles down County Road 44ZS from where the road intersects with Highway 145. The area where Buffy's remains were discovered was on the north side of Mountain View Lane, just east of County Road 44ZS. They spotted the broken fishing rod the witnesses used to mark the site stuck in the ground on the north side of the road and parked the car. From there, they hiked through the dense oak brush, pinion pine, and juniper vegetation that hid the site from the road. The body dump site was in a small clearing with a drainage ditch containing some standing water cutting through the center of it.

There were numerous bones scattered about in the drainage ditch and the area east of it. The bones were clearly human, and a white clothesline-type rope tied in knots was visible, wrapped around what appeared to be a leg bone. As I read Deputy Westcott's report fourteen years after he wrote it, I could clearly visualize those knots, even though I was never at the dump site in Norwood that night. The reason for this was I had seen the same type of rope and knots wrapped around the legs of Kathy Powell when her body was discovered in a dump site in Reno two months before Buffy's remains were discovered in Norwood. There are some things cops see that remain engraved in their memories forever…

Deputy Westcott also found remnants of plastic garbage bags strewn about the area, and some of the bones were still inside of garbage bags that remained intact. There appeared to be yellow plastic tie straps wrapped around the bags that were possibly used as handles to carry the body. A large clump of brown hair and more knotted rope were also located near the bones. Deputy Westcott had seen enough to know he was dealing with a crime scene, and since it was now getting dark, he secured the area and notified Sheriff Masters. The decision was made to keep the scene secure and search it further during daylight hours.

A meeting was held at the Sheriff's Office at 7:00 A.M the next morning to discuss the dump site and how it would be processed. According to the Sheriff's Office reports detailing this meeting, Lieutenant Tom Chinn and Detective Kevin Walters from the Montrose Police Department attended this meeting, in addition to the Sheriff's deputies and crime scene investigators who would perform the search of the dump site.

The identity of the body discovered at the dump site had not yet been determined, and I was not given any documentation from the Montrose Police Department in order to research this, so why the representatives of their department were at a meeting to discuss the investigation of a crime scene out of their jurisdiction is unknown. The likely conclusion was they assumed the body belonged to a person who had gone missing from their jurisdiction eighteen months earlier. Regardless of the reason for their attendance, these detectives were aware of the discovery and participants in this aspect of the investigation.

A Medical Examiner named Dr. Canfield examined the skull later that day. He determined through dental records that the body was, in fact, Buffy Rice-Donohue. Buffy was no longer a missing person, but she was also no longer a living person either. Based on the cause of death, it was determined she died at the hands of another, and her death was listed as a homicide. Over the course of the next two days, the dump site was meticulously searched, and numerous items of evidence were collected. Evidence confirmed this was a dump site and not a murder scene and that Buffy's body had been tied up and wrapped in plastic bags prior to being dumped. The description of the bags and size of the body bore a striking resemblance to the witness descriptions given to Montrose Police of the bag Middleton and Haley were seen carrying out of their apartment the night Buffy went missing.

One anomaly in the subsequent investigation that stuck out to me was the fact the Sheriff's Office took over the active murder investigation after Buffy's remains were discovered. No actual crime scene where the murder took place was ever located, and the crime originated in the jurisdiction of the Montrose Police Department since that is where Buffy went missing. Since Detectives from the Montrose Police Department participated in the search of the dump site, I was curious as to why they did not continue with the lead on the investigation with assistance from the Sheriff's Office for processing of the crime scene. Without access to any of the Montrose Police Department reports, I was not able to determine the reason for this.

During a phone conversation with Sheriff Masters on May 3, 2019, I asked him about the reasons why his department took over the lead on the homicide investigation instead of the Montrose Police Department. After a long pause, Sheriff Masters told me, "That girl's body was found in my jurisdiction, and if nobody else was going to investigate it, I would." I'd been a cop long enough to know not to push this topic. Who investigated the murder of Buffy Rice-Donohue didn't matter as long as someone spoke for her when she could no longer speak for herself.

The Sheriff's Office did an excellent investigation on this case. This included investigators taking a trip to Quantico, Virginia, to meet with the F.B.I. Violent Criminal Apprehension Program, (V.I.C.A.P.), for assistance in analyzing evidence and comparison to similar crimes and evidence. Their investigation was both thorough and comprehensive, including DNA evidence, trace evidence, and circumstantial evidence. As a matter of fact, the evidence in the Buffy Rice-Donohue murder case was much stronger than the evidence used to convict the same killer of the murders of Kathy Powell and Thelma Devilla in Reno, Nevada.

Among the evidence collected from inside one of the plastic bags Buffy's body had been concealed in was a partial hair. This hair sample later tested positive for Mitochondrial DNA (mtDNA), which was traced back to a single common ancestor. That ancestor was the natural mother of David Middleton.

Sheriff Masters felt that was strong evidence to convict Middleton of Buffy's murder, but he did not get the information on the DNA match till about a year after he submitted it. According to Sheriff Masters, the day his office submitted the hair sample to the F.B.I. lab for analysis was the same day the infamous blue dress worn by Monica Lewinski during her "meeting" with then-President Bill Clinton was submitted to the same lab for analysis of a mysterious stain on the dress. The DNA report from the dress took three days to come back, while the analysis report on the hair took a year. Present-day DNA analysis moves a little faster, but there is probably still case prioritization...

Another piece of trace evidence was carpet fibers later matched to Evonne Haley's car. The car was a two-door hatchback, and Buffy had been last seen in the passenger seat of the car with Evonne Haley driving.

The carpet fibers found on Buffy's remains came from the carpet in the rear hatchback storage area. This means at some point in time Buffy's body was in the rear storage area of Haley's car. In the same rear storage area, witnesses saw Middleton and Haley loading a large plastic bag after they carried it out of their apartment late on the same night Buffy was last seen in Montrose.

The knots in the ropes that were apparently used to bind Buffy's body and also used for carry handles on the bags were examined by the same knot expert used in the Reno murder investigations of Kathy Powell and Thelma Davilla. John "J.J." Van Tassel of the Royal Canadian Mounted Police was able to say all the knots located in the dump site where Buffy's remains were found were tied by the same person. Since he also examined the knots in the Reno case, he was able to compare the two cases and say they were all most likely tied by the same person.

At the end of the Sheriff's Office investigation into the Murder of Buffy Rice-Donohue, they listed the cause of death as murder, and the primary suspect was David Middleton. Evonne Haley was also listed in this case, as she was the person last seen with Buffy, and the carpet fibers from her car were located on the body. The carpet fibers were matched after the car was searched under the search warrants in the Reno murder cases. Haley and Middleton had left Montrose prior to the discovery of Buffy's remains, so no search of the car was done in Colorado, as there was no probable cause to do so.

The Sheriff's murder investigative case was submitted to District Attorney Wyatt Angelo for review and possible issuance of an arrest warrant for David Middleton. According to Sheriff Masters, there was plenty of evidence in his case to put Middleton on trial for the murder and to subsequently convict him.

The District Attorney elected not to file charges on this case and issued what is known in legal terms as a "D.A. Non-File." This means the crime was committed, and the person listed as the suspect probably committed the crime, but no charges will be filed based on the information in the investigation.

Angelo did not reject filing murder charges against Middleton due to lack of evidence. His stated reason was that Middleton had just been found guilty of the Reno murders and given the death sentence in Nevada. He declined to file charges against Middleton for Buffy's murder due to the costs of trying a person who was already in prison for murders in another state.

During a phone conversation, Sheriff Masters confirmed with me that he did, in fact, give the District Attorney's office $50,000 out of asset forfeiture funds for use in trial proceedings against Middleton. He did so because he felt strongly about the case and knew his department's investigation would result in a conviction of at least Middleton, if not Haley. I asked Sheriff Masters why he thought Angelo didn't file charges against Middleton. There was no hesitation this time when he answered, "I don't know, but he should have."

My last question to Sheriff Masters was one I raised several times elsewhere in this book. I told the Sheriff we spent a great deal of time researching murder cases to try and find one where there was an arrest and conviction for Accessory to Murder but never an arrest or prosecution of a principal suspect in that same murder. This is what happened in Buffy's case with the arrest of Evonne Haley, and it was the only case like it we were able to find.

Bill Masters had been the Sheriff of San Miguel County for just shy of forty years and was the longest-serving Sheriff in Colorado history the day I spoke to him. Everyone I spoke to while researching this case told me he is not only a good lawman but a good man in general. With all of his law enforcement history in Colorado, Sheriff Masters told me he'd never heard of a similar case. I asked him what he thought about the fact Evonne Haley was allowed to plead guilty to Accessory to Murder and get a sweetheart deal. He said, "I've never seen anything like that, and nobody asked me about it."

The murder investigation case of Buffy Rice-Donohue is completed and sits in the Records Section of the San Miguel County Sheriff's Office. The cause of death is Homicide by blunt force trauma, and the Suspect is David Stephen Middleton. There is no statute of limitations on a murder case, so charges against Middleton can be filed at any time. It's just a matter of the D.A. dusting off the case and filing charges.

District Attorney Wyatt Angelo is long gone from his position, and I asked Sheriff Masters if he thought another D.A. would ever consider filing the murder charges against Middleton, especially based on the information his admitted Accessory Evonne Haley gave the court under oath. The Sheriff does not feel any other D.A. will go against this non-file decision, especially since Middleton is still on death row in Nevada.

It's also been a long time since the case was completed, and witnesses move, disappear altogether, or have difficulty remembering what they saw or said 24 years ago. Filing charges now could possibly result in Middleton being found innocent of Buffy's murder based on these witness statements being challenged by a good defense attorney, and an acquittal on Buffy's murder could give him ammunition for an appeal on his Nevada convictions.

Those of us who have spent enough time in law enforcement know it doesn't matter if we agree or disagree with decisions that are made on a case after it leaves our hands. We just know it is what it is, but we don't have to like it. One thing you'll never hear anyone who has crossed paths with David Middleton say is that you can't kill a dead man twice. You're more than likely to hear them say there are some people you can't kill enough.

Before I ended my call with Sheriff Masters, I thanked him for doing his job with Buffy's case. I will never agree with not prosecuting Middleton for Buffy's murder, and I got the feeling he never will either, but at least in the end, he investigated the hell out of this case and named the devil as the suspect. Sheriff Masters and everyone in his department involved in this case I either spoke to or read about spoke for the victim who could no longer speak for herself. That's about all we can ask from anyone who wears a badge…

Chapter 72:
Conclusion

This book is not about the murder of Buffy Rice-Donohue, but her case is an integral aspect of the systemic breakdown that allowed David Middleton to move through life causing harm, and sometimes death, to those whose lives intersected with his. This same systemic breakdown of our law enforcement and criminal justice systems allowed him to eventually end up in Reno and take the lives of Kathy Powell and Thelma Davilla.

Middleton went from Boston to Miami, where he became a cop and committed crimes. He went to prison, but not for long enough or for the right crimes. His early release from prison in Florida allowed him to move to Montrose, where he kidnapped and murdered Buffy. He left Montrose a free man, so he was able to move to Reno and kill again. That is the short, cyclical story of the criminal life of David Middleton. The longer story is how this was allowed to happen, and those questions may never be answered.

Since the initial police investigation, or lack thereof, into Buffy's disappearance possibly allowed Middleton to leave Montrose and get to Reno, it is an essential aspect of the story of the murders of Kathy Powell and Thelma Davilla. What happened the night Buffy disappeared is something we'll never know. What happened with the police investigation during the eighteen months between Buffy's disappearance and when her remains were discovered is something else we'll never know. One thing we do know, is that if Middleton doesn't leave Montrose, he doesn't make it to Reno. And if he doesn't make it to Reno...

The Montrose Press did a news story on my book in 2009 when it was first released.[9] I was interviewed over the phone for that story, and the quotes contained in it made by me are accurate. Montrose Police Chief Tom Chinn and U.S. Attorney Wyatt Angelo were also interviewed for that article. Both of them challenged some of the facts in the book as they pertained to the Montrose case, but neither of them offered any information to challenge those facts. Also, neither of them took my offer to contact me

---

[9] Montrose Press, May 15, 2009. Story by Senior writer Katharhynn Heidelberg

and correct any information they thought to be non-factual. Angelo is quoted as saying the idea that his office declined to prosecute Middleton is "not accurate." I do not know how else to describe this, since his office did not file charges on the case.

I do agree with one quote from Tom Chinn in this article. He says, "There were a lot of people who worked very hard on that case." I know there were, as I read about them in the reports I received from the San Miguel County Sheriff's Office. I just don't know what was done by the Montrose Police Department, since they haven't told me.

I waited an additional two weeks to submit this updated manuscript to my publisher, as I wanted to give the Montrose Police Department ample time to respond to my multiple requests for information. Even though I was on a deadline, I wanted to make sure I they had the opportunity to supply my requested documentation and to answer a couple of simple questions I posed to them. I did not hear back from the Montrose Chief of Police, Blaine Hall, the Department's official keeper of records, regarding my FOIA request. But I finally heard back from Commander Matt Smith through an email on May 9, 2019.

The reply I got from Commander Smith stated they would not be supplying any requested documents, or answering any questions I raised in my FOIA request. No reason was given, except that he wasn't around when this happened, so he didn't want to give answers he didn't have knowledge of. Colorado law saying open investigative reports are not subject to public information requests was also quoted. The Montrose P.D. case is for the original missing person report, and Buffy is no longer missing, so I'm not sure why this case is still open and active. No reference was made in this correspondence about the handling or location of the nude photos of Buffy. But I was invited to come to Montrose to take a look at what they would be allowed to show me regarding their case.

Commander Smith didn't tell me what it was they had for me to look at, or if there was anything at all to look at. Since it would require four days of travel and several thousand dollars to make this journey into the unknown, I declined the offer to go to Montrose. The phrase "Pig In A Poke" that District Attorney Dick Gammick was quoted as saying to Middleton in Reno earlier in this book came to mind when I considered this offer. They wanted me to buy into something without knowing its true nature or value, and without inspecting the items beforehand. With all things considered, I did not make the trip to Montrose. Since the department did not chose to honor any section of the FOIA request, I wasn't willing to roll the dice on what I'd find when I got there.

I hope anyone who comes out disputing the facts in this book as they relate to the Montrose Police Department's investigation into Buffy's disappearance and murder will keep in mind the efforts myself and my team went through to obtain reports and interviews regarding their investigation. We went above and beyond, but in the end I have to write about what I can source reference. A lot of what I got from witnesses regarding the Montrose investigation does not appear in this book, since it was either hearsay or I could not source reference it. I can only hope this witness information is not factual, because if it is true, it is even more disturbing than what I included in this book.

By contrast, my requests for information from the San Miguel County Sheriff's Office, as they related to Buffy's case, were handled much differently. My email and phone call requesting information about the case were returned by the Sheriff himself, and he took time out of his schedule to talk to me about the case. He put me in touch with staff members from his office who were familiar with the case, and they provided all information I requested. That included a lot of information I didn't know when first writing this book. I was told exactly what was in their case, and given options to have the entire case, or just the portions of the case I needed for reference in this book, copied and sent to me. The portions of the case I needed were copied and sent to me via email within a day of my request.

My impression of these dealings with the Sheriff's Office is they wanted to help me get facts right. That is the intent of the FOIA process when dealing with public agencies charged with our safety, and the Sheriff's Office seemed to understand that. There should be nothing hidden from the public when it comes to obtaining their trust. Why a police department for a city that lies within the same jurisdiction as the San Miguel County Sheriff's Office did not handle the request for records in this same expeditious manner, and actually denied all aspects of the request, is a question I'll leave up to the reader to consider.

One fact to keep in mind while giving this question thought is a Sheriff is an elected official who answers directly to the people in their community who vote for them. A Police Chief is an at-will appointed official who answers directly to the elected officials who appoint them. A

Sheriff has to be voted out of office, where a Police Chief can be fired without cause.

I am not saying that this came into play during requests for records referenced in this book. I'm just saying I've worked under Sheriff's, and I've worked under Police Chiefs in my career. Sometimes the policies, procedures, and more importantly the agendas of a law enforcement agency can differ when dealing with an elected official versus an appointed chief running an agency. Anyone who disagrees with this last statement has either never worked under both law enforcement systems, or is probably an appointed at-will law enforcement official themselves.

I will use for source reference on these last statements my one and only experience with a major conference geared specifically for Chiefs of Police and police administrators. In my position as Director of Public Safety with my school district after my retirement from the Reno P.D., I was eligible for membership in the International Association of Chiefs of Police. I was invited to their 2008 annual conference in San Diego by the Chief of Police for a city within the boundaries of my school district, who told me he would gladly sponsor me for membership in the group if I was interested. This was an excellent, well-respected organization I'd heard a lot about during my law enforcement career, and I was honored when I got this invitation.

I went to the San Diego conference with the full intent of becoming a member of the association. There were thousands of people in the conference room and three huge screens streaming videos of the presenters on stage. This was the who's who in International law enforcement, and I felt a buzz of adrenaline from being part of this high powered crowd. I imagined this would lead to new high points in my law enforcement career and looked forward to networking with other upper level administrators.

Shortly after the opening session started, one of the keynote presenters told the crowd, "If you're going to be successful as a Chief of Police, sometimes you have to forget about right versus wrong and good versus evil. When you get to the top, it's not about fighting crime or what's morally and ethically correct anymore. It's about the good of the organization." To drive this statement home, he then used the George H.W. Bush quote of "Whatever it takes." I was familiar with the quote the former President used when he was the C.I.A. Director, and knew this presenter used it out of its intended context to make his point. I looked around the crowd and hundreds of high ranking police officials were writing down what the speaker had just said in their notebooks so they could take this *wisdom* back to their departments with them.

I felt sick to my stomach sitting in that room. This just wasn't what I had signed up for when I put on a badge twenty-six years earlier, and I felt like a kid who just found out Santa didn't really exist. I leaned over to the Chief of Police who had invited me to the conference and told him this group wasn't right for me, and more importantly, I wasn't right for this group. I left that conference, never looked back, and didn't join the organization.

I walked the four blocks back to my hotel room at the Embassy Suites on Harbor Drive, took off my suit, and changed into some proper San Diego beach attire. I knew I would not be returning to the conference the next day, so I checked out of the hotel, retrieved my car from valet, and drove five miles to the Lahaina Beach House bar in Mission Beach.

There is a reason I picked that bar out of all the other beach bars in San Diego. Twelve years earlier, my old narcotics unit partner Dean Spurr and I sat with a group of "real cops" from the San Diego Police Department's S.W.A.T. Team on the deck of this same beach bar while we were in town for a DEA Meth Lab training school. Dean is one of the finest and most ethical cops I've ever worked with, and we'd met these San Diego cops in the DEA class. We earned their respect working in this arduous school with them, and they invited us to their "debriefing" at Lahaina after the class. We were honored to accompany them, as that invitation meant more to us than any DEA diploma ever would.

Dean and I didn't do much talking as we sat there on the outdoor deck of Lahaina with these brave warriors, but we did a lot of listening. These cops were the best of the best tactical cops in what I consider to be the finest police department in the United States. There was none of the macho conversation seen on T.V. when these cops were talking to us. They told us they loved their department, loved their city, and felt pride every time they put on their uniforms. It was a great day for Dean and I to be a cops, and one I'll never forget. I needed to feel like a cop again after what I just heard at the Police Chief's conference, so I headed to that same beach bar for some ocean therapy. And it worked...

As I sat on the deck of the Lahaina Beach Bar on that sunny afternoon, looking out at the beautiful Pacific Ocean, sipping on a cold Red Hook IPA, and doing my best to forget about the conference I'd just left, something Detective Dave Jenkins once said to me popped into my head. While interviewing Dave for the first edition of this book a few months earlier, he said, "It's easy to keep your ethics and morals when you're at the bottom of the organizational chart. That's why all the real police work gets done at the bottom, and not the top." I call that bit of wisdom *"Cop Logic,"* and in that moment, everything made sense to me again.

I am by no means inferring that any law enforcement organization or that Police Chiefs as a group are unethical or immoral. I'm just repeating what I heard at this conference, which can be source referenced from the group's website if need be. I have met some very good Police Chiefs during my career, but I've met some pretty bad ones too. You can probably say that about CEO's in any industry, but it is my belief that law enforcement is the one industry where ethics can never be sacrificed for any reason. When the good of the organization rises above the good of the people we're sworn to protect, we've lost sight of our purpose.

I end this book with this story for a reason. Law enforcement is a noble profession, but sometimes mistakes happen. Even worse, sometimes unethical and immoral decisions are made by persons charged with the safety of the public. And sometimes those decisions are made intentionally, with no mistakes involved, by persons at high positions in their organizations. I make no allegations of any type against any law enforcement agency or person referenced in this book. I just ask the reader to keep this last story in mind when reading this book, and when looking at our justice system in general.

Blind faith in any system, including law enforcement, is a recipe for disaster. Who polices the Police? That is an often asked question in our society, but the answer has been around for a long time. In 1829 when Sir Robert Peel created the London Metropolitan Police Force, better known as *Bobbies*, he said, "The police are the public, and the public are the police. It is incumbent upon every citizen to ensure the interests of the community welfare and existence are best served by the police whose responsibility it is to serve us."

There is nothing new in this world. There is only history we're not familiar with. Who polices the Police? According to Sir Robert Peel, we do. Sometimes it's O.K. to question authority, as long as it's done properly, respectfully, and safely. It's our job.

The main premise of this book is we all need to watch out for ourselves because no one else really can. We should always be aware of our surroundings, never blindly give away our trust, be careful who you let into your inner circle of life, and always remember that evil exists in this world. If you turn your back on evil, it might just sneak up behind you and kick you in the butt to get your attention. If you look evil in the eye, it will find someone who isn't paying attention to prey on and leave you alone. It has been my experience that evil people are basically cowards, and they won't come at you head on. We can empower evil, or we can tamp it down in our society by our own actions. That choice is up to us.

David Middleton brought evil into people's lives by gaining their trust, and his victims gave him this precious possession because of a perception they had of people who perform a job in our society. He used his badge and uniform to lure a sixteen-year-old girl into his police car in Miami, sexually assault her, and change her life forever at this young age. He used the fact he was an ex-cop to gain people's trust wherever he went, including death row in Ely, NV. He said he was *"one of us,"* even though he never was. That was his mantra, and a lot of folks let him into their lives because of it without checking into it. It's human nature to trust cops, and Middleton was well aware of this.

The vast majority of the cops I've worked with or crossed paths with in the thirty-six years I've been involved in public safety have been honest, ethical, and would lay down their lives to protect the public they are sworn to serve. But I've met some bad ones too, and I am by no means naïve enough to think that a person's profession lends credibility to their honesty, no matter what that profession is.

When this book was first released in 2009, I said that David Middleton was the only cop in American history who was known to be a serial killer. That changed in 2018 when seventy-two-year-old Joseph James De Angelo was arrested in Citrus Heights, California for serial rapes and murders he committed in southern California during a ten-year crime spree between 1976 and 1986.

He is suspected of committing fifty-one rapes and at least a dozen murders. The suspects in these cases were known as the East Area Rapist and the Golden State Killer, and the cases were not connected during their investigations. A cold case DNA match in 2016 found the suspect in these cases was one in the same, and De Angelo was arrested for these crimes. He was a police officer with the Auburn, CA. police department during this crime spree. This case is still on-going, but the popular belief is the suspect used his police training, and possibly his position, to help him commit these crimes and avoid arrest for so long.

Law enforcement is not the only position people tend to blindly give their trust to. Who does not open their door for the cable guy, the carpet cleaner, the plumber, or anyone else who comes to our homes to perform a service? We're Americans, and we're busy. We want these folks to come into our homes, work quickly, and get the hell out of there so we can watch T.V. in rooms with clean carpets, and no leaky faucets to disturb us. And to make sure the workers aren't bothered, we give them free reign of our homes while we're usually occupied in another area of the house, because like I said, we're busy. We take it for granted that these folks have been properly vetted by their employers, and this would include a criminal history check.

That is not always the case. David Middleton was not given a sufficient background check when he took his job as the Cable Guy in Reno, NV. Had that been done, his felony conviction would have precluded him from holding that position, and he probably would not have crossed paths with either Kathy Powell or Thelma Davilla. Another systemic breakdown? Probably, but we'll also never know the answer to that question. The lawsuit against the cable company was settled out of court so it is sealed from the public.

And criminal history checks only show those persons who have been caught, arrested, and convicted. The vast majority of the people committing crimes in our society are still waiting to get caught so they will not show up in a criminal history check.

We cannot live in fear, but we must always live in a state of awareness. David Middleton has been on Death Row since 1995 and his murders are in the past, but as long as the murder of Buffy Rice-Donohue remains open and unsolved in Montrose Colorado, this story will always remain current. We can only hope that someday that wrong is righted. We owe it to ourselves as a society, and law enforcement as a profession, to ensure justice to the victims. We are their voices when they speak to us from the grave…

Acknowledgments

I'd like to thank all the members of the law enforcement community who contributed information for this book. There are too many of you to name here, and some of you did not want your names released for personal reasons, but I especially want to thank Dave Jenkins and John Douglas for the contributions you made to this book, and for the tireless work you did on this case. I'd also like to thank Paul Kuiper for his contributions regarding the Florida aspects of this case. The three of you spent many hours of your own time talking to me about this case, and also working on documentaries on this story after the initial release of the first book I wrote on the Middleton murders, *BEWARE OF THE CABLE GUY, From Cop to Serial Killer.*

A special thanks go to Bonny Rice for the information she provided on the Montrose, Colorado, aspects of this case. I cannot fathom what it is like to lose a child, especially to a senseless act of murder committed by a serial killer who shows no remorse for his crimes. I also cannot fathom how it must feel to live with the fact the law enforcement community let her and her family down by not prosecuting the person who took Buffy away from them at such a young age before she had a chance to realize her dreams. I was a member of the law enforcement community for twenty-five years, and the fact David Middleton, to this day, has not been charged with this heinous crime will never make sense to me. There is no statute of limitation on the crime of murder, so my one hope is that at some point, someone in the Montrose Colorado Police Department takes a hard look at the open case on the disappearance of Buffy Rice-Donohue and decides to have the suspect in her murder prosecuted. I can tell them where to find the suspect on any given day. If this book helps to get that done, then I've done my job.

I never personally met or talked to Buffy's father, Walt Rice. But from one father to another, I would like to thank him for inspiring me to write the two books about the murders committed by David Middleton. The Rice's sent me a photo of Buffy's tombstone when I started writing the first book about these murders in 2007. When I read the words Walt Rice had inscribed on the tombstone, I knew this was a story that had to be told. I'll include those words here:

Buffy, what a special treasure you are to me. A beautiful young lady not only in appearance but also in spirit. I know that you loved life and loved your family and friends.

On November 21, 1993, Buffy was abducted and murdered. For over 18 months, we desperately searched for you, sweetheart exhausting all our time, energy, and resources. We never gave up looking for you or gave up hope until your body was found on May 24, 1995. On June 30, 1995, we laid you here to rest. You are my only daughter, my special sweetheart, your mother's best friend, and your brother's only sister. Buffy, we all love you so much and miss you deeply.

I promise you, Buffy, that your mom and dad will never stop fighting for you and this injustice. I love you, sweetheart.

- Dad

My biggest thanks go to you, the reader. If reading this book, especially the words from Buffy's tombstone, moved you at all, then you can assist in righting this injustice. The only way to get Buffy's murder prosecuted is to generate publicity about it. Law enforcement agencies work for the public, not the other way around. They are also the only ones who can speak for the victims, so the public has the responsibility to hold them accountable for their actions. Sometimes, we have to remind them of that. It's easy to do. The contact information for the Montrose Colorado Police Department is on their website.

Lastly, my thanks go out to Melissa Blake from Melissa Kay Photography (www.melissakphotography.com) for the cover work done at PETCO Park, my home away from home…

The author.

www.ingramcontent.com/pod-product-compliance
Lightning Source LLC
Chambersburg PA
CBHW062115020426
42335CB00013B/977